THE FILMS OF
HENRY FONDA

Books by Tony Thomas

The Films of Errol Flynn (with Rudy Behlmer and Cliff McCarty)
The Busby Berkeley Book
Ustinov in Focus
Music for the Movies
Cads and Cavaliers
The Films of Kirk Douglas
Sam Wood: Hollywood Professional
Song and Dance: The Films of Gene Kelly
Harry Warren and the Hollywood Musical
The Films of the Forties
Burt Lancaster
The Films of Marlon Brando
Gregory Peck
Hollywood's Hollywood (with Rudy Behlmer)
The Great Adventure Films
The Films of 20th Century-Fox (with Aubrey Solomon)
Film Score
From a Life of Adventure (The Writings of Errol Flynn)
The Films of Ronald Reagan
Hollywood and the American Image
The Films of Olivia de Havilland

THE FILMS OF HENRY FONDA

by Tony Thomas

CITADEL PRESS • *Secaucus, N.J.*

For my son David

First edition
Copyright © 1983 by Tony Thomas
All rights reserved
Published by Citadel Press
A division of Lyle Stuart Inc.
120 Enterprise Ave., Secaucus, N.J. 07094
In Canada: Musson Book Company
A division of General Publishing Co. Limited
Don Mills, Ontario
Manufactured in the United States of America by
Halladay Lithograph, West Hanover, Mass.
Design: Holly Johnson at the
Angelica Design Group, Ltd.

Library of Congress Cataloging in Publication Data

Thomas, Tony, 1927-
    The films of Henry Fonda.

    1. Fonda, Henry, 1905-1982.   I. Title.
PN2287.F558T48   1983   791.43'028'0924   83-15081
ISBN 0-8065-0868-X

CONTENTS

★★★★★★★★★★★★★★★★★★★★★★★★ ACKNOWLEDGMENTS

A book of this kind cannot be written without the help of others. In the case of this particular book I am especially indebted to John Springer, whose own book *The Fondas* was published by Citadel Press in 1970. In order to allow for this updated and complete account of Henry Fonda's career, Mr. Springer agreed to the withdrawal of his book and for the use of a great many of its photographs. His book became the basis for this one, and I am grateful for that. Most of my research was done at the library of The Academy of Motion Picture Arts and Sciences in Los Angeles and I am indebted to Linda Mehr and her staff. In collecting the illustrations I must thank Eddie Brandt and Mike Hawks at Saturday Matinee (North Hollywood), Larry Edmunds Bookstore (Hollywood), and Collectors Bookstore (Hollywood).

For the opportunity to view a number of Fonda films I am thankful to Aubrey Solomon and to Robert Rosen, the director of the Film Archives of the University of California, Los Angeles.

— Tony Thomas

HENRY FONDA–
AMERICAN ORIGINAL

IN THE WORLD OF ENTERTAINMENT there are seldom any certainties, but on the evening of March 29, 1982, at the Academy Award presentations in Los Angeles, there was barely a doubt about Henry Fonda's receiving an Oscar for his performance in *On Golden Pond*. It is likely that even his competitors in the Best Actor category voted for him. Why? Was his work in this film so much better than anything else he had done? The simple answer is that Fonda's work in *On Golden Pond* was like everything else he had done in the respect that it was excellent. But there was a finality about this film, and Hollywood had become almost painfully aware that this 77-year-old actor, possibly one of the finest stage and film actors America had ever produced, had never won an Oscar for any of his performances.

Not only had Fonda never won an Oscar but he had only once been nominated—for the classic *The Grapes of Wrath* in 1940. His friend James Stewart won that year, for *The Philadelphia Story*, and Stewart was shocked. He had voted for Fonda. Hollywood has a peculiar history of awarding Oscars by compensation. In 1940 the industry was perhaps a little ashamed that Stewart had the previous year missed out on winning for *Mr. Smith Goes to Washington*—the Oscar went to Robert Donat for *Goodbye Mr. Chips*. In 1982 Hollywood must have felt very ashamed about Fonda. They had given him an Oscar in 1981 for Lifetime Achievement, but that was not the same thing. By that time Fonda had already been similarly honored by The American Film Institute, The Kennedy Center for the Performing Arts and numerous other worthy arts organizations.

Fonda had never cared much for the Oscar business, although at the end he, too, shared the general sentiment of the occasion and shed a tear when his daughter brought him the famed stat-uette. In 1941 he had not cared to attend the ceremonies, a fact that indicated his regard for the glitter of the movie business. Fonda despised the glitter. He was a major movie star who never thought of himself as being one. He was an actor, and he truly loved being an actor. He appeared in 85 films, not including those made for television, but he much preferred the stage. No other American actor maintained a constant standing in film for so many years while at the same time managing a reputation on the stage.

He was pragmatic in his attitude to film. He never sloughed off a performance, no matter how inferior the film; but he did most of his films because he knew it was necessary to keep his name alive and provide him with the income that enabled him to indulge himself on the stage. Fonda liked to live well but he was never a social creature and he avoided the parties that tend to be a vital part of the off-camera life of Hollywood. He never "went Hollywood." He was a quiet man, except when angry, when he did plenty of *cussing*, and his hobbies were painting and needlepoint. Among film crews and stage hands he preferred to be called Hank and not Mr. Fonda, and anyone who gave him the "star treatment" was usually advised to "cool it."

It was typical of Fonda that he resisted offers from publishers to do his autobiography. He was a very private man. Eventually he gave in and agreed to work with Howard Teichman on *Fonda: My Life*, published by Orion in 1981. Now a man who had undergone several serious bouts of ill health, he must have realized that it was time. It was also typical of Fonda that he did not want a glossy account of his life. It had to be the truth, warts and all.

The truth is that he was a far more complex and complicated man than his gentle, placid image led people to believe. His drawling Nebraska voice and loping walk tended to give the impression of an easygoing fellow. Fonda was both more and less than that.

He shocked people in his later years by admitting that he had never really liked himself very much. Those nearest to him confirmed that he could be hard on his loved ones, that he found it difficult to communicate on the very personal level and that he was not quite as affable as *Mister Roberts,* an image so perfectly wrought by Fonda that admirers tended to think *that* was the man himself.

Fonda was married five times and said he was ashamed to admit it. He also said he was sorry it had taken him so long to find in marriage the kind of rapport and contentment he had always needed. As a youngster he had been very shy and ill-at-ease, but found his solution in acting. "It occurred to me that for a self-doubting man, this was the answer. Writers can give you words and you can become another person."

Fonda never considered himself a good interview. Despite all the years of appearing before the public he never completely lost a sense of shyness and a certain diffidence about himself. He claimed he was not articulate enough to do a good interview and it took much persuasion to get him to appear on television talk shows. But when he did get on them he always came off well. Fonda had more charm than he realized

Baby Henry.

Henry at fourteen.

and no one other than himself criticized his ability to express himself.

An interviewer's best chance with Fonda came with any intelligent questions about the art of acting. When asked about the length of his career he would point out that despite his distinct image—the image of a quiet, generally decent and well-behaved American Everyman—he had tried all along to avoid getting typecast. "It's fun for me as an actor, for any actor I guess, to do a diversity of parts and not get stuck in any one. You're apt to get stuck if you let yourself, because if you're good in one thing, you find they'll ask you to do it over and over again. So I've resisted that. After *Mister Roberts* I was offered a lot of navy lieutenant parts, but none of them were as good, so it was easy to say no. I've been lucky. I've been able to pick and choose."

To those who saw Fonda in Broadway plays, and in places where those plays may have toured, he was obviously as much a master of the stage as of the screen. But to the world in general Henry Fonda was a motion picture star. They may have heard that he sometimes appeared on the stage but to most moviegoers in that very long career period between *The Farmer Takes a Wife* in 1935 and *On Golden Pond* in 1980 he was a man of Hollywood, a reference that caused him to shudder a little. "I've never made it a secret that I prefer the theatre as work for myself. It's a much more personally gratifying and satisfying medium. For me the reasons are obvious, but they may not be for other people. If it's brought up they say, 'Oh, because you have a live audience?' That's not it at all. It helps to have a response at the moment you do something, especially with comedy, but that isn't the reason. As simply as I can put it: in the theatre you prepare extensively with rehearsals and try-outs out of town. Then when you open on Broadway you begin at the beginning and play it to the end, consecutively, building emotion on emotion."

When Fonda left Hollywood in 1947 to return to Broadway it was partly because he was not pleased with the way his postwar movie career had developed, but mostly because he had not been on the stage in years and yearned to get back to it. At the time he said he was tired of playing scenes for camera crews and sound stage workers. It was not snobbism, simply a desire to play to a paying audience. He was quite articulate about the difference between building a part during the course of an evening in the theatre and trying to build one for a movie. "For the camera you do short scenes, anywhere from thirty seconds to a couple of minutes—three minutes is a long scene on film. You do these scenes hours apart and sometimes out of continuity and not in context—and over a period of weeks. Somebody else puts it all together. If they like it—you're happy. But you don't have the memory of having created it, because you never did. But in the theatre you get a chance to do it all again. In film you don't get the opportunity to rehearse very much, and no matter how many times you do a scene, you're usually left wishing you had another chance."

How could a man with so little apparent passion for movies appear in 85 of them over a 45-year period and gain a reputation as one of the world's foremost film actors? The answer is simply that Fonda was an actor. He may have disliked some of his pictures but there were some of which he was proud and he was well aware that his success on the screen abetted his prestige in the theatre. Many people would come to a Fonda play because they wanted to see a famous movie star in person, but most of them would leave the theatre realizing they had seen an actor. Fonda was also pragmatic about his film work. It paid well and it enabled him to have an enviable standard of living, and to pretty well chart his own course. Fonda did not wallow in wealth but he lived well, and had since the time of his first movie. He never forgot, however, that the first 30 years of his life were modest and frugal.

Fonda's plain, ordinary background served him well as an actor because it made him aware of his range. He seldom played anyone other than Americans and even at that they were never *way-out*, flamboyant characters. As a cowboy, a naval lieutenant, as young Abe Lincoln, as the president in *Fail Safe*, or as the retired old professor in *On Golden Pond*, they were all credible, grass roots men. He always seemed to be exactly the man he was playing, which led people to assume that acting was easy for him. The truth is that Fonda worked very hard as an actor and it is the ultimate tribute to his talent that he never, as he put it, let the seams show. "About the only goal I set for myself was to disguise acting, and I learned to do that simply by watching other actors. It seemed to me that no matter how good an actor performed, if you could see the wheels going round it destroyed the illusion. If you can see what he's trying to do, then it doesn't work.

Henry (age about seven) standing between his parents. His two sisters stand at the right. The other child is unidentified.

Fonda's first pay as an actor—appearing with Lincoln impersonator George Billings in the Spring of 1928.

So I said to myself, 'Don't let 'em see you working, don't let it show.' "

In later years Fonda would be forced into discussion about *The Method*, even by his children, but he claimed he never knew any method other than watching and listening. He had no formal training as an actor and felt that the only way to learn acting was by experience, by being with an audience and getting their reactions. For him it was all a matter of instinct and intelligence. "A lot of it has to do with having a good ear—and I *do* think I have a good ear. You hear a line and your ear tells you if it rings true. Would the character say that? You're lucky if what you're playing has been written by a writer who has a good ear, like John O'Hara. He had a great ear for dialogue. Ours is a medium of the spoken word and what you say has to sound as if you just made it up. Everytime you say a line in a play it has to sound as if it's the first time you've said it. So I go by my ear—do the words *sound* right? If they don't, then you discuss it with the director, or better still, the writer, and juggle the words a little. Really, it has a lot to do with having a good ear."

Fonda not only had good ears but good eyes as well. He always looked as if he was looking and thinking. Critics often made that point. His characters appeared to be thinking things over.

Few actors have ever been more adroit with the soulful look, the gaze of a man with something on his mind. This ability served him well on the screen. In the 45 years between *The Farmer Takes a Wife* and *On Golden Pond*, Fonda never received a bad review, even in pictures that were generally regarded as stinkers. How was it possible for a man who had no coaching in the art of acting and no thought of being an actor until he tried it as a twenty-year-old—how was it possible to be so good? He had no family tradition on which to draw—his could hardly have been a less showbiz family. They were conservative, emotionally constrained, well-behaved mid-Westerners of Dutch stock, hardly the most expressive people in the world.

Fonda's Italian name stemmed from ancestors who left Italy around the year 1500 and went to Holland. They emigrated to America at some point in the mid-seventeenth century and settled in the Mohawk Valley of New York State. Eventually they founded the township of Fonda and it was there that both of Henry Fonda's paternal grandparents were born. They became westward pioneers and trekked to Nebraska, thereby giving Fonda genuine claims to being an American of classic stock. He was born in the prairie town of Grand Island on May 16, 1905, the first child and only son of William Brace Fonda and Herberta Jaynes. When Fonda was six months old the family moved to Omaha, where, after a number of residences, they settled in the suburb of Dundee, the spot he always regarded as home. Here were born his sisters Harriet and Jayne.

Fonda senior was a printer who operated his own small company, and his son inherited his characteristics of being quiet and introverted. The mother, a Christian Scientist, was affable and outgoing, and enjoyed singing and playing the piano. Fonda's upbringing was conventional, but because he was small of stature as a child he tended to be even more withdrawn and quiet. In his early teens he quickly grew to six feet and one inch, which gave him the confidence to partake of sports. In those years he became good at swimming, basketball and track events. He had by this time revealed some talent for drawing and painting but his only career notion was in the direction of journalism, a notion spurred by his having won a short-story contest when he was ten.

In his high school years Fonda had worked part-time for the telephone company and when he graduated in 1923 he enrolled in journalism at the University of Minnesota because North-

In 1933, at the Mount Kisco Playhouse.

western Bell in that city had assured him of work, which he needed in order to pay his way through college. The job fell through after a while and he received another as a physical training instructor at a settlement house. The meager salary was supplemented by a few dollars from home, and in this fashion Fonda drifted through the next two years. At the end of that time he was not at all certain of continuing and went home to ponder his uncertain future.

As a 20-year-old hanging around the house in the summer of 1925 his fortunes took a definite turn when his mother's friend Dorothy Brando, an avid member of Omaha's Community Playhouse, invited him to do a part in a play. Mrs. Brando was at that time the mother of a one-year-old son named Marlon. The Playhouse needed a youth to play the part of Ricky in *You*

and I by Philip Barry. Being painfully shy, it was torture for young Henry to get through the part, but somehow he did, and liked the theatre enough to stay on as an odd-job boy. Since it paid no money he had to look for work elsewhere, and after a variety of menial labors managed to get work as a clerk with a credit company at 18 dollars per week. His parents did not encourage his interest in amateur theatrical life but he became more and more enchanted with the smell of the theatre. He painted scenery, helped construct sets and did walk-on bits in plays.

In the summer of 1926 the director of the Playhouse, Gregory Foley, shocked Henry by telling him he wanted him to play the title role in *Merton of the Movies*. Up until that time Fonda had looked upon what he had been doing in the

First Broadway lead—with June Walker in The Farmer Takes a Wife *in 1934.*

theatre purely as fun. After his opening night he returned home, where his sisters debated about the virtues of his performance. After some minutes of loud discussion, Fonda senior emerged from behind his newspaper and said, "Shut up, he was perfect!" This piece of paternal approval was clearly a signal point in his life—Fonda never tired of relating this incident—and now at the age of 21 he had some notion of ambition. With the good notices as Merton, he decided that being an actor was what he would do for a career, much to the consternation of his family.

Fonda was put on salary at the Playhouse as an assistant to the director, at a wage of five hundred dollars for the whole season, from September to May. At the end of that season another stroke of luck came his way when an Omaha dowager, Mrs. Hunter Scott, Sr., engaged Henry to accompany her son Hunter, Jr., back to Princeton University, a bonus of which job was an all-expense-paid week in New York. Exposed to the wonders of Broadway, Fonda saw nine plays in six days. On returning to the Omaha Community Playhouse he was now really fired up about being an actor. A variety of parts at the Playhouse helped build up his confidence, and when he heard that traveling vaudevillian George Billings was looking for an assistant, Fonda jumped at the job. Billings specialized in playing Lincoln and for a couple of months Fonda toured around with him, writing sketches and performing bit parts. It also paid him a hundred dollars a week, something Fonda considered a fortune at the time.

In June of 1928 Fonda's interest in going East to try his luck was aided by being hired as a driver for a lady who wished to spend the summer in Cape Cod, Massachusetts. Once there he decided to tackle the various summer stock companies. At the first he was warded off by no chance of employment, but at the second, the Cape Playhouse in Dennis, he managed to get a job as an assistant, which provided room and board but no salary. After a few weeks of laboring, a young actor quit and Fonda was given his part. Some weeks later he happened to visit Falmouth, where the University Players Guild staged their plays, and they liked him enough to invite him to join the company. One of the actors was young Joshua Logan, playing a comedy part, and he was grateful when Fonda's loud and peculiar laugh guided the audience into gales of laughter. He wanted to meet the laugher afterwards, and from that meeting came the offer to join the group; since it paid five dollars per week

In 1937 Fonda returned to the Mount Kisco Playhouse to appear in The Virginian, *with Dan Duryea and Henry Morgan, both of whom would soon turn up in Hollywood.*

With bride Frances on September 16, 1936, at Christ Episcopal Church in New York.

plus room and board, Fonda had no hesitation in quitting his position at Dennis.

After the summer season ended Fonda went to New York, confident that his experience was now sufficient to get him work in the theatre. He found there were multitudes like himself and that work for actors was hard to come by. His first job came in December when he and his friend Kent Smith, a colleague in the University Players, were offered five dollars a week, plus board, to appear with the National Junior Theatre in Washington. This, his first professional engagement, carried him through until April of 1929.

Fonda next appeared in Boston to play a small comic part in *Close Up*, in a scene which also featured an 18-year-old fledgling actress named Margaret Sullavan. The play was a college production staged by one of the University Players and Sullavan later joined the group. It was also the start of a fiery romance between her and Fonda. They were together all through the Players' 1929 summer season and when he went back to New York, she followed. That winter he got his first Broadway job, doing a walk-on in *A Game of Love and Death*, which starred Claude Rains, and then went back to eking out a living until the Players' 1930 season. Sullavan was again with him and this time they were playing leads together. By this time the group was calling itself University Repertory and gaining a good reputation. In the winter of 1931–32 they did a season in Baltimore, and on Christmas morning Henry Fonda and Margaret Sullavan were married in the dining room of the Kernan Hotel.

Their friends had noted that as lovers Fonda and Sullavan quarreled continuously. As a married couple they apparently quarreled even more, and in February of 1932 they separated. She had a mercurial, temperamental nature and Fonda often said she was Scarlett O'Hara long before Margaret Mitchell invented the character. For all that, they would remain attracted to each other and would sometimes work together. At about the same time the marriage broke up, so the University Players disbanded, yet one more victim of the Depression. In their last season they had been joined by a graduate of Princeton University, James Stewart. He and Fonda would strike up a friendship for life.

Now a bachelor again, Fonda shared a small New York apartment with Stewart, Joshua Logan and Myron McCormick, all of them desperately trying to find work as actors. By the summer

With one-year-old Peter and four-year-old Jane.

Enlisting in the navy, 1942.

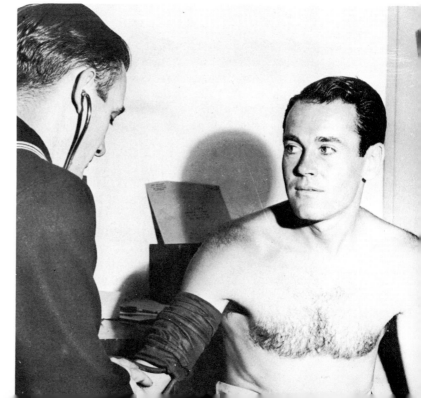

Fonda was desperate enough to accept a job as a workman at a theatre in Surrey, Maine. Fortunately, the scenic director quit half-way

Lieutenant (jg) Fonda, home on leave in 1944 with Jane.

through the season and Fonda got his job. In the autumn he returned to New York. His most conspicuous employment that winter was a season with a stock company in East Orange, New Jersey. Things picked up in the summer of 1933 when he joined the Westchester Players in Mount Kisco, New York, as a scenic designer, with occasional parts in plays. Back in New York

things got worse and by the end of the year Fonda took a job working for a florist. He was in his 29th year and with barely a dollar to his name. It was not much to write home about.

Luck smiled upon Fonda in March of 1934 when young producer Leonard Sillman chose him for a part in *New Faces*, which ran for five months and paid him 35 dollars a week, his highest salary to that point. He returned to the Mount Kisco company that summer as a full-time actor. He had also signed a contract with Leland Hayward to represent him. Hayward also represented Margaret Sullavan, whom he later married.

*Another naval lieutenant—*Mister Roberts, *on Broadway in 1948. Fonda served more time in this uniform than in his own.*

16

Fonda donned yet another naval uniform in 1954 for his Broadway hit The Caine Mutiny Court Martial, *with Lloyd Nolan and John Hodiak.*

offer Fonda, he went back to New York until such time as Wanger needed him.

Because of his having played the lead in the Mount Kisco production of *The Swan*, Fonda was considered for the lead in Max Gordon's production of Marc Connelly's play *The Farmer Takes a Wife*. June Walker had been signed for the female lead, and because her husband Geofrey Kerr was in *The Swan* she had seen the play several times and became impressed with Fonda. After they had seen him in *The Farmer Takes a Wife*, the critics and the public were also impressed. It had taken him eight rough years of struggling, but Fonda had finally broken through to success—and that success would stay with him for the rest of his life. However, this joyful experience was marred by the death of his mother, who had developed a fatal blood clot as the result of a fall. His father died the following year and so neither parent saw their son become a major success.

The Farmer Takes a Wife opened on October 30, 1934, and ran for 104 performances. The reviews were kind and Fonda felt that he had given a good account of a role he completely understood. When Fox purchased the property

With Jane in 1955, helping her make her stage debut in The Country Girl *at the Omaha Community Playhouse.*

In the Fall of that year Fonda, with a few dollars in his pocket, decided on a vacation with his family in Omaha. While there he received a telegram from Hayward informing him that it would be possible to get Fonda work in Hollywood. He replied that he was not interested; he was interested only in work as a stage actor. Hayward kept on at him until Fonda took a trip to Hollywood, with Hayward paying all the expenses. He was introduced to independent producer Walter Wanger, who liked the look of Fonda and asked him how much he wanted to sign a contract. The 35-dollar-a-week actor still had no desire to be in the movies and he thought that if he asked for an outrageous salary they would laugh at him and send him away. Fonda asked for one thousand dollars a week. To his shock, Wanger agreed and the two men shook hands. Since there was nothing immediate to for filming they followed the then-common practice of ignoring the original cast. It was bought for Janet Gaynor, and Fox hoped to get Gary Cooper to play opposite her. When he was not available they tried Joel McCrea, who also had other commitments. Walter Wanger, who had Fonda under contract, then sold Fox the idea of using the actor who had made such an impression in New York. They agreed and Fonda left

talent to studios, most independent producers made hard deals for themselves and kept most of the profit. From the start Wanger told Fonda that whatever he received for his services he would divide with the actor. On these generous terms Fonda was able to receive three thousand dollars a week while making *A Farmer Takes a Wife*, a considerable salary for any Hollywood figure in 1935.

In 1955 Fonda made his first major television appearance playing Emmett Kelly in Clown, *with whom he here poses.*

In 1955 Fonda also appeared with Humphrey Bogart and Lauren Bacall in the television version of The Petrified Forest.

early in February of 1935 to make the trip to Hollywood that would change his life.

Fonda had not been especially lucky in the first 29 years of his life. Now he became very lucky indeed—an instant movie star, with no period of striving, and fortunate in being under contract to a man like Walter Wanger, who seldom leaned on him to take roles he hated and who behaved decently in regard to money. In loaning their

Fonda quickly learned the price of success in Hollywood. His original idea of dividing his time between the stage and the screen was put aside as Wanger arranged for him to go from one movie to another. Wanger may have been generous with money but he knew the film business and the need to keep a new young star on a steady swing. It was not until his fourth film that Fonda actually worked for Wanger, with the popular *The Trail of the Lonesome Pine*. Wanger then had the idea of uniting Fonda with his former wife Margaret Sullavan in the comedy *The Moon's Our Home*, a device that not only worked with the public but rekindled the pair's feelings about each other. But her temperament was still volatile and the flames subsided.

Fonda's personal life was about to take another direction, one which would have great bearing.

took off on a European tour together. On September 16, 1936, they were married in New York in a high society wedding, with Josh Logan as best man. Fonda, the boy from Omaha, found himself decked out in swallow-tail coat, striped trousers and silk top hat.

Had he chosen to do so, Fonda at this point could have retired from acting and gone into some other business. His bride had acquired a

Fonda's first television series, The Deputy, *in 1959, with Allen Case in the title role.*

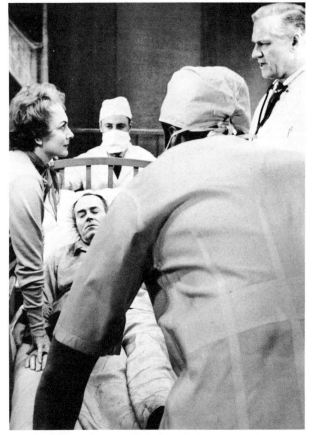

With Olivia de Havilland and Rufus Smith in A Gift of Time, *on Broadway in 1962.*

In the summer of 1936 he happily accepted an offer to appear in the first British Technicolor film, *Wings of the Morning*, which gave him his first trip overseas. While filming in the Denham Studios near London, a party of upper-crust American tourists visited the set to take a look at picture making. One of them was the beautiful young divorcée Frances Seymour Brokaw. After completing his work on the film he and Frances

considerable sum from her previous husband and she was familiar with the world of stocks, bonds and investments. Because of this Fonda allowed her to take over the management of his own financial affairs, which she handled very well. She had very little interest in matters theatrical but she had to adapt to the fact that her new husband was not only an actor but a workaholic actor. Within days after the wedding the pair

With Eddie Hodges and Mildred Natwick in Critics Choice, *on Broadway in 1960.*

flew to California, where Fonda began work on his first important film, Fritz Lang's *You Only Live Once.*

After two years of movies Fonda's urge to get back into the theatre caused him to ignore the advice of his agents and go back to Mount Kisco in the summer of 1937 to appear in *The Virginian.* Since he was not under contract to a studio, as were most leading men at the time, and since Walter Wanger was more understanding than most producers, Fonda was able to follow the Mount Kisco engagement with a Broadway appearance in *Blow Ye Winds,* which ran five weeks. Frances was now pregnant and she stayed in New York to have her child while Fonda returned to Hollywood. In making *Jezebel* at Warners he specified in his contract that he would have to leave by the middle of December in order to be with his wife. Despite the film's runnng over schedule, Fonda left when he wished and was with Frances when she gave birth to Jane on December 21.

Fonda's hope of doing plays as well as films was now shelved for a period of 11 years. His success in films made it hard for him to decline the continual offers, and since he was now a family man he bought property and settled down. He purchased a house in Brentwood, a district just beyond Beverly Hills in the direction of the ocean. In 1937 it was still fairly rural and Fonda enjoyed the fact that he now owned eight acres of land, which he cultivated for farming. Whatever frustration he felt in making films he could now work out in his land.

Fonda was clear of his commitment with Walter Wanger by 1938 and free to make his own selection of jobs. His career took a turn for the better when John Ford persuaded him to play *Young Mr. Lincoln,* a role that at first scared Fonda because he considered Lincoln almost sacrosanct. It was the start of a profitable association with the great Ford, who considered Fonda an exceptional actor. When Ford was signed by 20th Century-Fox to make *The Grapes of Wrath,* he knew precisely the actor he wanted for Tom Joad. The gruff, irascible Ford got his way. But Fonda paid a price for the celebrated role. Darryl F. Zanuck, in need of male stars for his roster, coerced Fonda into signing a long-term contract. No contract, no Joad. Fonda signed, and spent years cursing the fact that he did. He thereafter appeared in a number of Fox movies which he later claimed to loathe. On the other hand, none of them seemed to hurt his growing popularity, and Zanuck was wise enough to loan him to other studios for first rate films like *The Lady Eve* and *The Male Animal.*

The Grapes of Wrath helped forge Fonda's image as a quintessential American figure—the uncommon common man, who seemed to symbolize the decency and integrity with which Americans ideally saw themselves. The image fit Fonda as well off-screen as on. He was not a social sophisticate. He preferred to spend his spare time tilling his land and growing crops. Years later, Jane said that as a child she never knew her father was an actor and always assumed he was a farmer. On February 23, 1940, Fonda became a father for the second time when Peter was born. He was born in New York because the birth was by cesarean and Frances was always tended by the same surgeon. She had had a daughter by her first marriage and all the children were born by cesarean. There were complications this time and her recovery was slow. Not long after her return to California, Fonda bought nine acres in Bel Air and built a new home, called Tigertail. It allowed him even greater play as a farmer.

The war brought a great change in Fonda's life, although it was a change created of his own volition. In August of 1942 he joined the U.S.

Navy. As a 37-year-old family man he would not have been called to duty. He chose to go because he did not like the idea of spending the war years making movies that would doubtless present him as a cardboard hero. Whatever his reasons, Fonda joined up as an ordinary seaman and trained at

In his first movie made for television, Stranger on the Run, *in 1967.*

With bride Shirlee on December 3, 1965.

the naval base in San Diego. As a quartermaster third class he was assigned to the destroyer *Satterlee,* with later duties as a signalman. After about a year of this he was ordered to report for officer training.

After receiving his stripes as a junior grade lieutenant, Fonda was ordered to Washington, where the Navy wanted to use him in the pro-

duction of training films. His complaints fell on a few sympathetic ears and he was assigned to the naval air station at Quonset, Rhode Island, where he learned to be an air combat intelligence officer. As such Fonda spent the final year and a half of the war in the South Pacific, on the staff of Admiral John Koover. He was awarded a Bronze Star and at the time of his discharge in October of 1945 was a full lieutenant.

Returning to civilian life was problematical for Fonda, as for many ex-service men. He was not enthusiastic about returning to films, feeling that the three years away had weakened his image. However, he was still under contract to Zanuck and had no choice but to return. He was fortunate with his first postwar picture. John Ford still had one more contractual obligation to Zanuck and chose to make a western, *My Darling Clementine,* for which he wanted Fonda as Wyatt Earp. It could hardly have been a better way for a star to reappear before the public. But Fonda was much less lucky with the films that followed. The only pleasure he found in

21

Hollywood by 1947 was that his contract with Zanuck had run its course. Now desperate to get back to the stage, he went to New York in the summer of that year to look for a play.

A large part of Fonda's discontent at this point in his life was due to the decline in his marriage. Frances had taken a long time to recover from her third cesarean operation and afterwards became obsessively interested in her business affairs, while at the same time becoming an overly protective mother. There were also increasing signs of hypochondria, which in time developed into forms of mental illness.

Fonda's professional life took an enormous turn for the better when he landed the play *Mister Roberts*. With the help of Joshua Logan, Tom Heggen adapted his novel into a stage play and both he and Logan had Fonda in mind for the lead. The play opened in Philadelphia to glowing reviews on December 26, 1947, and then settled into the Alvin Theatre in New York for a long run. Fonda sent for his family and rented a house in Greenwich, Connecticut. His Californian children found the change of lifestyle a jolt, and this accented the strain upon their mother.

The joy of being praised for his work in a smash hit play contrasted with the gloom on the homefront. Frances became more erratic and she was placed in a rest home for several months.

With John Beal and Mildred Natwick in the Plumstead Playhouse production of Our Town *in 1968.*

Soon after release she asked to be committed to the Craig House Sanitarium in Beacon, New York. On April 14, 1950, her 42nd birthday, she committed suicide by slashing her throat. By this time Fonda had been spending most of his time in New York, where he kept an apartment. On the evening of his wife's death he went on and gave his usual flawless performance as Roberts. He claimed that it was the only way of saving his own sanity at that point.

Fonda's third wife was Susan Blanchard, some 20 years his junior. She was the daughter of Dorothy Hammerstein, the wife of lyricist-

Henry Fonda — painter.

playwright Oscar, but a child by a previous marriage. She and Fonda were married on December 28, 1950. *Mister Roberts* continued to delight the theatregoers and when it closed on Broadway, Fonda went on a tour of all the major American cities with it. He claimed he played the role almost 1700 times and never tired of it. With no interest in returning to Hollywood, he then accepted the lead in John P. Marquand's play *Point of No Return*, which opened in December of 1951 and ran for two years. He followed that

in their views about making the film. Fonda felt the material should be left as it was but Ford believed the play should be opened up for the screen and with greater accent on comedy. The two men came to blows in their dispute. Shortly afterwards Ford was taken ill with a gall bladder condition. *Mister Roberts* did well with the public but Fonda regretted that it was never the film it should have been.

Henry Fonda broadened his horizons in 1955 by resolving to do television as well as stage and film. He had often vowed to maintain a balance between the theatre and the movies, and now he was in a position to do so; this he did for the rest of his life. In March of 1955 he played Emmett Kelly in the half-hour TV production of *The Clown*. He had long wanted to play Kelly and to this end he had bought the rights to his autobiography. In May he appeared with Humphrey Bogart and Lauren Bacall in a live television production of *The Petrified Forest*, with Bogart reprising the role of Duke Mantee, with which he had come to fame 20 years previously. Fonda then went back to Omaha to make a joyous return to the Playhouse where he had started, to appear in Odets' *The Country Girl*, with Dorothy McGuire, who had also started her career at the Playhouse, and with Jane Fonda making her theatrical debut. Immediately after that Fonda accepted an offer from Dino De Laurentiis to go to Rome and play Pierre in a mammoth production of *War and Peace*.

Rome proved to be another turning point in Henry Fonda's life. Due to the long production schedule of *War and Peace*, he sent for his children, which proved to be another cultural shock for them, and a boring one. This in turn placed a strain upon another marriage that was heading downhill. Susan enjoyed the social life offered by the international set in Rome; Fonda did not. She left and a year later obtained her divorce. Years later she told biographer Howard Teichman, "I think there's a scream inside Hank that's never been screamed, and there's a laugh that's never been laughed." However, in spite of his distaste for the social set, it was in Rome that Fonda fell in love with a 24-year-old member of that set, Afdera Franchetti, the daughter of a Venetian baron.

When Fonda returned to New York to make Alfred Hitchcock's *The Wrong Man*, he courted Afdera by telephone and by mail. She spent Christmas of 1955 with him and came again the following summer when Fonda had rented a house at Cape Cod, which pleased his children.

with *The Caine Mutiny Court Martial*, which took up another year of his life. On the personal side of the ledger Fonda had been enjoying his time with his wife, who won the affections of Peter and Jane. In November of 1953 they adopted a daughter, whom they called Amy and whom Fonda always referred to as "the white sheep of the family."

After seven years of success and constant praise as a stage actor, Fonda looked with doubt upon the resumption of his film career. Things had changed greatly in the movie business and now a 50-year-old he doubted if his name still had any box office value. He was about to be proven very wrong. *Mister Roberts* was bought by Warners for filming and John Ford was hired to direct it. Warners did not want Fonda, despite his obvious association with the part. Ford, on the other hand, refused to budge until he got Fonda. This reunion should have become a happy chapter in both their lives, but unfortunately they differed

Jane now decided to join the Cape Theatre at Dennis, which prompted Fonda to accept their offer to star in *The Male Animal* and repeat the role of Tommy Turner, which had been a hit for him in the 1942 film. Jane played Patricia, and the pairing of the Fondas gave the theatre a definite boost in prestige. At the same time Fonda and Afdera decided upon marriage, with the ceremony taking place in New York in March of 1957.

Fonda's next stage play was *Two for the Seesaw*, which brought him good reviews from the New York critics but which he himself did not like very much, feeling that playwright William Gibson had come up with a part that was less than promised. He was much happier with his next play, *Silent Night, Lonely Night*, with Barbara Bel Geddes, which opened at the Morosco on December 3, 1959. This story of a nice but unhappily married man seemed to fit in with his own situation. Since marrying Afdera there had been numerous travels between Europe, New York and Hollywood, none of which helped close the taste gap between the couple. A few months after the opening of *Silent Night, Lonely Night* they were divorced and Afdera returned to her Roman social life. It was the least probable of all the Fonda marriages.

In 1959 Fonda's agents persuaded him to do a television series, *The Deputy*. He agreed when they sold NBC the idea of Fonda being the narrator-host for the series, with occasional

With Darlene Carr, Janet Blair, Michael James Wixted and Ronny Howard on the TV series The Smith Family.

appearances as the star. This allowed him time to travel and engage in other projects at the same time. Allen Case played the title role, with Fonda as a town marshall in the Arizona of the 1880's. The series started in September and was renewed for a second and final year. NBC claimed they would have done better had Fonda been the star of each episode but he was not about to tie himself down to a series. He preferred to do what he thought were interesting films, with an eye ever peeled for good plays. In December of 1960 he did the comedy *Critic's Choice* on Broadway and enjoyed himself.

Fonda appeared in 20 films during the 1960's, more than most stars of his vintage. Whenever possible he returned to the stage and occasionally appeared on television if he was interested. In February of 1962 he starred on Broadway in *The Gift of Time*, as a man dying of cancer and trying to persuade his wife (Olivia de Havilland) to give him the means to enable him to commit suicide. The play was so harrowing that audiences were too shaken to applaud at the closing curtain, and it closed after ten valiant weeks of trying to keep it afloat. He was much luckier two years later with the comedy *Generation*, which poked fun at the contemporary generation gap and which drew some comment because of the apparent gap between Fonda and his own children, Jane and Peter, both of whom were now actors themselves and getting a little newspaper coverage because of their off-screen lives. In 1968 Fonda indulged himself as an actor by appearing with the Plumstead Playhouse in their revival of Wilder's *Our Town*. He played the Stage Manager and the critical concensus was that no actor was more suited to the part. He also did a small role in their *The Front Page*, following which he went back to Hollywood to earn more of the money that enabled him to do things like his stint with the Plumstead Playhouse.

In 1960 Fonda had met airline stewardess Shirlee Mae Adams and dated her steadily thereafter. His pronouncements about no more marriage went by the board on December 3, 1965, and for the rest of his life Fonda never stopped telling people that this was the girl he should have been married to all along. He had finally found the right one, someone who knew how to manage his moods and silences, and who thoroughly understood him. Shirlee was the balance wheel, and with time she helped Fonda find a more expressedly loving relationship with his children.

In 1967 Fonda made his first film directly for

television, *Stranger on the Run*, directed by Don Siegel, with Fonda as a drunken derelict who gets thrown out of a western town and hunted down by a posse for sport. The reviews were good and it encouraged him to spend more time with the medium. The following year he signed to do a series of commercials for GAF and obviously earned a lot of money. He thus became one of the first major Hollywood names to appear as a commercial spokesman, and since it seemed to do his image no harm at all, other celebrities followed in his wake.

Fonda took another crack at a TV series in 1971 with *The Smith Family*, which presented him as a 25-year veteran of the Los Angeles Police Department, balancing his dangerous work

With Larry Hagman in the 1973 telefilm
The Alpha Caper.

With Maureen O'Hara in the 1973 telefilm The Red Pony.

retaliates by becoming a master criminal. It was considered good enough to release as a theatrical feature outside the United States, retitled *The Inside Job.* There were also cameo roles in two successful TV productions, both limited series, *Roots: The Next Generation* and *The Captains and the Kings.* Much more important than his work in either of those superior soap operas was his portrayal of General Douglas A. MacArthur in *Collision Course,* for ABC Theatre (January 4, 1976), which pitted him against the Harry S. Truman of E. G. Marshall. It was an impressive restaging of an historical battle of wits, with Fonda coolly transmitting MacArthur's imperious manner and his disdain for the civilian mind.

The customary retirement age of 65 meant less than nothing to Henry Fonda. For him it occurred in 1970 and all it seemed to do was act as a challenge. His final decade would be full of activities. In that year he toured with a one-man

As Clarence Darrow.

against a normal home life with a wife and three children. It did only moderately well in the ratings and staggered to a close at the end of its second season. Much more to his credit was the TV version of John Steinbeck's *The Red Pony* in 1973, co-starring Maureen O'Hara as the wife and Clint Howard as son Jody, a boy who finds more rapport with his pony than with his gruff father. Again a few critics pointed out that there seemed to be some parallel between fiction and fact as Fonda's embarrassments with his own children drew headlines. It was in these years that Fonda was perplexed by Jane's political activism and with Peter's publicized bouts with narcotics.

Fonda's films in the Seventies seldom drew much box office business, although critics constantly pointed out the quality of his work in films which did not merit his involvement. As the decade progressed he did more and more cameo roles, clearly good pieces of business arranged by his agents. His television films were more impressive. In 1973 he appeared in *The Alpha Caper,* as a parole officer who becomes embittered when forced into retirement and who show he called *Fathers Against Sons Against,* reading passages from authors as disparate as Shakespeare and Bob Dylan. It all touched upon the generation gap and Fonda quipped that he was an authority. The following year he directed *The Caine Mutiny Court Martial* in Los Angeles and the year after that he went on a national tour of Saroyan's play *The Time of Your Life.* But the real triumph for Fonda in the early Seventies was his performance as Clarence Darrow.

David W. Rintels had written a one-man play about the career of the famous lawyer, illustrating it with material from some of his trials. Fonda received a copy of the script through his agents and had decided to accept it even before he got to the end. It was too long, but by working with the author and director John Houseman, they were able to bring it down to a workable two hours. The play opened on Broadway on March 24, 1974, and the reception from the critics and the public was one of total approval. *The New*

With Cloris Leachman in the televised version of the play The Oldest Living Graduate.

With E. G. Marshall in the 1976 telefilm Collision Course.

York Times reviewer said, "If Darrow was not like this, he should have been." Apart from his performance, which seemed to bring the folksy-liberal, shambling lawyer back to life, people were amazed that Fonda could memorize two hours of dialogue. Those who knew him were not amazed. It was well known among his colleagues that Fonda had an incredible memory; he could commit pages to memory with just a few readings. Now, just short of his 69th birthday, he showed he had lost none of that facility.

Clarence Darrow was televised in September of 1974, but by that time there had been an important change in Fonda's life. Four weeks after playing Darrow on Broadway, he collapsed with exhaustion. Examinations proved fibrillations of the heart and a pacemaker was installed. Previously Fonda had been a healthy man who always looked younger than his years. Now things changed—but only physically. He was as stubborn and determined as ever. As soon as he felt well enough he took *Darrow* to Los Angeles and performed it there with equal success.

Aside from his films and his television plays, Fonda was always available for work as a narrator, and he did many such jobs. He also appeared at benefits within the industry and seldom refused to do promotional TV spots for worthy art endeavors for the likes of PBS and educational film makers. When asked why he worked so constantly he admitted that he had a fear of failure, that people would stop asking for him. "No matter how many calls I get, it's still there. Sounds ridiculous, but that's why I sometimes take jobs I probably should pass by. But maybe fears aren't all bad. Mine never let me down. I'm still that new kid, fighting his way on up, proving himself."

In 1976 Fonda submitted to what he considered another indignity of the aging process and finally agreed, after much urging by his wife, to wearing a hearing aid. Neither this nor the pacemaker had any affect on medical advice that he retire from work. Not long after the installing of the hearing aid Fonda went on location for six weeks in northern California to make what would be his last movie with top billing, *The Great Smokey Roadblock.* It required him to play the role of a feisty old truck driver who knows his days are numbered but who nevertheless is determined to make one glorious last drive. In Fonda's case it was art imitating life. He became increasingly angry about his physical frailty but utilized that anger on the stage and screen in his remaining roles. He now became a kind of animated spokesman for the rights of the frail and the infirm.

Fonda spent much of his time in his last years at home, tending to his garden, keeping bees, doing needlepoint and painting. His talent as a painter was considerable and several of his works now hang in art galleries, as well as in the homes of friends. He accepted cameo roles in films but always kept his eye open for plays. A good one came his way in December of 1977 with *First Monday in October* by Robert E. Lee and Jerome Lawrence. It offered him the role of a crusty old Supreme Court judge, who at first opposes a woman being appointed to the court but gradually becomes her ally. The play opened in Washington and Fonda relished the part, as did the audience and the critics.

First Monday in October ran six weeks, precisely the length of time Fonda's doctors had allowed. It could have run longer but the company shut down and sent the actor home. A few months later he went to Canada to make the television film *Home to Stay,* yet another booster for the aged. Directed by Delbert Mann, it told the story of a grandfather who runs away from home with his supportive granddaughter rather than submit to being placed in an old folks' home by his family. They are chased across the country and caught, but the old boy at least surrenders on better terms.

Feeling stronger by the summer of 1978, Fonda told the producers of *First Monday in October* he was ready to play the part again. After several weeks with the Los Angeles presentation he took a rest and then went to Broadway for a three-month run. The company afterwards went to Chicago for what Fonda hoped would be another long run but his health let him down after a few

As Clarence Earl Gideon in the 1979 teleplay Gideon's Trumpet.

weeks. He injured his left hip and in being hospitalized for that it was also discovered that he had a cancerous tumor. The doctors were able to arrest this condition and by the end of April, 1979, Fonda was back in his hilltop home in Bel Air. In December of that year he was a recipient of the Kennedy Center Honors and he was reduced to tears when a chorus of naval midshipmen ended their serenade by saluting him and saying "Thank you, Mr. Roberts."

Fonda struck a couple of more blows for the dignity of the elderly with the telefilm *Gideon's Trumpet* and the play *The Oldest Living Graduate*. The former was a Hallmark Hall of Fame production which told the story of Clarence Earl Gideon, a Florida handyman who was convicted of petty larceny in 1961. Denied free legal representation at his trial, he defended himself and lost, and was sentenced to five years. In jail he constantly petitioned the U.S. Supreme Court, claiming his rights had been violated. His eventual courtroom victory resulted in a landmark decision in America jurisprudence, and another landmark performance by Fonda as the common man pitted against the system. Before *Gideon's Trumpet* was broadcast, Fonda went to Dallas to appear in a live televising of his performance as the cantankerous, invalided Colonel Kinkaid in *The Oldest Living Graduate*. This was staged at Southern Methodist University and the telecast received such approval that Fonda was asked to do the role again for a limited run at the Wilshire Theatre in Los Angeles.

The 75-year-old Fonda grudgingly obeyed his doctors' advice regarding his health—more importantly, his wife saw to it that he did—but there was no stopping his desire to keep working. Once he had read the script of *On Golden Pond* it instantly became a project that he *had* to do. And so in the summer of 1980 he went to New Hampshire to make what proved to be his last movie. But it was not his last work. Right after completing the film he did a 60-minute teleplay called *Summer Solstice*, co-starring Myrna Loy, and dealing with a couple reviewing the 50 years of their marriage.

The year 1981 started off well for Fonda. On the evening of January 10, the marquee of the Omaha Community Playhouse read, "Welcome Home, Mr. Fonda." He had been back many times through the years but this would be the last and most joyous time. The 500 seats had been sold at 50 dollars each in order to raise funds for the house, and there was no cause to which Fonda was more emotionally attached. This is where it had all started for him 55 years ago. And

With Myrna Loy in the teleplay Summer Solstice.

it was also the stage where Jane and Peter had made their debuts. Before the evening was through Fonda had called Peter's 13-year-old son Justin on stage, so that he could proudly tell the audience that a third-generation Fonda was also making a debut. Fonda's long-time friend and business associate John Springer arranged a program of film and television clips, encompassing all of the actor's most famous roles, and ranging from home movies made when he was with the University Players at Cape Cod in 1932 right up to the Kennedy Center tribute. The ovation given him when he then walked out onto the stage of the Omaha Community Playhouse was, as expected, deafening. Afterwards he answered questions from the audience and reminisced with them about his life and career and the many people he had known. He told them, "I really feel that I was a lucky boy to have grown up in Omaha."

If Fonda had chosen to conclude his career with that evening in Omaha he could hardly have picked a more glowing occasion. But he still wanted to work. Even before he went to Omaha he had started rehearsals on a play titled *Showdown at the Adobe Motel* by Lanny Flaherty at the Hartman Theatre in Stamford, Connecticut. He opened there on February 8 and amazed the audience not only with his perform- ance but with the fact that the role required him to be on stage for almost the entire play. The role was that of Clyde Lee, an old former rodeo star who meets up with a pal (Art Lund) after not having seen him for 30 years, and talks about the old days. The critical concensus was the same one that Fonda had received for every play and every film—that he seemed to be the character he was playing. To Fonda that was the ultimate tribute. He never went before the cameras or the footlights as himself.

In Omaha Fonda had been asked many times about his health and he replied to every query that he was in better shape than the newspaper accounts may have led people to believe. This may have accurately reflected his feelings at the time but sadly, after the performance in Stam- ford, there was a decline. When the public next saw him it was on the evening of March 31, at the Academy Awards, when Robert Redford pre- sented him with a Lifetime Achievement Oscar. When Fonda slowly walked to the podium with the aid of a cane he was obviously frail, and he lacked the gusto he had shown only a few months previously in Omaha.

"As an actor he is the definition of dedication and professionalism," said Redford in introduc- ing a montage of celebrated Fonda film clips, a montage which ended with a scene from the as- yet unreleased *On Golden Pond.* The lights went up and there stood the man who had played Tom Joad, young Abe Lincoln, Wyatt Earp, Mr. Roberts, and all kinds of Americans from farmers and cowboys to admirals and presidents. Perhaps it occurred to those who stood in ovation that they were seeing the last appearance of an actor who was a symbol of his country, an image of common American integrity.

After thanking Redford, Fonda said, "When I realized—and I really have to remind myself— that I've been working in films for 46 years, I feel I'm a very, very lucky man; not just because I survived but because, over the years, I've had the opportunity to work with some of the best directors, best producers, best writers, best actors in motion pictures. It's been a very rewarding 46 years for me and this has got to be the climax." It was, however, not quite the climax. That would come exactly one year later when the members of the Academy voted him an Oscar as Best Actor for *On Golden Pond.* Unfortunately, by then, Fonda was far too weak to attend. He sat at home and watched, and possibly took a little satisfaction in knowing that he had achieved

As Norman Thayer in On Golden Pond, *the role which finally brought him his Oscar.*

something few veteran actors ever achieve—to end a career at the top of the business, to end with a performance that was a victorious valedictory.

In the last year and a half of Fonda's life he fought to stay alive. He was hospitalized a half- dozen times during that period and another pacemaker was installed to give greater aid to his heart. He resented the way his body was let- ting him down and as a symbol of defiance he grew a beard, claiming that he would not shave it off until he got better. There was no deteriora- tion of his mind. He enjoyed the company of his visitors and he welcomed talk about future work projects. Since he was too weak to travel he de- cided to do a television project in his home—a one-man show as Walt Whitman. To this end he studied the writings of Whitman, made his selections and rehearsed himself. Sadly it was a project that would never be.

On Sunday, August 8, 1982, Fonda was taken to Cedars-Sinai Medical Center in Los Angeles. He was no longer responding to medication and his heart had weakened to the point where nothing further could be done. Fonda died at 8:15 on the morning of the following Thursday. His wife Shirlee was with him at the time and she reported that it was a quiet and peaceful ending.

Receiving the special Oscar in 1981 from Robert Redford. Photo: Academy of Motion Picture Arts and Sciences.

He had been able to talk through most of the time in the hospital and his final night was without pain and restful. In the morning he woke up, sat up in bed and then just stopped breathing. Jane and Peter were called and arrived shortly thereafter.

Fonda had specified in his will that there was to be no funeral. He said he did not like funerals and did not want one. His wishes were observed to the letter. His body was cremated a few hours after he died and his eyes, at his request, were donated to the Manhattan Eye Institute. The family asked that in lieu of flowers, contributions be made to the Henry Fonda Theater Center at the Omaha Community Playhouse.

None of the many tributes paid Fonda after his death could sum him up better than he did himself. "I'm an actor. I guess if you really want a little honest self-definition, it all comes back to that. I'm an actor. Never claimed to be anything else." In his honesty he admitted that he was not greatly impressed with himself as a man and that he was not as nice as Mr. Roberts, even though that strong image tended to lead people to think so. He once said, "I've never been through psychoanalysis but maybe I should have. You become an actor maybe because there are these complexes about you that aren't average or normal, and these aren't the easiest things to live with. You can be easily upset, or short-tempered, or lack patience . . . but if I can project a certain kind of person—something in the eyes, a kind of honesty in the face—then I guess you could say that's the kind of man I'd like to be, the man I always wanted to be. . . ."

Despite what he may have said about himself, Fonda was liked and respected by all who worked with him. He invariably behaved well. He was patient and helpful with his co-workers, he never *lorded* it over them or pulled rank. It was typical of Fonda that when he was making *Gideon's Trumpet* he lined up with everybody else at the meal breaks and refused attempts to push him to the head of the line. "No," he said, "I'll take my turn." It is difficult to think of many other stars of his magnitude who behaved as modestly as Fonda. In his later years he was the subject of salutes and tributes and the recipient of important awards, but it never seemed to alter his modesty.

Henry Fonda would probably have been embarrassed to hear himself referred to as *unique*. But if a man cannot be replaced, then there is no more appropriate word to describe him.

THE FILMS OF
HENRY FONDA

☆☆☆☆☆☆☆☆☆☆☆☆☆☆

THE FARMER TAKES A WIFE

1935

A Fox Film, produced by Winfield Sheehan, directed by Victor Fleming, written by Edwin Burke, based on the stage play by Frank B. Elser and Marc Connelly, and the novel *Rome Haul* by Walter D. Edmunds, photographed by Ernest Palmer, music by Oscar Bradley, 94 minutes.

CAST:

Molly Larkins, *Janet Gaynor;* Dan Harrow, *Henry Fonda;* Jotham Klore, *Charles Bickford;* Fortune Friendly, *Slim Summerville;* Elmer Otway, *Andy Devine;* Sam Weaver, *Roger Imhof;* Delia, *Jane Withers;* Lucy Gurget, *Margaret Hamilton.*

36

With Janet Gaynor

Henry Fonda's movie career started off with a great advantage—with a film version of a play in which he had recently starred on Broadway. He therefore knew his characterization thoroughly, which is an enormous help for an actor beginning in another medium. It also meant that Fonda could start in Hollywood as a leading player and not as a struggling actor going from bit part to bit part, ever in hope of a lucky break. Be that as it may, it was still luck that started Fonda in Hollywood. He was not, as most people assumed, brought from Hollywood to appear in *The Farmer Takes a Wife*. The Fox studio wanted Gary Cooper for the role of Dan Harrow and when they could not get him they went after Joel McCrea, who was also not available. It was Walter Wanger, who had Fonda under contract, who suggested to producer Winfield Sheehan that the man who played the part on Broadway would be a logical choice. After meeting Fonda, Sheehan agreed. It was rare in 1935 for an unknown to be cast as a lead but Sheehan, who had been with Fox since 1912, had a reputation for being right in his decisions. And he certainly was in this one.

The Farmer Takes a Wife is set in New York State in 1850, when the Erie Canal was the most important transportation route through that area. The railroad would in time render the canal of diminishing value and it was already becoming a rival force. Conflict also came from the farmers along the canal who considered its workers roughnecks and its boating population somewhat gypsy in its lifestyle. The film tells about a pretty young girl named Molly Larkin (Gaynor), who is the cook on the boat of tough, pugnacious Jotham Klore (Charles Bickford). She shares the view that farmers are weak, dull folks but she falls in love with young Dan Harrow (Fonda), a farm boy who has taken a job as a canal driver in order to save up money for a farm. Molly gets mad at the drunken Klore and leaves his boat, and goes to work for Dan, who has won an interest in a boat in a lottery. Their love grows with time but they refrain from talking about the future because each knows how the other feels about farm life and canal life. Klore is still sore at Dan for taking Molly away from him and after Klore and a band of his roughneck canal men beat up a group of railroaders, he sets after Dan, who runs away.

Eventually Dan gets his farm but Molly has been disillusioned by his apparent cowardice and stays away from him. A friend tells Dan that Molly is subject to ridicule in town because her

man ran away from Klore. Dan then goes to town and as a band of excited citizens stand around he challenges Klore. The long fist fight ends with the astonished Klore conceding defeat and telling Dan he lost to a real man. Later, as Dan tills

his fields, Molly comes running over the furrows and asks him the way to the kitchen. The farmer has won himself a wife.

The plot is simple and the film is leisurely paced but it has charm and recalls a particular chapter in American folk history. By 1935 Janet Gaynor's long popularity as a Fox star was beginning to wane but *The Farmer Takes a Wife* gave her career a lift. Both the critics and the public found the movie pleasing and the reaction to Fonda was favorable in all quarters. Many critics

With Charles Bickford and Janet Gaynor.

remarked on Fonda's quiet charm and unusual screen presence, pointing out that he somehow combined simplicity with strength. Eileen Creelman in *The New York Sun* put her finger on his mystique, "One of Mr. Fonda's most outstanding assets is his appearance of sincerity." That appearance would be a dominant factor in Fonda's career in the movies. No matter the part, from simple farm worker to Admiral of the Fleet, he always appeared believable. The farm worker and the admiral may have looked and sounded like Fonda but they were entirely believable—and being believable is what acting is all about.

The Farmer Takes a Wife was a fine first film and launched Fonda on a screen career that would span 46 years. He received star billing in this his first film and he received star billing in his final film, *On Golden Pond* in 1981. An incredible record of success. And it was all done with apparent ease. He never let the study and effort show. He made the transition from the stage to the screen fairly quickly, but Fonda always admitted that he learned one essential, basic lesson from director Victor Fleming while making *The Farmer Takes a Wife.* "I had been playing it as I did on the stage—*projecting* to the audience. After the first day, Fleming took me aside. 'Hank,' he told me, 'you're hamming.' Well, that was a dirty word to me. He made me see the difference between playing to an audience and playing for the camera."

WAY DOWN EAST

1935
A Fox Film, produced by Winfield Sheehan, directed by Henry King, written by Howard Estabrook and William Hurlbut, based on the play by Lottie Blair Parker, photographed by Ernest Palmer, music by Oscar Bradley, 85 minutes.

CAST:
Anna Moore, *Rochelle Hudson;* David Bartlett, *Henry Fonda;* Constable Seth Holcomb, *Slim Summerville;* Lennox Sanderson, *Edward Trevor;* Martha Perkins, *Margaret Hamilton;* Hi Holler, *Andy Devine;* Squire Bartlett, *Russell Simpson;* Mrs. Bartlett, *Spring Byington;* Kate, *Astrid Allwyn;* Cordelia Peabody, *Sara Haden;* Hank Woodwine, *Al Lydell;* Mr. Peabody, *Harry C. Bradley;* Doc Wiggin, *Clem Bevans;* Mrs. Poole, *Vera Lewis.*

Way Down East (1920) is one of the classic American silent films, produced by D. W. Griffith and starring Lillian Gish, especially remembered for its scenes on a frozen river in which the poor, long suffering heroine is trapped on the shifting ice floes. With Gish as the wistful girl subjected to a lot of hardships, it was fairly dated material even in 1920 but the magic of Griffith and Gish made it compelling. In 1935 the Fox studio, looking for a follow-up to the success of *The Farmer Takes a Wife,* decided to remake *Way Down East* as a similarly bucolic picture for Janet Gaynor and Henry Fonda. Unfortunately, Gaynor was involved in a traffic accident just as the film was going into production and, rather than halt the project, they decided to proceed, with Rochelle Hudson as a replacement. Hudson was a lovely girl but a limited actress and the film suffered as a result. However, her role was of such melodramatic tissue that it

would have leaned heavily upon even a major talent.

The story is set in New England in the early years of the century and deals with a young girl,

With Rochelle Hudson.

Anna Moore (Hudson), who is taken advantage of by a wealthy cad, Lennox Sanderson (Edward Trevor). Their marriage ceremony turns out to be false and her baby dies shortly after it is born. Penniless, she heads for the farm of a lady who was a friend of her mother. The lady (Spring By-

With Clem Bevans, Margaret Hamilton,
Spring Byington, Astrid Allwyn, Russell Simpson
and (in bed) Rochelle Hudson.

the critics enjoyed themselves pointing out the ludicrous plotlines. Some allowed that the production values were good, giving a good account of New England farmlife of the period, and most singled out for praise the performance of the young Margaret Hamilton as the venomous gossip. Henry Fonda came off well as the genial farmboy, especially in the review in *The New York Times* by Andre Senwald: ". . .this is a personal triumph for Henry Fonda, whose immensely winning performance as the Squire's son helps

With Astrid Allwyn, Russell Simpson and
Spring Byington.

ington) is kindly and talks her stern, puritanical husband, Squire Bartlett (Russell Simpson), into hiring her. The son of the family, David (Fonda), is soon smitten with the pretty girl but she is cautious about returning his affections. She comes under the suspicious eye of the local gossip, Martha Perkins (Margaret Hamilton), who ferrets around until she digs up the story. It turns out that Lennox Sanderson is also a friend of the Bartletts and when he arrives at their farm for a visit he and Anna agree to be silent about their relationship. But one evening Martha maliciously spills the beans to the family. The Squire is horrified and tells Anna she is fired. He also orders Lennox out of his house. While the family are arguing Anna slips out of the house and makes her way through a snow storm. In trying to cross a river she is suddenly in danger when the ice breaks up and heads for a waterfall. David arrives in time to save her, and later asks her to be his bride. By now even the hard-hearted Squire approves of her and decides to build a new wing to the farmhouse.

This hokum was hard to swallow in 1935 and

to establish an engaging bucolic mood for the drama in its quieter moments." The best that can be said for this version of *Way Down East* is that it did Fonda no harm. It might even have helped. If he could perform credibly in a picture like this, he could perform in anything.

☆☆☆☆☆☆☆☆☆☆☆

I DREAM TOO MUCH

1935

An RKO Radio Film, produced by Pandro S. Berman, directed by John Cromwell, written by James Gow and Edmund North, based on a story by Elsie Finn and David G. Wittels, photographed by Vernon Walker, songs by Jerome Kern and Dorothy Fields, music direction by Max Steiner, 85 minutes.

With Lily Pons.

CAST:

Annette, *Lily Pons;* Jonathan, *Henry Fonda;* Roger, *Eric Blore;* Darcy, *Osgood Perkins;* Mr. Dilley, *Lucien Littlefield;* Mrs. Dilley, *Esther Dale;* Gwendolyn Dilley, *Lucille Ball;* Boy on Merry-Go-Round, *Scotty Beckett;* Pianist, *Miscah Auer;* Tito, *Paul Porcasi.*

In the Thirties Hollywood tried to turn a number of the more beautiful operatic stars in-

to screen attractions and, although the attempts were interesting, the results merely proved that the mass audience was not ready for cultured voices. Grace Moore came off best, especially with *One Night of Love* (1934), but after another three pictures the public lost interest. Paramount tried to make a movie star out of the glamorous mezzo Gladys Swarthout but could not, and in 1935 Columbia gave the diminutive French coloratura soprano Lily Pons a crack at Hollywood

with *I Dream Too Much*, for which Henry Fonda agreed to play leading man. Perhaps to break the bucolic strain of his first two films he thought it wise to try something sophisticated. RKO Radio, who were then turning out the marvelous Astaire-Rogers musicals, assigned Max Steiner as music director and Hermes Pan as choreographer, as well as hiring Miss Pon's famous husband Andre Kostelanetz to conduct the film's operatic sequences. To give the picture an even better shot

With Osgood Perkins and Lily Pons.

at popularity, they commissioned Jerome Kern to write four new songs, with lyricist Dorothy Fields.

Like all the movies with opera stars, this one bases its humor on the problems of balancing love life with professional life. *I Dream Too Much* puts an immediate strain on the audience by asking it to believe that a woman with such an incredible voice as Pons's would not be interested in a singing career. Annette (Pons) has to be pushed by her adoring husband Jonathan (Fonda) into auditioning. Success quickly comes to the perky little French wife and she finds she likes it. As she ascends the top ranks of opera the husband is overshadowed and he finds he does not like it, especially since he is a struggling composer. After a while Annette tires of fame and decides to help her pouting husband, but without his knowing it. Through her machinations, Jonathan's unsuccessful opera is turned into a successful musical comedy. With his music bringing him offers for more of the same, Annette can now have what she wants, which is to have a happy home and a baby, and perhaps a little singing on the side.

I Dream Too Much did moderately well at the box office but soon faded into movie limbo. Today it is an item of study for film musicologists, as well as a pleasing reminder of Lily Pons in her vocal prime, as she sings the "Bell Song" from *Lakme* and "Caro Nome" from *Rigoletto.* Of the four Kern songs only the title tune and "Jockey on the Carousel" have any sustaining life. Most of the reviews favored Fonda, with the word *likable* being well in evidence. He managed to make something out of the role of the supportive and then disgruntled husband and Hollywood took note that he was more than just another handsome young leading man.

THE TRAIL OF THE LONESOME PINE

1936

A Paramount release of a Walter Wanger Production, directed by Henry Hathaway, written by Grover Jones, based on material adapted by Harvey Thew and Horace McCoy from the novel by John Fox, Jr., photographed in Technicolor by Robert C. Bruce, musical direction by Boris Morros, 100 minutes.

CAST:

June Tolliver, *Sylvia Sidney*; Dave Tolliver, *Henry Fonda*; Jack Hale, *Fred MacMurray*; Judd Tolliver, *Fred Stone*; Thurber, *Nigel Bruce*; Melissa Tolliver, *Beulah Bondi*; Buck Felin, *Robert Barrat*; Buddie Tolliver, *Spanky McFarland*; Tater, *Fuzzy Knight*; Corsey, *Otto Fries*; Sheriff, *Samuel Hinds*; Clayt Tolliver, *Alan Baxter*; Lina Tolliver, *Fern Emmett*; Ezra Tolliver, *Richard Carle*; Wade Falin, *Henry Kleinbach*.

The Trail of the Lonesome Pine was not only Henry Fonda's first film in color but it was the first American movie to use the newly perfected three-strip Technicolor in an outdoor setting. The public responded to this visual improvement and also responded to the film for its story values and its action. It helped Fonda with his steadily growing popularity and satisfied his doubts about whether Walter Wanger would ever use him in one of his own productions instead of hiring him out. Wanger knew what he was doing in starring Fonda in this one.

The film opens in the picturesque mountains of Kentucky in the early years of the century, where "old woods, old ways and old codes live unchanged." A band of mountain men are ringed around a homestead and firing at it. They are members of the Falin family and they have been feuding for generations with the Tollivers. Inside the house the mother (Beulah Bondi) gives birth to a daughter and prays, "Give her strength to be good, Lord, but don't let her carry the burden of fear. Oh, the killing, the killing! Why has it got to be?" No one can give her much of an answer. Years pass and the daughter, June (Sylvia Sidney), grows up. Civilization starts coming to the area in the form of railroad and construction engineers, one of whom, Jack Hale (Fred MacMurray), takes a liking to June, which does not please her brother Dave (Fonda), despite the fact that Jack saved his life after Dave was wounded in a fight with the Falins. Dave thinks the Tollivers should stick to their own kind, a

With Sylvia Sidney.

With Spanky McFarland.

view not shared by his little brother Buddie (Spanky McFarland), who idolizes Jack.

Jack's company, opening up the area, brings new wealth to the local population and Dave gradually sees the advantages, but his resentment at Jack wells up again when Jack sponsors June to a school in Louisville, which she accepts. One day the two men get into a fist fight, but they combine forces when the Falins attack Jack's camp. The site is wrecked and burned, and the workers are scared off. When June returns from Louisville she learns that Buddie has been killed as a result of the Falin attack. She reverts to her former self and turns her anger on Jack as well as the Falins. Dave comes to realize that the feud must come to an end and volunteers to shake hands with the head of the Falins, Buck (Robert Barrat), who accepts. But another Falin disagrees and shoots Dave. Buck himself is appalled at this and appears at the Tolliver home to say the feud is finished. Dave smiles as he and Judd Tolliver (Fred Stone) shake hands. Before he dies, Dave also causes Jack and June to join hands.

The Trail of the Lonesome Pine is a good account of a vanished era of American lore and, because of its splendid color photography of the southern mountains, still a pleasure to see. Fonda's portrayal of the sullen hillbilly who finds a change of heart gives the film some poignancy, but Fred MacMurray is very much the hero figure. By now Fonda was getting a little tired of playing the rustic.

With Fred MacMurray, Robert Barrat, Sylvia Sidney, Fred Stone and Beulah Bondi.

With Sylvia Sidney and Fred MacMurray.

☆☆☆☆☆☆☆☆☆☆☆☆☆☆
THE MOON'S
OUR HOME

1936

A Paramount release of a Walter Wanger Production, directed by William A. Seiter, written by Isabel Dawn and Boyce DeGaw, based on the serial by Faith Baldwin, with additional dialogue by Dorothy Parker and Alan Campbell, photographed by Joseph Valentine, musical direction by Boris Morros, 80 minutes.

CAST:

Cherry Chester, *Margaret Sullavan;* Anthony Amberton, *Henry Fonda;* Horace Van Steedan, *Charles Butterworth;* Mrs. Boyce Medford, *Beulah Bondi;* Mitty Simpson, *Margaret Hamilton;* Lucy Van Steedan, *Henrietta Crosman;* Hida, *Dorothy Stickney;* Ogden Holbrook, *Lucien Littlefield;* Lem, *Walter Brennan;* Babson, *Brandon Hurst;* Abner Simpson, *Spencer Charters;* Chauffeur, *John G. Spacey;* Miss Manning, *Margaret Fielding.*

The fact that Henry Fonda and Margaret Sullavan had been married and divorced was an obvious titillating factor in the public wanting to see them in *The Moon's Our Home,* as its producers and publicists were well aware. What the public might not have known is that the couple were still friends and occasionally dated each other, and enjoyed making a film together. The fascination that Fonda and Sullavan had for each other was ended only by her death in 1960. That plus their talents as actors made anything they did together of special interest. Sullavan, with her slightly husky voice and her beautiful eyes, had a beguiling, seductive quality and Fonda was not the only man who found her fascinating. The public was not to know that she could also be difficult, temperamental and ultimately

On the set with Sullavan.

With Margaret Sullavan.

48

With Margaret Sullavan and Walter Brennan.

unstable. *The Moon's Our Home* is a fine example of the comedic Sullavan and a film in line with the "screwball" comedies that pleased moviegoers in the Thirties.

In this swiftly paced romp Fonda and Sullavan play celebrities who use their own names instead of their celebrity names when they are not working, in order to enjoy privacy. She is Cherry Chester, movie star, but Sarah Brown once she leaves the job. He is Anthony Amberton, a traveling writer of adventure books, but plain John Smith when he is at home. Both impulsive by nature, they meet, fall in love and get married, but with neither informing the other of their celebrity status. Unfortunately they are both volatile in temper and flare up at each other at the slightest provocation, thus their relationship is a seesaw of mad love and loud arguments. At their wedding they bicker and the hard-of-hearing Justice of the Peace (Walter Brennan) has a hard time keeping track of the ceremony. On their honeymoon night in a New Hampshire lodge, Cherry douses herself with musk perfume, to which Anthony is violently allergic, and she

assumes his revulsion to the perfume is an expression of his regard for her. And off she goes. His searching for her proves fruitless, but one day they bump into each other in New York. More loving, more bickering and then a fade-out as the madcap couple fall into each others arms.

Dorothy Parker and her husband Alan Campbell were hired to perk up the script with additional dialogue and since they were expert with man-woman bickering (apparently they did plenty of it themselves) it is easy to see where *The Moon's Our Home* got some of its most stinging quips, such as she yelling "I'll leave you constantly" and he replying "I'll always find you." The Fonda-Sullavan relationship must have had something to do with their spirited delivery of these lines. The film brought good notices to them both, although with some comment on the implausibility of the material. Many years later Fonda happened to see the film on television and commented, "It was fun. It had pace and charm and I found myself laughing and enjoying it, too. It has held up so much better than a lot of those pictures of the Thirties."

49

SPENDTHRIFT

1936

A Paramount release of a Walter Wanger Production, directed by Raoul Walsh, written by Raoul Walsh and Bert Hanlon, based on a story by Eric Hatch, photographed by Leon Shamroy, music by Gerard Carbonara, 80 minutes.

CAST:
Towndsend Middleton, *Henry Fonda;* Boots O'Connell, *Pat Patterson;* Sally Barnaby, *Mary*

With Edward Brophy, Mary Brian and Pat Patterson.

With Pat Patterson and Mary Brian.

Brian; Topsy, *June Brewster;* Uncle Morton, *George Barbier;* Beuhl, *Halliwell Hobbs;* Colonel Barnaby, *Spencer Charters;* Popsy, *Richard Carle;* O'Connell, *J. M. Kerrigan;* Bill, *Edward Brophy;* Enrico, *Jerry Mandy;* Hilda, *Greta Meyer;* Valet, *Miki Morita.*

The only distinction *Spendthrift* has in the Henry Fonda catalogue is that it was the first film in which he received top billing, but unfortunately with a pair of leading ladies whose names meant little at the box office. The film was in keeping with Hollywood's policy in the mid-1930's of poking fun at the idle rich, hopefully in order to keep the audience from thinking too seriously about the Depression. The script was based on a story by Eric Hatch, who had the reputation of being a kind of American P. G. Wodehouse, with his humorous yarns about the doings of the American upper crust. This one did not translate well to the screen.

In *Spendthrift* Fonda is a giddy young fellow named Towndsend Middleton, who has light-heartedly dwindled away 23 million dollars. Not knowing what to do about it, he keeps giving parties and having fun. A pretty southern girl (Mary Brian) marries him for his name value and then drops him when he can no longer aid her social climbing. Now shocked, Towndsend looks for a job and finds one as a sports announcer on the radio at a thousand dollars a week (a considerable achievement in 1936). Working for a living brings him new values, including the love of the daughter (Pat Patterson) of an Irish stableman.

Spendthrift failed to impress the critics or the public and Fonda can be excused for claiming that he barely had any recollection of making it.

With Pat Patterson.

WINGS OF THE MORNING

1937

A 20th Century-Fox release of a New World Film, produced by Robert T. Kane, directed by Harold Schuster, written by Tom Geraghty, based on stories by Donn Byrne, photographed in Technicolor by Ray Rennahan, music by Arthur Benjamin, 88 minutes.

CAST:

Marie, *Annabella*; Kerry, *Henry Fonda*; Lord Clontarf, *Leslie Banks*; Sir Valentine, *Stewart Rome*; Marie, *Irene Vanbrugh*; Malrik, *D. J. Williams*; Padly, *Harry Tate*; Jenepher, *Helen Haye*; Don Diego, *Teddy Underdown*; Jimmy, *Mark Daly*; Angelo, *Sam Livesey*; with John McCormack and Steve Donoghue as themselves.

Wings of the Morning was the first Technicolor film made in the British Isles and Henry Fonda jumped at the chance to appear in it because it gave him his first trip overseas. It is doubtful if he would have otherwise jumped, because the script was old-fashioned even by 1936 standards. Seen today the film is interesting because so much of it was filmed amid beautiful scenery in Ireland and truly does justice to the subject. For music lovers it is of interest because of the appearance of the famed Irish tenor John McCormack, who appears during a party sequence and sings three Irish ballads. It was the first English-speaking movie of the French actress Annabella, and was successful enough for 20th Century-Fox to put her under contract and bring her to Hollywood.

It begins with a dramatic prologue, set around the beginning of the century in Ireland, during which a member of the landed gentry (Leslie Banks) falls in love with a beautiful young Spanish Gypsy, Marie (Annabella), and marries her, despite the disdain of his social set. After he is killed in a riding accident, she returns to Spain with her people. In 1936 her granddaughter Marie (also Annabella) visits Ireland and, because she wants to ride as a jockey, disguises herself as a boy. As such she comes into contact with a Canadian trainer, Kerry (Fonda), who roughhouses with the boy and soon finds him to be a girl. When he next sees her at a party she is beautifully gowned and he instantly falls in love with her.

The two now team their forces, his expertise and her ownership of a racehorse, to enter and

With Annabella.

win the Derby. After surviving the usual number of complications in stories of this kind, their plans are successful. *Wings of the Morning* is of more interest to British viewers than American because it contains a well covered account of the 1936 Derby Day at Epsom Downs, with all its myriad attractions, plus a few color shots of London of the period. And for anyone interested in Ireland the film retains its value with photography of landscapes and estates that would do credit to any travelogue producer. On the other hand, it is a film hard on the American ear, with a spectrum of accents—French, Spanish, Gypsy, English and Irish, and with Fonda delivering in straight Midwestern drawl.

There was nothing about Fonda's role in *Wings of the Morning* that put any strain on his talent; it was a simple yarn requiring him to be a little angry at times, a little bashful at others, but he always looked back on it with affection because of the fun he had making it in Ireland and England. It was during a session in the London studios that he first met the woman who would be his second wife, Frances Seymour Brokaw, and with whom he shortly thereafter enjoyed a European tour.

With John McCormack and Annabella.

53

☆★☆★☆★☆★☆★☆

YOU ONLY LIVE ONCE

1937

A United Artists release of a Walter Wanger Film, produced by Walter Wanger, directed by Fritz Lang, written by Gene Towne and Graham Baker, photographed by Leon Shamroy, music by Alfred Newman, 86 minutes.

CAST:

Eddie Taylor, *Henry Fonda*; Joan Graham, *Sylvia Sidney*; Stephen Whitney, *Barton MacLane*; Bonnie Graham, *Jean Dixon*; Father Dolan, *William Gargan*; Mugsy, *Warren Hymer*; Ethan, *Charles "Chic" Sale*; Hester, *Margaret Hamilton*; Rogers, *Guinn Williams*; Dr. Hill, *Jerome Cowan*; Warden, *John Wray*; District Attorney, *Jonathan Hale*; Guard, *Ward Bond*; Policeman, *Wade Boteker*; Kozderonas, *Henry Taylor*.

The expatriates of the pre-Hitler German film industry made a profound impression on Hollywood. The many actors, directors, writers, composers and cameramen were a vital contribution to the American cinema. Foremost among them was Fritz Lang, whose imaginative direction of such films as *Dr. Mabuse* (1922), *Die Niebelungen* (1924), *Metropolis* (1927), and *M* (1931) made him famous while still a young man. He was a major force in the remarkable German film world of the time—a distinction Germany would have to forfeit with the uncompromising dictatorship of the Nazis. Lang left and came to Hollywood, where he made a brilliant new start to his career with *Fury* (1936), one of the first film studies of American mob violence. Next he made *You Only Live Once*, which brought him into contact with Henry Fonda. They were entirely different kinds of men and they would never like each other. Lang was a bit of a dictator—Fonda was then and always a genial, democratic fellow.

With Sylvia Sidney.

You Only Live Once met with critical but not much public approval in 1937. It was a little too harsh in its treatment of young, innocent people caught up in crime, and stylistically it was a departure from the Hollywood norm. It was

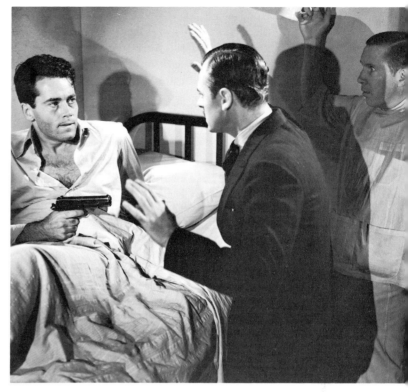

quite Germanic—intense, full of symbolism, dramatic lighting and bizarre camera angles. Among film students it is still an item for examination. Critic Andrew Sarris once said of Lang that he was "the cerebral tragedian of the cinema." This film is right in line with that view.

It is the story of a doomed young man, Eddie Taylor (Fonda), jailed for a petty crime and released after a short sentence. He rejoins his sweetheart Jo (Sylvia Sidney) and marries her. But when their landlord finds out that Eddie is an ex-convict they are ordered out. When he loses his job with a trucking company, Eddie turns bitter about his prospects in society. Eddie's hat is found at the scene of a bank robbery and he is arrested for the crime, which includes murder. Unable to offer anything in his own defense, Eddie is convicted and sentenced to death. He escapes Death Row by feigning illness and being taken to the prison hospital, where he pulls a gun, takes a doctor as hostage and makes his way across the prison yard. News comes that evidence has been found which exonerates him. Eddie greets this as a tactic to get him to surrender, and in making his break he kills the prison chaplain. Now a wanted fugitive, he and his wife head for the Canadian border. Just as they cross the border the pair are caught in the telescopic sights of a New York State policeman's rifle. The shots mortally wound Eddie and Jo, and as they lie dying in each other's arms the voice of the dead chaplain is heard, "You're free now, Eddie."

The trouble with working for Fritz Lang is that he was meticulous and demanding and drove his workers as hard as he drove himself. Hours and effort meant nothing to him. He seemed to have little regard for actors. As Henry Fonda saw it, he and others were merely puppets to be manipulated. Lang would do anything to get the right effect. If it meant that his actors were tired and uncomfortable—wet, cold, miserable, whatever—that was unfortunate, but the picture came first. Fonda was himself meticulous in his work and fully prepared when he arrived on a set. But he considered *You Only Live Once* a tortured nightmare to make.

SLIM

1937

A Warner Brothers–First National Film, produced by Hal B. Wallis, directed by Ray Enright, written by William Wister Haines, based on his novel, photographed by Sid Hickox, music by Max Steiner, 86 minutes.

CAST:

Red Blayd, *Pat O'Brien;* Slim, *Henry Fonda;* Cally, *Margaret Lindsay;* Stumpy, *Stuart Erwin;* Pop, *J. Farrell MacDonald;* Tom, *Dick Purcell;* Wilcox, *Joseph Sawyer;* Gambler, *Craig Reynolds;* Wyatt Ranstead, *John Litel;* Stumpy's Girl, *Jane Wyman.*

In the 1930's Warner Bros. had the reputation of being the studio that most supported the

With Pat O'Brien.

With Margaret Lindsay, Pat O'Brien and Dorothy Vaughan.

American working man, in the sense that they made so many pictures about the men who joined the armed forces, or excelled in the sports world or worked the land or made a living in factories. If steel workers or truck drivers were to be recognized, it was usually in a Warner movie. Henry Fonda made his Warner debut in 1937 in just such a setting, as a lineman in *Slim*. This kind of movie usually commenced with a montage view of its subject and a stentorian narrator, in this instance saluting the skill and daring of

the men who erect the high towers and string the power lines across the country.

Slim is a farmboy anxious to leave the farm once he spots linemen setting up their towers. He applies to the company and cheerfully informs a veteran gang boss, Red Blayd (Pat O'Brien), "It seems like I'm obliged to be a linesman." Red likes him enough to hire him and teach him the hazardous job of climbing towers, stringing up high voltage electrical cables and the constant work of maintaining them. Slim is scared stiff as he climbs his first steel tower but he comes to like the challenge the work offers. The friendship between the two men undergoes a tremor when Red's girlfriend Cally (Margaret Lindsay) takes a shine to Slim, but Red gradually gives way because he knows in his heart that he is married to his dangerous job and will never give it up for a woman.

Despite Cally's love, Slim still carouses with Red in the evenings. Both of them enjoy drinking and brawling, and in one elaborate barroom fracas Slim is stabbed while protecting Red. Even after leaving the hospital he refuses to heed Cally's pleas to give up the job. One stormy winter night Slim and Red are called upon to repair power lines that have been blown down. Red climbs the tower as the blizzard swirls, but touches an open wire and falls to his death. Slim completes the job, and Cally realizes that the man she loves will always be a power lineman.

Fonda enjoyed making *Slim* because it had something to say about real people and not the supposed silly antics of high society folks. As a "man's picture" it had a limited box office appeal, although it is worth seeing today for its coverage of its subject matter rather than its somewhat square story. But with his next movie Fonda would swing to the other end of the Warner scale, with a true-blue "woman's picture."

With Stuart Erwin and Jane Wyman.

THAT CERTAIN WOMAN

With Bette Davis and Donald Crisp.

1937

A Warner Brothers–First National Film, produced by Hal B. Wallis, directed and written by Edmund Goulding, photographed by Ernest Haller, music by Max Steiner, 91 minutes.

CAST:

Mary Donnell, *Bette Davis;* Jack Merrick, *Henry Fonda;* Lloyd Rogers, *Ian Hunter;* Flip, *Anita Louise; Donald Crisp; Katherine Alexander;* *Mary Phillips; Minor Watson; Ben Welden; Sidney Toler; Charles Trowbridge; Norman Willis; Herbert Rawlinson.*

Bette Davis had met Henry Fonda when she was a teenage fledgling actress in summer stock and she admitted years later that she had had a crush on him. By 1937 she had enough sway with Warners to specify actors she would like to

With Bette Davis, Dwane Day and Anita Louise.

have in her movies. Davis took some pleasure in asking for Fonda as her co-star in the very romantic, soap-operish *That Certain Woman*. Director-writer Edmund Goulding had made it in 1929 with Gloria Swanson and called it *The Trespasser*. Apparently he felt he could do better by the material with Davis in 1937. He may have done better but it is not a prime item in the Davis career.

That Certain Woman is Mary Donnell (Davis), the young widow of a gangster. Striving for a better life she becomes the secretary of a posh but unhappily married lawyer (Ian Hunter), who soon falls in love with her but keeps his feelings to himself. Jack Merrick (Fonda), the son of a wealthy client (Donald Crisp), falls for Mary and elopes with her. The father has the marriage annulled and Mary promises to give up Jack, who thereafter marries again. But his new bride (Anita Louise) is terribly injured in a traffic accident on the honeymoon. In the meantime Mary finds she is pregnant with Jack's child, a fact she confides only to her loving employer. When *he* dies from fever he leaves Mary and her son well provided for, which leaves the widow to believe her husband was probably the father of Mary's child. Because of this, Mary decides it is time Jack knew that the child, a boy, is his.

When Jack's father learns of this he swings his weight and has the boy legally taken from Mary and placed with his father. Jack's injured but no-

With Dwane Day and Bette Davis.

ble wife dies and then Jack is free to go after Mary, whom he traces to her secluded spot in Europe and tells her he loves her. Happy ending.

Henry Fonda often claimed he could barely remember some of his early films. In the case of *That Certain Woman*, he could be forgiven for claiming he never appeared in it.

With Bette Davis.

I MET MY LOVE AGAIN

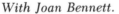
With Joan Bennett.

1938

A United Artists release of a Walter Wanger Production, directed by Arthur Ripley and Joshua Logan, written by David Hertz, based on the novel *Summer Lightning* by Allene Corliss, photographed by Hal Mohr, music by Heinz Roemheld, 79 minutes.

CAST:

Julie, *Joan Bennett*; Ives Towner, *Henry Fonda*; Aunt William, *Dame May Whitty*; Michael, *Alan Marshall*; Brenda, *Louise Platt*; Tony, *Alan Baxter*; Budge, *Tim Holt*; Mrs. Towner, *Dorothy* Stickney; Carol, *Florence Lake*; Agathe, *Alice Cavenna*.

Henry Fonda could hardly have been pleased with having to follow one "woman's" movie with another but he was under contract to Walter Wanger, who had been good to him, and he was not in a position to refuse, especially since it starred Joan Bennett, the lady with whom Wanger was in love and would soon marry. It was very much a Bennett film, and required little from Fonda in playing the role of a scholarly

moviegoers in 1938 and gives a well-produced account of life in a small Vermont town of the period, with a few good digs at the gossipy elements. But as a Fonda film it must have been one that quickened his growing resentment at the course of his career on the screen and his desire to get back to the stage. *I Met My Love Again* brought Fonda into contact with his friend Joshua Logan, who was assigned to it as a co-director, along with Arthur Ripley. It could hardly have been a happy Hollywood debut for Logan because George Cukor was later brought in to re-direct a few scenes. Logan would not return to the movies until 1956, when he directed the successful *Picnic*. It is a fair assumption that during the making of *I Met My Love Again*, Fonda and Logan spent some time together commiserating with each other.

With Louise Platt.

young man who becomes embittered when dumped by his girl friend.

I Met My Love Again begins in a small Vermont town in 1927 and tells of a lovely, spirited girl, Julie (Bennett), who is eager for a more exciting life and who is thrilled when she meets a handsome young writer (Alan Marshall), who is much more suave and worldly than studious Ives Towner (Fonda). She jilts Ives and goes off to Paris with the writer, marries him and has a daughter. But the Bohemian life isn't as much fun as she imagined because her husband is a heavy drinker; after ten years he dies in a drunken accident. Julie returns to Vermont, where she seeks out Ives, who is now a professor of biology, as well as being a glum bachelor. Her desire to win him back is complicated by one of his students, a spoiled brat of a beauty (Louise Platt), who threatens to kill herself if Ives doesn't return her love. Making matters worse is the general resentment around town about Julie and her past behavior. But the complications settle down and the ending finds Ives and Julie picking up their lives together after a ten-year lapse that has, hopefully, made them better people.

The film is a good example of the kind Hollywood so carefully tailored for the female

JEZEBEL

1938

A Warner Brothers–First National Film, produced by Hal B. Wallis and Henry Blanke, directed by William Wyler, written by Clement Ripley, Aben Finkel and John Huston, based on the play by Owen Davis, Jr., photographed by Ernest Haller, music by Max Steiner, 100 minutes.

CAST:

Julie Marston, *Bette Davis;* Pres Dillard, *Henry Fonda;* Buck Cantrell, *George Brent;* Dr. Livingstone, *Donald Crisp;* Aunt Belle, *Fay Bainter;*

With Bette Davis, Fay Bainter and Henry O'Neill.

Amy, *Margaret Lindsay;* General Bogardus, *Henry O'Neil;* Jean La Cour, *John Litel;* Dick Allen, *Gordon Oliver;* Mrs. Kendrick, *Spring Byington;* Stephanie Kendrick, *Margaret Early;* Ted Dillard, *Richard Cromwell;* Zette, *Theresa Harris;* Molly Allen, *Janet Shaw;* Huger, *Irving Pichel;* Gros Bat, *Eddie Anderson.*

As any self-respecting film buff knows, Bette Davis was not only one of the many actresses who yearned to play Scarlett O'Hara in David O'Selznick's *Gone With the Wind,* but she stood a good chance of getting the role. Her boss, the shrewd Jack L. Warner, was in favor of a loan-out but on his terms, which would be a package deal. If Selzneck wanted Davis, then he would also have to take Errol Flynn as Rhett Butler. Selznick was at least willing to consider that offer but Davis was not. Much as she wanted the part she felt that Flynn would be entirely wrong. On that point she would not budge. Warner, well aware of all the publicity whipped up by Selznick and the nearness of Davis getting the coveted part, came up with a profitable solution—*Jezebel,* a southern romance with more than a little similarity to *GWTW,* especially since its heroine was a willful beauty who wrapped men around her finger.

Jezebel had been a moderately successful play on Broadway, starring Miriam Hopkins, who rather resented the fact that she was not chosen to repeat the role on the screen. Resentment also came from Tallulah Bankhead, a genuine southern beauty and the daughter of a prominent Alabama family. Bankhead would undoubtedly have been good in the film but the moviegoers had not responded to her work on the screen, and there was no way Warners would give the part to anyone other than their leading female star.

Warner Bros. knew precisely what they were doing in making *Jezebel*, giving it top production values and releasing it months ahead of *GWTW*. Whatever disappointment Davis may have felt was more than compensated when the film brought her an Oscar, her second. She had been adamant about Flynn not getting cast as Rhett Butler and she was adamant about Henry Fonda appearing with her in *Jezebel*. Since he had been doing well with the moviegoers, Warners had no objection. It was a break for Fonda. This, his 12th film, would be a box office winner and bring him a lot of attention.

Jezebel is set in some unspecified part of New

With Bette Davis and Margaret Lindsay.

With Bette Davis and George Brent.

Orleans, except that it is obviously very upper class; the story begins in 1852. Julie Marston (Davis) is a self-centered beauty, ever intent on having her own way in everything, but her fiance, the young banker Pres Dillard (Fonda), is just as strong willed and frequently angered by her haughty manners. He is especially angered when she decides to attend the high society Olympus Ball in a flaming red dress instead of the white dress traditionally worn by unmarried ladies. He covers his embarrassment at the ball by being abrasive to whomever they meet and he insists on dancing with Julie, even though she by this time is herself embarrassed and desirous of leaving. All the other couples withdraw from

Brent), which causes Pres to break their engagement and take off for Philadelphia, where he joins one of his family's banks. Three years pass and Julie, ever confident that Pres will one day return to her, learns that he is coming back to New Orleans, which is beginning to feel the effects of a fever epidemic called Yellow Jack. The city has suffered from it before and a recurrence is always feared. When Pres does return to pay his respects, Julie is shocked to discover he has married, indeed he proudly presents his wife Amy (Margaret Lindsay) to Julie and their friends. Julie later creates a fuss about her wounded pride and her violated honor, and Cantrell, ever eager to defend her, finds himself faced on the duelling field by Pres's young brother Ted (Richard Cromwell), who shoots and kills Cantrell. The plague worsens in New Orleans and one of its victims is Pres, who must, like all the other victims, be shipped to a nearby island for isolation. Julie, now aware of the errors of her ways, begs Amy to let her accompany Pres to the island and spare Amy the misery she will encounter there. After much persuasion Amy agrees. *Jezebel* ends with the sad spectacle of

With Bette Davis.

With Bette Davis.

the floor and Julie becomes painfully conspicuous as Pres leads her on and on in the dance (a beguiling waltz by Max Steiner, who scored this and so many of Davis's best Warner films).

Julie thereafter gives attention to her long-time admirer, the dashing Buck Cantrell (George

With Henry O'Neill, Fay Bainter, George Brent, Gordon Oliver, Margaret Lindsay and Richard Cromwell.

Julie and a large parade of victims leaving town. She and Pres may survive—maybe they will not. But at least Julie has atoned for playing the wicked Jezebel of the bible.

Jezebel is, of course, a Bette Davis picture, with all other actors in support. But Fonda, with his portrayal of the proud, unbending Pres, made an impact on the critics and the public. He may have had a little trouble with the southern accent, but so did the entire cast. Upon signing his contract with Warners he specified that his work on the film should end by early December of 1937, or whatever time his pregnant wife felt she needed him. Warners, a studio used to swift and efficient production methods, had not reckoned on the slow, painstaking style of director William Wyler. The film went weeks over schedule and

Fonda received a call from New York at the end of the second week in December. He left, leaving Davis to do some of their pick-up shots alone (scenes in which the camera cuts back and forth with close-ups) but after rushing to New York Fonda had to sit around for a few days before his wife Frances gave birth to their first child, daughter Jane, on December 21st. In the meantime Davis pacified the brothers Warner, who were threatening Wyler with a lay-off and the bringing in of another director to finish the picture, by promising to spend any amount of time at the studio, day and night. She wisely valued the talents of Wyler, despite his snail-like pace, and with him she would make two more of her finest films, *The Letter* (1940) and *The Little Foxes* (1941).

69

BLOCKADE

1938

A United Artists release of a Walter Wanger Production, directed by William Dieterle, written by John Howard Lawson, photographed by Rudy Mate, music by Werner Jansson, 73 minutes.

CAST:

Norma, *Madeleine Carroll*; Marco, *Henry Fon-*

da; Luis, *Leo Carrillo*; Andre, *John Halliday*; Basil, *Vladimir Sokoloff*; Edward Grant, *Reginald Denny*; General Vallejo, *Robert War-*

rick; Commandant, *William Davidson*; Pietro, *Fred Kohler*; Magician, *Peter Godfrey*; Major, *Carlos de Valdez*; Peasant Girl, *Katherine DeMille*; Troubador, *George Byron*.

Despite all the drama offered by the Spanish Civil War (1936-1939) it was not a subject that Hollywood cared to touch, mostly because of the confused political sympathies it touched off in America as in the rest of the world. Franco's rebellion was clearly fascistic but the resisters, the so-called loyalists, were made up of socialists, communists and various idealists (including some Americans who joined the International Brigade), and Hollywood could not be sure of a market for such a convoluted subject. Nonetheless, Walter Wanger took it upon himself to make a movie about the trouble in Spain and decided to star Henry Fonda in it.

Blockade required Fonda to play a Spanish peasant, Marco, a farmer devoted to his native soil and a willing fighter against the opposition. As a reward for his bravery, Marco is sent to headquarters and promoted, where he falls in love with a beautiful girl, Norma (Madeleine Carroll), whom he comes to realize is working for the enemy. But when he points out to her the suffering that her side is causing, the slaughtering of civilians, the starvation and the injustice, she gradually has a change of heart and leads him to the headquarters of the group of spies for whom she works. With her help Marco manages to bring a supply ship into port, escaping the blockading submarines and coming to the relief of the hungry masses.

The problem with *Blockade* is that it fails to clearly identify the opposing forces. The producers were so wary of offending political sympathies that it hardly seems like a film about a civil war. Fonda's Marco is obviously a man of the people engaged in a noble fight against oppression, but the military machine they oppose appears almost like an invading force from another country. Wanger apparently wanted to take a stand against fascism, particularly the kind that was emerging in Europe. He has Fonda trying to halt the terrorized peasants as they flee the military advance, "Stop—turn back! This valley is ours, it's part of us. We were born here. . .our fathers were, and their fathers before them. . .turn back and fight!" At the end of the film the actor has to make an impassioned plea directly to the audience, "It's murder. . .murder of innocent people. There's no sense to it. The world can stop it. Where's the conscience of the world?"

Unfortunately *Blockade* did little to halt the

With Madeleine Carroll.

rising tide of fascism in 1938. The film did well at the box office, greatly helped by the fact that it was banned in several American cities and was condemned by the Catholic Church. It raised more controversy than it really merited because its anger was defused by any specific identification of the enemy. Seen today *Blockade* is an interesting curiosity item, with some well directed crowd and battle scenes, but for anyone hoping to learn something about the Spanish Civil War it is hopeless. And it was yet another of his films that Fonda did not like, feeling that his characterization was synthetic, with lines that belonged more in the mouth of a political activist than a farmer.

☆☆☆☆☆☆☆☆☆☆☆☆
SPAWN OF THE NORTH

With Louise Platt.

1938

A Paramount release of an Albert Lewin Production, directed by Henry Hathaway, written by Jules Furthman, based on the novel by Barrett Willoughby, photographed by Charles Lang, music by Dimitri Tiomkin, 105 minutes.

CAST:

Tyler Dawson, *George Raft;* Jim Kimmerlee, *Henry Fonda;* Nicky Duval, *Dorothy Lamour;* Red Skain, *Akim Tamiroff;* Windy Turion, *John Barrymore;* Diane, *Louise Platt;* Jackson, *Lynne Overman;* Lefty Jones, *Fuzzy Knight;* Dimitri, *Vladimir Sokoloff;* Ivan, *Duncan Renaldo;* Tom, *Richard Ung;* Fisherman, *Lee Shumway;* Patridge, *Stanley Andrews.*

If *Spawn of the North* had been made in more recent years, Henry Fonda would have spent quite some time on location in Alaska. In 1938, however, he had to roam no further than the Paramount backlot for this adventurous yarn about Alaskan salmon fishermen and their battles with Russian pirates. The studio built a wharf and sundry rough buildings to approximate an Alaskan fishing town of some 60 years ago and augmented it with a lot of location footage of salmon fishing runs, Indian rituals relating to the spawning season and some spectacular sequences of mighty icebergs in the act of breaking up. Randolph Scott had been set for the film but when he had to cancel due to another commitment, Paramount asked Fonda to step in. It was a good step. The picture was popular and harmed him not at all.

The story centers on a pair of friends who have grown up together, Jim Kimmerlee (Fonda) and Tyler Dawson (George Raft). They fish together and they have fun together, but they are men of different character. Jim is a square shooter and Tyler isn't. Since he wants to acquire some money fast in order to buy a boat, Tyler accepts an of-

With Louise Platt.

fer from the head (Akim Tamiroff) of the Russian pirates to work for them. In the eventual battle between the fisherman and the pirates, Jim ends up shooting Tyler. Tyler pretends not to forgive him but he sees the error of his ways and with his last strength he guides the pirate boat into an iceberg, causing the boat to be demolished in a cascade of ice. Tyler had sent a friendly message to Jim beforehand on the ship's hooter, so Jim understands what his old friend has done.

The plot of *Spawn of the North* is somewhat lean, particularly in view of all the time and expense Paramount invested in location filming and backlot sets. The film had been on the planning boards for three years. Director Henry Hathaway summed up the script right away and concentrated on action and character. One of the film's assets is John Barrymore, as the editor of the town newspaper, who spends most of his time in the saloon. Since Barrymore was by this time in his life a man truly in his cups, the part was a

natural, and he played it with his usual cavalier flair. For Fonda it was a welcome chance to act with the legendary Barrymore and ask him many things about the art they both preferred—the art of the stage actor.

In reviewing the film, Frank Nugent in *The New York Times* commented, "Director Hathaway has built excitement steadily in the two-man and free-for-all battles between the pirates and the honest fishermen. Scorning such effeminacies as fists or marlin spikes, the picture's huskies go at it with harpoon guns, sealing knives, lengths of chain and gaffs. The bloodshed is beautiful; in Technicolor it would have rivaled Remington. But the battles are not all of it, although they happen to be the best parts. There are some impressive shots of crumbling icebergs, of the salmon run and of Henry Fonda's puzzled brow." Perhaps the puzzled brow came from having to work against so many process shots (rear projection) and wondering what was going on.

THE MAD MISS MANTON

1938

An RKO Radio Film, produced by P. J. Wolfson, directed by Leigh Jason, written by Philip G. Epstein, based on a story by Wilson Collinson, photographed by Nicholas Musuraca, music by Roy Webb, 78 minutes.

CAST:

Melsa Manton, *Barbara Stanwyck*; Peter Ames, *Henry Fonda*; Lt. Brent, *Sam Levene*; Helen Frayne, *Frances Mercer*; Edward Norris, *Stanley Ridges*; Pat James, *Whitney Bourne*; Kit Beverly, *Vicki Lester*; Lee Wilson, *Ann Evers*; Dora Fenton, *Catharine O'Quinn*; Myra Frost, *Linda Terry*; Jane, *Eleanor Hansen*; Hilda, *Hattie McDaniel*; Sullivan, *James Burke*; Bat Regan, *Paul Guilfoyle*; Frances Glesk, *Penny Singleton*; Sheila Lane, *Leona Maricle*; Gloria Hamilton, *Kat Sutton*; Mr. Thomas, *Miles Mander*.

Henry Fonda always said that his favorite actress was Barbara Stanwyck and that she was a joy to work with. This view was a virtual concensus. In an industry not noted for kind opinions, Stanwyck seems to have been everybody's favorite co-worker. She and Fonda made three films together and the pity is that they did not make more. However, the first one they made, *The Mad Miss Manton*, did not please him at all.

With Barbara Stanwyck.

With Barbara Stanwyck

With Barbara Stanwyck and Stanley Ridges.

tor. Leigh Jason was the man who steered this madcap caper through its paces and the credit is his for making it move and amuse. But it is, essentially, Stanwyck's film and her performance as the lively Melsa, saucy as well as bright, helped make her a popular star. She and Fonda had a particular chemistry between them, although Fonda apparently did not realize this until they worked together three years later on *The Lady Eve.* Whatever his reservations may have been about the *Manton* script—perhaps he disliked the idea of a half dozen squealing young ladies fluttering around him—it does not show in the performance. He has one especially good scene; as Peter lies in a hospital bed after having been shot, although not badly, he pretends to the visiting Melsa that he is dying. He does this to squeeze some information out of her, but then she notices his finished dinner tray under his bed. She leads him up to the climax of her revelation and then jabs him with a fork, "You black-hearted faker!" Like most leading men in "screwball" comedies, he gives in at the end, and tells her, "We'll take a honeymoon to Europe—with your money."

He disliked the script and asked Walter Wanger, who still had him under contract, not to send him out on this one. But Wanger had his own dealings to contend with and Fonda dutifully turned up at RKO for work. Later he said, "I was so mad at this picture. I resented it." This may be one instance where Fonda was off the mark in his judgment. *The Mad Miss Manton* is generally regarded as a good and typical example of Hollywood's celebrated "screwball" comedies of the Thirties.

Melsa Manton (Stanwyck) is not really mad, she's just a spirited, enterprising heiress who leads a group of six high society debutantes in what they consider public duties. This includes meddling in police affairs and winning the printed disdain of a newspaper editor named Peter Ames (Fonda). Once Peter meets the delightful Melsa he falls in love with her, but that doesn't stop him from lambasting her in print when he thinks she and her girls have behaved outrageously. When the group set about solving a murder that has the police baffled, they receive notes threatening their lives, plus sarcasm from Peter and disgust from the cops. But they solve the murder.

In this kind of "screwball" comedy, much of the effectiveness was in the hands of the direc-

With Frances Mercer and Barbara Stanwyck.

JESSE JAMES

1939

A 20th Century-Fox Film, produced by Darryl F. Zanuck, directed by Henry King, written by Nunnally Johnson, based on material assembled by Rosalind Shaffer and Jo Frances James, photographed in Technicolor by George Barnes, music by Louis Silvers, 110 minutes.

CAST:

Jesse James, *Tyrone Power;* Frank James, *Henry Fonda;* Zee Cobb, *Nancy Kelly;* Will Wright, *Randolph Scott;* Major Rufus Cobb, *Henry Hull;* Jailer, *Slim Summerville;* George Runyan, *J. Edward Bromberg;* Barshee, *Brian Donlevy;* Bob Ford, *John Carradine;* McCoy, *Donald Meek;*

Mrs. Samuels, *Jane Darwell*; Jess James, Jr., *John Russell*; Charles Ford, *Charles Tannen*; Pinky Washington, *Ernest Williams*; Bill, *Harold Goodwin*; Tom Colson, *Arthur Aylesworth*; Mrs. Bob Ford, *Claire Dubrey*; Clark, *Willard Robertson*; Lynch, *Paul Sutton*; Roy, *George Chandler*; Preacher, *Spencer Charters*.

The western had been a staple of the picture business right from the start but in the late Thirties the Hollywood studios found a market, an international market, for super westerns in which they could showcase their top male stars. Darryl Zanuck decided in 1938 that the story of the fabled Missouri bandit Jesse James would be a likely vehicle for the 24-year-old Tyrone Power, whose popularity was soaring. As always, Zanuck knew what he was doing.

Jesse James was all that Zanuck and his shareholders had hoped for, although as American historians were eager to point out, neither Power nor the screenplay came very close to accuracy. The only really accurate thing about the film was the choice of location. Zanuck took his cast and crew to Missouri, to shoot in the picturesque countryside in which James and his men had grown up. Missourians were well pleased to see their fabled outlaw come to life as a handsome, dashing Robin Hood. In casting the role of Jesse's brother Frank, Zanuck was a little more restrained and offered it to Henry Fonda, whose performance, as Zanuck probably realized, brought in the only critical approval.

According to history, Jesse James was a teenager when he joined the guerrilla band known as Quantrill's Raiders in the years following the Civil War. He was 20 when he and Frank formed their own band and he spent the remaining 15 years of his life leading them in raids on banks and trains. According to Nunnally Johnson's screenplay, the boys are happy on the farm, living with their mother, when a group of representatives from the St. Louis Midland Railroad turn up to shove them off their land, after first making a pittance of an offer. All the other farmers have been bullied into submission, but the James boys stand their ground. The leader of the railroad group, the unscrupulous Barshee (Brian Donlevy), later returns to the farm and sets off a fire that results in the death of the boys' mother (Jane Darwell). Jesse goes after Barshee and guns him down. From then on he and Frank are wanted men, although with the sympathy of the citizenry. Jesse's fiancée Zee (Nancy Kelly) and her cantankerous father Major Cobb (Henry

With Tyrone Power and Nancy Kelly.

Hull) lend support in their newspaper and even the U.S. Marshall, Will Wright (Randolph Scott), understands the facts in the case. But it is his job to bring the boys to justice.

Jesse and Frank make life miserable for the railroad with their robberies, and McCoy (Donald Meek), the local head of the railroad, instructs the marshall to make a deal with the boys, promising them a light sentence if they will give themselves up. Jesse agrees but when the deal proves a fraud and Jesse is set to be hanged, Frank and their friends ride in and rescue him. From here on they are bandits. Jesse marries Zee and they have a child but she goes back to her father when Jesse's exploits make home life im-

With John Carradine, Nancy Kelly,
Tyrone Power and Spencer Charters.

possible. Eventually, he says, he will stop and then they will have a real home. In the meantime he and Frank are fugitives with the marshall always in pursuit.

The James boys decide on one last, big raid before retirement and proceed to Northfield, Minnesota, to knock over the First National Bank. What they don't know is that one of their gang, Bob Ford (John Carradine), has made a deal with a Pinkerton detective (J. Edward Bromberg) to turn the brothers in. The raid is a disaster but Jesse and Frank manage to escape. Later Frank appears to be swept away while crossing a river and the wounded Jesse makes his way alone back to his wife. After recuperating Jesse and Zee make plans to leave Missouri and head for California, but Bob Ford turns up and kills Jesse with a bullet in the back.

Jesse James, beautifully photographed, full of action and briskly directed by the veteran Henry King, became 20th Century-Fox's biggest money-maker for 1939. Anyone who criticized its interpretation of history was reminded of that fact. Tyrone Power was obviously a pleasingly absurd choice as Jesse but Fonda was just as obviously

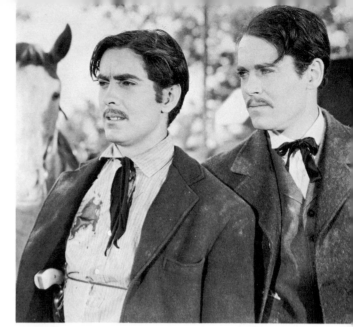

With Tyrone Power.

a right choice for Frank, a man said to be a quiet, saturnine Missouri farmer, given to chewing tobacco and speaking only when spoken to. Midwesterner Fonda clearly knew that kind of man, and the slow drawling accent and the laconic manner made the part ring true.

LET US LIVE

1939
A Columbia release of a William Perlberg Production, directed by John Brahm, written by Anthony Veiller and Allen Rivkin, based on a story by Joseph F. Dineen, photographed by Lucien Ballard, music by Karol Rathaus, 66 minutes.

CAST:
Mary Roberts, *Maureen O'Sullivan;* Brick Tennant, *Henry Fonda;* Lt. Everett, *Ralph Bellamy;* Joe Linden, *Alan Baxter;* District Attorney, *Stanley Ridges;* Chief of Police, *Henry Kolker;* Joe Taylor, *Peter Lynn;* Ed Walsh, *George Douglas;* Frank Burke, *Philip Trent;* Jimmy Dugan, *Martin Spellman.*

Henry Fonda was back in prison for *Let Us Live* and again unjustly accused, as he had been in *You Only Live Once,* and would be again many years later in *The Wrong Man.* Fonda's screen *persona* seemed ideal for the quietly bewildered and wronged innocent. *Let Us Live* was based on an actual near-miscarriage of justice when two taxi drivers in Lynn, Massachusetts, in 1934 were identified by witnesses as being men who held up a theater and killed a man in making their getaway. Their trial was in its third week when the real culprits were apprehended. *Let Us Live* took that situation and dramatically extended it.

Brick Tennant (Fonda) and his pal Joe Linden (Alan Baxter) are identified as robbers and murderers. They are tried, convicted and sentenced to death. Brick's fianceé Mary (Maureen O'Sullivan) takes it upon herself to save him. She finally enlists the aid of a police lieutenant (Ralph Bellamy) and the pair of them ferret out the actual criminals. They present their evidence to the State only an hour before the scheduled execution.

Hollywood waged a good many celluloid battles on behalf of American justice, especially the lack of it in times gone by, and *Let Us Live* was greeted by the critics as just a routine entry. Columbia edited the film to not much more than an hour, the shortest of all Fonda's films, and released it as something the theaters could use as either the top or the bottom of a double bill. The fact that the Commonwealth of Massachusetts threatened action if they leaned too heavily on the Lynn case may have had something to do with it.

With Alan Baxter.

With Maureen O'Sullivan and Charles Lane.

THE STORY OF ALEXANDER GRAHAM BELL

1939

A 20th Century-Fox Film, produced by Kenneth MacGowan, directed by Irving Cummings, written by Lamar Trotti, based on a story by Ray Harris, photographed by Leon Shamroy, music by Louis Silvers, 97 minutes.

CAST:

Alexander Graham Bell, *Don Ameche;* Mrs. Bell, *Loretta Young;* Thomas Watson, *Henry Fonda;* Gardner Hubbard, *Charles Coburn;* Thomas Sanders, *Gene Lockhart;* Mrs. Hubbard, *Spring Byington;* Gertrude Hubbard, *Sally Blane;* Grace Hubbard, *Peggy Ann Garner;* Berta Hubbard, *Georgiana Young;* George Sanders, *Bobs Watson;* Barrows, *Russell Hicks;* Chauncey Smith, *Paul Stanton;* Western Union President, *Jonathan Hale;* Judge, *Harry Davenport.*

If Henry Fonda had made this film after signing his long-term contract with Darryl Zanuck, he would probably have dismissed it as something in which he had to appear. Since he did it while still a freelance actor it is puzzling why he would accept third billing in a popularized account of Alexander Graham Bell's inventing of the telephone. It would have made dramatic sense if Fonda had played Bell and brought a deeper understanding of the inventor, but Zanuck knew that the market for such a film would rest on a more popular actor playing the role. It is, of course, the one film by which Don Ameche is remembered.

The Scottish born Bell (1847–1922) settled in Boston and became a professor in the physiology of speech and continued the pioneering work of his father, A. M. Bell, in teaching speech to deaf-mutes. The film ignores his origins and begins with the young Bell, a struggling inventor, eking out a living by teaching deaf-mute children. He comes to the attention of a prominent citizen,

With Don Ameche.

Gardner Hubbard (Charles Coburn), who hires him to teach his daughter Mabel (Loretta Young), whom Bell is pleasantly surprised to find a lovely young lady. They are soon in love and she persuades her father to advance money to Bell so that he may continue his experiments with a multiple telegraph system. This leads to Bell thinking of the possibility of transmitting the human voice through wire and he hires a young electrician, Tom Watson (Fonda), to help him.

Living in their attic workshop Bell and Watson labor relentlessly with their equipment and experiments. Bell asks Mabel to marry him but her father refuses consent. Now discouraged by his failure to make his invention work, Bell decides to become a full-time teacher and he tells Mabel this by writing the words on the back of a paper on which he has drawn his plans for the telephone. She refuses to let him quit and the two men struggle on. One day Bell pours sulphuric acid into the transmitter and spills some on his leg. In agony he cries out, "Mr. Watson, come here, I want you." In another room Watson is startled to hear the words coming over the equipment. Thus, in 1876, the telephone was born. Bell marries Mabel and her father backs him, but Western Union takes him to court with a charge that they perfected the device previously. Bell looks like he will lose the case because he has no proof—until his wife turns up with the message he wrote her on the dated set of his telephone designs.

The Story of Alexander Graham Bell did a lot for the career of Don Ameche and for years thereafter he was the butt of jokes about his having invented the telephone, but his performance, while earnest, is limited. Fonda's role as Watson comes close to being comedy relief, especially the scene in which he hears Bell's voice coming over the apparatus, "It talks!" It is not a film by which Fonda is remembered, and he may have been a little depressed by the apparent drift in his film career. However, that career was about to take a considerable upward swing.

With Loretta Young and Don Ameche.

82

YOUNG MR. LINCOLN

1939
A 20th Century-Fox-Cosmopolitan Film, produced by Kenneth MacGowan, directed by John Ford, written by Lamar Trotti, photographed by Bert Glennon, music by Alfred Newman, 101 minutes.

CAST:
Abraham Lincoln, *Henry Fonda;* Abigail Clay, *Alice Brady;* Mary Todd, *Marjorie Weaver;* Hannah Clay, *Arleen Whelan;* Efe Turner, *Eddie Collins;* Ann Rutledge, *Pauline Moore;* Matt Clay, *Richard Cromwell;* John Palmer Cass,

With Pauline Moore.

Ward Bond; John Felder, *Donald Meek;* Judge Bell, *Spencer Charters;* Adam Clay, *Eddie Quillan;* Carrie Sue, *Judith Dickens;* Stephen S. Douglas, *Milburn Stone;* Sheriff Billings, *Cliff Clark;* Juror, *Robert Lowery;* Ninian Edwards, *Charles Tannen;* Sam Boone, *Frances Ford;* Scrub White, *Fred Kohler, Jr.;* Mrs. Edwards, *Kay Linaker;* Woolridge, *Russell Simpson.*

Abraham Lincoln as a young man, and upon seeing himself in that guise, Fonda was almost unnerved. It was uncanny, and it made his reaction against doing the film even stronger. A few days later he received a call asking him to meet John Ford, who was assigned to direct the film and whom Fonda had never before met. The gruff Ford appeared angry at Fonda's attitude

When Henry Fonda was offered *Young Mr. Lincoln* his response was quite negative. Producer Kenneth MacGowan and writer Lamar Trotti approached Fonda not only because they thought him the logical choice but because they had heard he was a Lincoln buff. But with persuasion, including that of his wife, Fonda agreed to at least test for the part. The test was in full Lincoln costume and included makeup which altered Fonda's hair style, deepened his eyes and changed the shape of his nose. The result was that Fonda startlingly resembled the photos of

and explained that this was not a picture about a great president but about a young, small-town lawyer and with no reference to his later fame. There was no reason to feel modest or cowed about playing a renowned historical figure. In this manner Ford shamed Fonda into playing a role that would be a milestone in his career.

Young Mr. Lincoln begins in 1832, when Lincoln was 23 and the part owner of a general store in New Salem, Illinois. On their way west the Clay family stop by the store in need of supplies but explain that all they can do by way of payment is barter. Since they have some books, Lincoln is more than willing. One of the books is *Blackstone's Commentaries*, the reading of which whets Lincoln's appetite for the law. In this he is encouraged by his first sweetheart, Ann Rutledge (Pauline Moore). She dies a few years later and one wintry day, while kneeling at her grave, Lincoln resolves to become a lawyer. After studying he goes to live in Springfield and gradually picks up a little business. He comes to the attention of the ambitious Mary Todd (Marjorie Weaver), socially prominent and a constant companion of politician Stephen Douglas (Milburn Stone), the man who in later years became Lin-

Lincoln agrees to represent the Clay boys in their trial and after a long session of confusing evidence he manages to prove that the real killer is Palmer Cass. His success wins Lincoln much approval, including that of the admiring Mary Todd. He also receives a handshake and congratulations from Stephen Douglas, who vows never to underestimate him again. Lincoln replies that it would be better if neither of them underestimate the other. The film ends with Lincoln, still not yet 30, giving some thoughts to politics, and as the sound track swells with "The Battle Hymn of the Republic," the audience is reminded of the man's eventual destiny.

With Alice Brady and Eddie Quillan (right).

With Marjorie Weaver.

coln's bitter opponent. He also comes into contact again with the Clay family. At the end of a day of celebration (Illinois Admission Day) in Springfield, Matt Clay (Richard Cromwell) and his brother Adam (Eddie Quillan) become involved with a pair of roughnecks, Scrub White (Fred Kohler, Jr.) and Palmer Cass (Ward Bond), in which Scrub dies from a knife wound. Cass fingers the Clay boys as the murderers and they are hauled off to jail. A drunken mob storms the jail with the idea of a lynching, but the calm and humorous Lincoln talks them down.

Young Mr. Lincoln is slowly paced and almost as ambling as Fonda's long-legged walk. The script is accurate and Fonda's resemblance to the subject is astonishing. It is easy to see why he felt aghast when he heard his own voice coming from this image. Fonda *is* the film, and it is a prime item in any study of either the actor or the statesman. It also was the film which triggered his long and fruitful association with John Ford, resulting in a half-dozen films that are highlights in Hollywood history.

DRUMS ALONG THE MOHAWK

1939

A 20th Century-Fox Film, produced by Raymond Griffith, directed by John Ford, written by Lamar Trotti and Sonya Levien, based on the novel by Walter D. Edmonds, photographed in Technicolor by Bert Glennon and Ray Rennahan, music by Alfred Newman, 103 minutes.

CAST:

Lana Borst Martin, *Claudette Colbert;* Gilbert Martin, *Henry Fonda;* Mrs. McKlennan, *Edna May Oliver;* Christian Reall, *Eddie Collins;* Caldwell, *John Carradine;* Mary Reall, *Dorris Bowden;* Mrs. Weaver, *Jessie Ralph;* Father Rosenkranz, *Arthur Shields;* John Weaver, *Robert Lowery;* General Herkimer, *Roger Imof;* Joe Boleo, *Francis Ford;* Adam Hartman, *Ward Bond;* Mrs. Demooth, *Kay Linaker;* Dr. Petry, *Russell Simpson;* Blue Back, *Chief Big Tree;* Inn-keeper, *Spencer Characters;* George, *Arthur Aylesworth;* Jacobs, *Si Jenks;* Amos, *Jack Pennick;* Robert Johnson, *Charles Tannen;* Capt. Mark Demooth, *Paul McVey.*

The success of *Young Mr. Lincoln* made Henry Fonda an obvious choice for John Ford's next foray into American history, *Drums Along the Mohawk.* The director and the actor would never be close friends but their professional regard for

each other was considerable—they were clearly the right men with the right material. *Mohawk* would be more commercial than *Lincoln*, with rich Technicolor, a huge cast and a large budget. Ford wanted to make an exciting epic about frontier life in the Mohawk Valley during the Revolutionary War and Zanuck backed him all the way.

With Claudette Colbert.

87

The principal characters are a pair of newly-weds, Gil Martin (Fonda) and Lana (Claudette Colbert), a city girl who finds rural life in 1776 far rougher than she had imagined. As time goes by she becomes accustomed to their crude log cabin and learns how to be a farmer's wife. At the nearby fort Gil and the other locals drill as militia because the Colonies have revolted against the Crown and the British are encouraging the Indians to harass the settlers. In the first attack by the savage Indians Gil and Lana lose their home and their crops, and they also lose their prematurely born baby. In order to earn money for a fresh start they go to work for a crusty but kindly neighbor, Mrs. McKlennan (Edna May Oliver). The Indians attack again and the militia march out to face them. Gil does not return with the others but Lana searches and finds her wounded husband, and nurses him back to health.

During the next two peaceful years Gil and Lana enjoy their life with Mrs. McKlennan and Lana gives birth to their son. Then the Indians again appear, this time in greater numbers and led by British officers. Again the settlers lose their homes and their crops by fire, and retreat to the fort where they desperately manage to ward off the savages. Struck by an arrow, Mrs. McKlennan assigns all her property to Gil and Lana before she dies. The attacks become more ferocious and one of the settlers decides to make a run for it and reach the American military at Fort Dayton. The man is cut down and Gil volunteers to take his place. He is a fine runner and outpaces his pursuers, who finally drop with exhaustion as the fleet Gil speeds on. In the meantime the Indians resume their attack on the fort, now in desperate condition with many casualties and ammunition running low. The situation worsens and at last the women and children are herded into the church as the point of last defense. Hours pass and the Indians are about to break into the church when Gil and the soldiers arrive to turn the tide of battle. The British give up on their plans to control the Mohawk Valley, and with the British surrender in 1781, Gil and Lana look forward, with the other settlers, to a peaceful life in their beautiful valley.

Drums Along the Mohawk made no great demands on Fonda's talents. Suffice it to say that he was completely believable as a young pioneer. It is more the director's film than a vehicle for actors. Ford painted a rich canvas of early frontier life and gave excitement to the scenes of the

With Claudette Colbert.

Indian attacks. This is the kind of material Ford loved and he believed in the basic values of early American life—independence, hard work and faith—and when the preacher at the embattled fort yells to the men, "Trust in the Lord and don't shoot until you can make every shot count," the words could very well have come from Ford himself. In one of the film's most satisfying scenes, when Fonda runs and outpaces the savages, it affirms the audience's belief in Ford's views. *Drums Along the Mohawk* is more than an enjoyable movie, it is a good history lesson, dealing with an area of American experience seldom touched by Hollywood.

With Ward Bond

THE GRAPES OF WRATH

With Eddie Quillan, Dorris Bowden, Jane Darwell, Russell Simpson, Frank Darien, O. Z. Whitehead, and John Carradine.

1940

A 20th Century-Fox Film, produced by Darryl F. Zanuck, directed by John Ford, written by Nunnally Johnson, based on the novel by John Steinbeck, photographed by Gregg Toland, music by Alfred Newman, 129 minutes.

CAST:

Tom Joad, *Henry Fonda*; Ma Joad, *Jane Darwell*; Casey, *John Carradine*; Grandpa, *Charley Grapewin*; Rose, *Dorris Bowden*; Pa Joad, *Russell Simpson*; Al, *O. Z. Whitehead*; Muley, *John Qualen*; Connie, *Eddie Quillan*; Grandma Joad, *Zeffie Tilbury*; Noah, *Frank Sully*; Uncle John, *Frank Darien*; Winfield, *Darryl Hickman*; Ruth

Joad, *Shirley Mills*; Guardian, *Grant Withers*; Policeman, *Ward Bond*; Tim, *Frank Faylen*; Accountant, *Joe Sawyer*; Bert, *Harry Tyler*; Conductor, *Charles B. Middleton*; Davis, *John Arledge*.

There are certain roles in the history of the movies that are so perfectly cast that it is difficult to imagine them being played by anyone else. Who else but Clark Gable as Rhett Butler, James Cagney as George M. Cohan, Errol Flynn as Robin Hood or Spencer Tracy as Father Flanagan? Also in that select company is Henry Fonda's performance as Tom Joad in *The Grapes*

of Wrath. When Darryl Zanuck purchased the screen rights to the John Steinbeck novel he had only two male stars he could possibly assign to the film—Tyrone Power and Don Ameche, and it is doubtful if he seriously considered them. Once John Ford was signed to direct the film there was no doubt about who would play Joad. Ford wanted Fonda and nobody else, a choice that was underlined by the fact that Steinbeck himself thought Fonda would be ideal.

Steinbeck's novel had been a best-seller through most of 1939, despite its searing treatment of poverty and distress. It told a story alarmingly out of keeping with The American Dream, the plight of huge numbers of mid-western tenant farmers forced from their land by soil erosion and the desire of the land owners, mostly the banks, to clear them out. They became displaced people, many of whom headed for California because they were led to believe they could find work on the fruit and vegetable farms. Traveling west in rickety cars and trucks they became a 1930's version of the wagon train pioneers of the previous century. The novel had displeased some Americans because it seemed like an indictment of capitalism and a cry for socialism, as well as an ugly depiction of the failure of such American values as independence and free enterprise. In selling his book to 20th Century-Fox, Steinbeck demanded and received an unusual clause in his contract—that the film version "fairly and reasonably retain the main

action and social intent of said literary property." Zanuck and scenarist Nunnally Johnson honored the clause and consulted with Steinbeck on whatever changes they felt necessary.

Since many of the displaced people came from Oklahoma they, and most others, begot the nickname "Okies." Tom Joad is an Okie and when first seen he is hitchhiking a ride home, having just completed four of seven years in

With Jane Darwell.

With Russell Simpson.

prison for manslaughter, and is now on parole. The first person he runs into is Casey (John Carradine), a preacher who says he has lost the call and is no longer fit to preach. With nowhere else to go, Casey accompanies Tom. They come across an old friend, Muley (John Qualen), now half out of his mind with grief about having lost his home and the right to work his land. The land has never really been his but he thinks it is because he and his family were born on it and grew up on it. But the owners now find that a

single tractor can do the work of dozens of men and there is no longer a need for sharecroppers. Tom learns that this miserable situation applies to his own people and he joins them in their decision to head west.

The long, slow trip to California along Route 66 is arduous and costs the lives of Tom's grandparents. But it is his strong-willed mother (Jane Darwell) who holds the family together. When they arrive in California they find it to be less than paradise, with thousands of their own kind huddled together in shabby camps and desperately in need of work. They pull into one of these so-called Hoovervilles and are shocked at the conditions. Hordes of hungry children hang around the Joads as they prepare a meal. The Californian encouragement to come to the state turns out to be a way of recruiting cheap labor. A group of deputy sheriffs arrive in the camp to arrest an Okie who had stood up for fair treatment, and Tom and Casey go to his aid. Tom aids

the man and in so doing knocks out a deputy. Casey proudly takes the blame and is hauled away. The Joads move on and find work on a farm, where they are given a hut in which to live and a payment of five cents an hour picking peaches. In doing so they find they are being used as strike breakers for men who have refused to work for less.

One night Tom, against the instructions imposed on the workers, sneaks out of the camp and finds a group of the breakers, one of whom is the released Casey. When a band of deputies surround them the outspoken Casey is clubbed to death and Tom strikes down the man who did it, but after first receiving a blow to the face that leaves an ugly gash. He escapes and leads the Joad family out of the camp. A little luck comes their way when they reach a government camp and find fair treatment and decent living conditions. Life picks up for them but Tom is a hunted man, and identifiable because of the scar on his face. He realizes that for the sake of his family he must leave. He doesn't know where but as he tells his tearful mother, "Maybe I can jus' find out sump'n. Jus' scrounge aroun' an' try to find out what it is that's wrong, an' then see if they ain't sump'n could be done about it." Ma worries about how she will ever know what has happened to him. He says he doesn't know, but like Casey says, maybe a man doesn't have a soul of his own, just a piece of a big one that belongs to everybody, "Then I'll be all aroun' in the dark. I'll be everywhere—wherever you look. Wherever there's a fight so hungry people can eat. I'll be there. Wherever there's a cop beatin' up on a guy, I'll be there. I'll be in the way guys yell when they're mad. . ." Tom says goodbye to his mother and promises that if there's a way to come back to her he will.

The Grapes of Wrath as written by Steinbeck gave little hope at its conclusion. Zanuck felt the film, obviously a moving experience for anyone to see, needed at least a hint of uplift at its ending. Steinbeck agreed. The movie ends with the family on the road again and with staunch old Ma Joad sitting up front in the truck and saying to her husband (Russell Simpson), ". . . we keep a-comin.' We're the people that live. Can't nobody wipe us out. Can't nobody lick us. We'll go on forever, Pa. We're the people." It was a good ending for an excellent film. And that ending was written by Zanuck himself.

The Grapes of Wrath is a classic American film and credit is due Zanuck. Steinbeck's novel had been banned in parts of the United States and

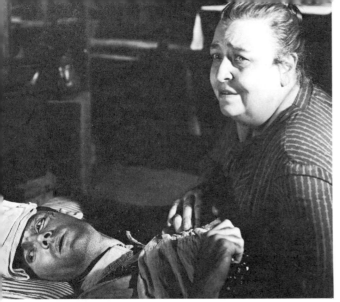

With Jane Darwell.

happy scene, the dance at the government camp, Tom dances and warbles "Red River Valley." The song would be identified with Fonda from then on, and for a man who admitted to having an atrocious singing voice, it was a compliment. Perhaps the best thing that can be said about his performance is that it doesn't fade with time. It remains clear and sharp.

John Steinbeck was well pleased with what Zanuck, Ford and Fonda had done. Many years later he took a reluctant look at the film, fearing that it had perhaps dated, but gritted his teeth and sat back. "Then a lean, stringy, dark-faced piece of electricity walks out on the screen, and he had me. I believed in my own story again. It was fresh and happening and good. Hank can do that. He carries with him that excitement which cannot be learned—as many an actor has found to his sorrow—but he backs up his gift with grueling, conscientious work and agony of self-doubt."

The success of *The Grapes of Wrath* was sweet but Fonda had to pay a price. In order to get the role of Tom Joad he had to sign a contract with Zanuck, who with only Tyrone Power and Don Ameche heading up his leading men department badly needed a star in that category. Fonda knew Zanuck had him trapped and he signed. As a result he made a number of Fox pictures over the next few years, but they were never quite as bad as he claimed, and the period of bondage would be less than he imagined.

some people assumed that when Zanuck purchased the screen rights it was to take them off the market. Whatever doubts Zanuck may have had about the bleak, severe account Steinbeck painted of the migrant workers and their plight vanished after he had sent some investigators out to check on them. They returned to say that Steinbeck had been reserved in his appraisal— the actual conditions were worse. With that in mind Zanuck launched into an honest and uncompromising film, with John Ford directing in an equally honest and uncompromising manner. No false heroics or sentiment. Indeed Ford's film is visually in line with the Depression era documentary *The Plow That Broke the Plain*, and the man who made that celebrated film, Pare Lorentz, said that he considered *The Grapes of Wrath* a magnificent achievement and that Fonda's performance was one of the finest he had ever seen; "In fact you may forget Fonda is in the company—his performance is so tough, undeviating and simple you may think he is one of the extras, or one of the actual migrants. . . ."

Fonda's portrayal of Tom Joad can be considered the triumph of his film career. He simply *is* Tom. The well remembered farewell scene with the mother is one of the most quoted scenes in American film literature, which is a direct tribute to Fonda because in the hands of a lesser actor the scene could have become maudlin and corny. The lines do not really make a great deal of sense—it is close to pop philosophy—but Fonda makes them seem true and real. And this applies to the whole performance. In the film's only

With Jane Darwell, Dorris Bowden

☆☆☆☆☆☆☆☆☆☆☆☆☆☆☆☆☆☆

LILLIAN RUSSELL

1940

A 20th Century-Fox Film, produced by Darryl F. Zanuck, directed by Irving Cummings, written by William Anthony McGuire, photographed by Leon Shamroy, musical direction by Alfred Newman, 127 minutes.

CAST:

Lillian Russell, *Alice Faye;* Edward Solomon, *Don Ameche;* Alexander Moore, *Henry Fonda;* Diamond Jim Brady, *Edward Arnold;* Jesse Lewisohn, *Warren William;* Tony Pastor, *Leo Carrillo;* Grandma Leonard, *Helen Westley;* Cynthia Leonard, *Dorothy Peterson;* Charles Leonard, *Ernest Truex;* Edna McCauley, *Lynn*

Bari; William Gilbert, *Nigel Bruce;* Arthur Sullivan, *Claude Allister;* Weber and Fields, *Themselves;* Marie, *Una O'Connor;* Eddie Foy, *Eddie Foy, Jr.;* Walter Damrosch, *Joseph Cawthorne;* President Cleveland, *William B. Davidson.*

Henry Fonda was stunned when Darryl Zanuck assigned him to *Lillian Russell.* Having just completed *The Grapes of Wrath* he assumed he merited first-class material instead of being given third billing in an Alice Faye musical. However, it must be said that Zanuck designed this as the most costly and elaborate of the Faye musicals, aiming for a blockbuster at the box office, and needed to give it all the strength he could. If Fonda's notices with the Steinbeck story could help, so much the better. Zanuck was in the business of making commercial movies.

Lillian Russell is a fairly good account of the famed American entertainer (1861–1922)—famed for her beauty and as the star of many musicals. She retired in 1922 after marrying newspaper publisher Alexander Moore, played in the film by Fonda. Russell was married four times but the movie opted to overlook two of her husbands. Running a half hour longer than most Fox musicals of the day, it shows the young Helen Leonard (Faye) being accepted as a pupil in New York by Walter Damrosch but advised that her voice, though good, is not suitable for opera. One evening her runaway carriage is stopped by a handsome young man, Alexander Moore, who then fades from her life. She is spotted by theatre producer Tony Pastor (Leo Carrillo) who hires her for his theatre and changes her name to Lillian Russell.

Lillian gradually becomes the toast of New

With Alice Faye.

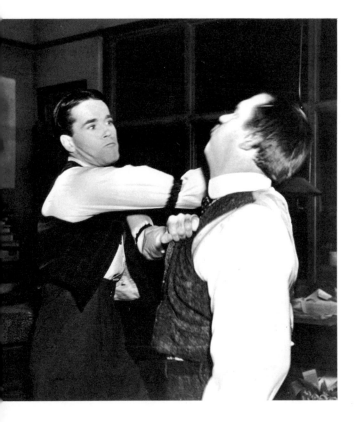

With Leo Carrillo.

With Edward Arnold, Don Ameche, Alice Faye and Warren William.

York, going from success to success and being courted by many men, one of whom is a serious young musician named Edward Solomon (Don Ameche), and he is the one she marries. Years later in London, where Gilbert (Nigel Bruce) and Sullivan (Claude Allister) are writing an operetta for her, she is approached by Moore, who is now a newspaperman and eager to write a series on her. Husband Edward dies while writing a musical for her and she returns to America, there to become more and more famous, appearing with all the contemporary greats of the American theatre. One night, after the opening of a show, Moore comes backstage to see her. Happy reunion, happy ending.

It is easy to see why such a shallow role should have displeased Fonda after having proved his calibre in *The Grapes of Wrath*. It is doubtful if he ever saw *Lillian Russell*, but any mention of it in his presence always brought forth a grunt of disgust. As a movie musical it is passing fair, although somewhat pedestrian, and the witty Bosley Crowther, in his *New York Times* review, could not resist this barb: "Miss Russell is said to have been a rather poor actress and Miss Faye—even granting the thinness of her material—does not violate that reputation."

95

THE RETURN OF FRANK JAMES

1940

A 20th Century-Fox Film, produced by Darryl F. Zanuck, directed by Fritz Lang, written by Sam Hellman, photographed in Technicolor by George Barnes and William V. Hellman, music by David Buttolph, 92 minutes.

CAST:

Frank James, *Henry Fonda*; Eleanor Stone, *Gene Tierney*; Clem, *Jackie Cooper*; Major Rufus Todd, *Henry Hull*; George Runyan, *J. Edward Bromberg*; McCoy, *Donald Meek*; Station Agent, *Eddie Collins*; Bob Ford, *John Carradine*; Judge, *George Barbier*; Pinky, *Ernest Whitman*; Charles Ford, *Charles Tannen*; Randolph Stone, *Lloyd Corrigan*; Agent, *Russell Hicks*; Preacher, *Victor Killian*; Colonel Jackson, *Edward McWade*; Roy, *George Chandler*.

The enormous success of *Jesse James* paved the way for some kind of sequel, clearly one that would have to deal with brother Frank and his desire to see assassin Bob Ford brought to justice. Darryl Zanuck, who now had Henry Fonda under contract, wanted a film that would stand on its own merits and not be an obvious follow-up. To this end he hired, somewhat to the astonishment of Hollywood, the meticulous Fritz Lang. Lang had, in fact, spent some time studying western life and had shot some documentary footage on Indians. He happily accepted Zanuck's offer and went off to scout locations in the California Sierras, near the towns of Bishop and Sonora, while sets were constructed at the studio. Zanuck had no desire to skimp with this production and looked to Lang for a different kind of western. He got it. *The Return of Frank James* has action and superbly photographed scenery, but it also had moods, details, attention to sound and lighting unusual for a western of its time. Lovers of conventional westerns prob-

With Gene Tierney.

ably found it a little strange and a bit slow. Henry Fonda blanched at the idea of having to work again with Lang but the director promised that this time he would be more considerate.

The characterization of Frank follows that set in the previous film. He is still quiet and laconic, and still chewing tobacco. Now a farmer happily working his fields in Missouri he is content to let the law take care of Bob Ford (John Carradine) and his brother Charlie (Charles Tannen). But the law decides that Bob Ford was justified in getting rid of the famous bandit and sets him free. Frank now makes his own deci-

With Jackie Cooper.

agonies of *You Only Live Once* again. Apparently Lang, with tears in his eyes, said he would be more compassionate toward Fonda and the rest of the cast, but such was not the case. Fonda claimed that Lang was just as inconsiderate of his actors as before, having little regard for their comfort or how long they were kept waiting while Lang considered his shots. Fonda also claimed that while on location Lang was responsible for the death of several horses, which he required to be galloped mercilessly in high mountain altitudes. At one point in the filming Lang spoke sharply to Gene Tierney, who made her movie debut in this film, and Fonda sprang to her defense, "Don't you dare speak to that girl in that way!" In her autobiography Tierney recalled having a crush on Fonda at the time because he was gentle and thoughtful, and somewhat in awe of him because he was always letter-perfect in his lines and because the crew referred to him as "one-take Fonda." Fonda would work with Tierney again but never with Lang.

sion—to take the law into his own hands. With his young friend and ward Clem (Jackie Cooper), he sets out for Colorado where the Fords, all the while boasting about how they cleared up the James gang, hope to start a new life. Major Rufus Cobb (Henry Hull) still prints the truth in his newspaper and a pretty young lady reporter, Eleanor Stone (Gene Tierney), pursues Frank to try and get an in-depth account of his life. Frank shows no interest in this but in time comes to feel affectionate toward her. In Colorado Frank and Clem catch up with the Fords. Charlie is accidentally killed but Bob escapes. When Frank returns to Missouri, he is charged with murder and robbery and put on trial in Liberty.

The smug Bob Ford turns up at the trial to gloat but is shocked when Frank is acquitted. Frank resumes his pursuit of Ford but it is the eager young Clem who engages him in a gun battle in the streets of Liberty. Both are killed, with Clem losing his life to save Frank. Now free of revenge Frank rides out of town to start life again as a farmer.

When Fonda started work on *The Return of Frank James*, he faced Fritz Lang in order to come to an understanding about their working together. He did not want to go through the

With Gene Tierney and Jackie Cooper.

CHAD HANNA

1940

A 20th Century-Fox Film, produced by Nunnally Johnson, directed by Henry King, written by Nunnally Johnson, based on the story *Red Wheels Rolling* by Walter D. Edmonds, photographed in Technicolor by Ernest Palmer, music by David Buttolph, 86 minutes.

CAST:

Chad Hanna, *Henry Fonda*; Albany Yates, *Dorothy Lamour*; Caroline, *Linda Darnell*; Huguenine, *Guy Kibbee*; Mrs. Huguenine, *Jane Darwell*; Bisbee, *John Carradine*; Fred Shepley, *Ted North*; Ike Wayfish, *Roscoe Ates*; Bell Boy, *Ben Carter*; Burke, *Frank Thomas*; Cisco Tridd, *Olin Howard*; Mr. Proudfoot, *Frank Conlon*; Fiero, *Edward Conrad*; Joe Duddy, *Edward Mundy*; Pete Bastock, *George Davis*; Budlong, *Paul Burns*; Mrs. Tridd, *Sarah Padden*; Mr. Pamplon, *Leonard St. Leo*; Mrs. Pamplon, *Elizabeth Abbott*; Mr. Mott, *Tully Marshall*; Mrs. Mott, *Almira Sessions*.

Walter D. Edmonds' novel *Rome Haul* had been the source material for Henry Fonda's debut movie, *The Farmer Takes a Wife*, and he had also starred in the film version of Edmonds' *Drums Along the Mohawk*. So when Darryl Zanuck decided to film Edmonds' novel *Red Wheels Rolling*, there was little doubt about the choice of actor to play the leading part of Chad Hanna, Zanuck assigned Nunnally Johnson to produce the film as well as script it and he agreed with Johnson's opinion that the name of the lead character would make a more intriguing title for the film.

Chad Hanna is a descriptive account of early 19th century Americana, seen through the adventures of a wagon circus moving through upper New York state. In 1841 the people of Canastota are elated by the arrival of Huguenine's International Circus, which is actually a rather tatty group. Chad Hanna (Fonda) is a chore boy in a tavern and he becomes smitten with Albany

With Guy Kibbee and Ted North.

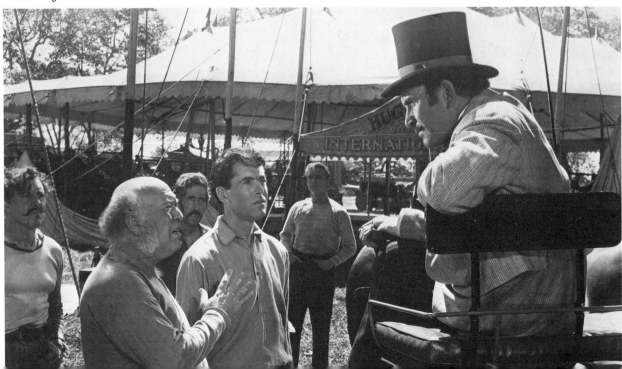

With Dorothy Lamour.

Yates (Dorothy Lamour), the beautiful bareback rider, so much so that he joins the circus as a roustabout. Also joining in order to escape her brutal father is Caroline Tridd (Linda Darnell), who becomes an understudy to Albany. Trouble erupts when a rival circus owner, Fred Shepley (Ted North), warns Huguenine (Guy Kibbee) to stay out of towns in which his group is performing. Shepley also steals Albany by offering her more money. This results in a battle between the two sets of employees, in which Huguenine is injured, and Chad takes his place as ringmaster.

Chad marries Caroline but things turn bad for Huguenine when his main attraction, a lion, dies. Huguenine blames Chad for the death and Chad angrily storms off to join Shepley's circus and deserts his wife, whom he doesn't know is pregnant. Chad almost has an affair with Albany but comes to his senses and realizes how much he loves Caroline. In the meantime Huguenine stages a show minus his lion and comes to grief when his audience of rough Erie Canal workers threaten to tear the place apart. The situation is saved by Chad, who strides in with an elephant he has acquired by promising its owner a quarter share in the circus. The audience is delighted and Chad resumes his happy life.

Chad Hanna, fortunately in Technicolor, is a pleasing picture but hardly something Fonda needed at this point in his career, especially since it required him to return to the old stamping

With Linda Darnell and Dorothy Lamour.

grounds of the Erie Canal for yet another portrayal of a good natured yokel. But it was a mark of Fonda's talent that he could make something of even that limited characterization. In his *New York Herald Tribune* review, Robert Dana made a good point: ". . . his portrait of Chad is something else, the something that proves an actor can be somebody else if he is good enough. Fonda makes Chad terribly ingenuous, almost stolid. It is the one clear-cut aspect of the film, perfect in every respect."

THE LADY EVE

1941

A Paramount Film, produced by Paul Jones, directed and written by Preston Sturges, based on a story by Moncton Hall, photographed by Victor Milner, music by Sigmund Krumgold, 97 minutes.

CAST:

Jean/Eve, *Barbara Stanwyck;* Charles Pike, *Henry Fonda;* Colonel Harrington, *Charles Coburn;* Mr. Pike, *Eugene Pallette;* Muggsy, *William Demarest;* Sir Alfred, *Eric Blore;* Gerald, *Melville Cooper;* Martha, *Martha*

With William Demarest and Robert Grieg.

O'Driscoll; Mrs. Pike, *Janet Beecher;* Burrows, *Robert Greig;* Gertrude, *Dora Clement;* Pike's Chef, *Luis Alberni.*

As time goes by it seems increasingly apparent that the brilliant, eccentric Preston Sturges (1898–1959) is not likely to be replaced. Or equalled as a writer-director with gifts as both a verbal and visual wit. Sturges had been a successful writer at Paramount for some years before he finally persuaded the studio to let him direct his own material. In 1940 he made two small-budget pictures—*The Great McGinty,* a political satire, and *Christmas in July,* a spoof on the

With Barbara Stanwyck.

advertising business. Both were minor gems and profitable enough for Paramount to trust him with a bigger budget and a pair of name players for his third venture, *The Lady Eve.* Some film buffs may argue that *The Palm Beach Story* or *Hail the Conquering Hero* are better, but there are many who claim that *The Lady Eve* is the most perfectly structured and trenchant Sturges comedy. Henry Fonda and Barbara Stanwyck certainly believed it to be so, and with good reason. It gave both of them a much-needed shot at comedy and a chance to show how well they could handle it.

This is a battle of the sexes, with woman very much the winner. Charles Pike (Fonda) is a nice but dull young millionaire, the son of a wealthy brewer (Eugene Pallette), whose slogan is "Pike's Pale, the Ale That Won for Yale." Innocent of guile but terribly wary of women because all they seem to be interested in is money, Charles has devoted his life to scientific explorations, with a particular study of snakes. After one such expedition he boards an ocean liner bound for America. Spotting him walking up the gangway is Jean (Stanwyck), who drops an apple on his head. It is symbolic of the tra??? t?e confused Charles is about to undergo. Jean is traveling in the company of her father (Charles Coburn), who calls himself Colonel Harrington. They are a pair of expert cardsharps who ply the luxury lines bilking the wealthy. Jean first gets Charles's

attention by tripping him in the dining room and then using all her guiles to get him to fall in love with her.

Her scheme is well underway when Pike's tough and vigilant bodyguard, Muggsy (William Demarest), exposes Jean as having a police record. The disillusioned Charles snorts, "Thought you were having a lot of fun with me, didn't you?"and wipes her out of his life. She, however, is not about to give up. She assumes another guise and next appears in Charles's life as a titled Englishwoman, Lady Eve. He accepts her once he convinces himself that she resembles Jean too much to actually be her.

The naive millionaire falls into the same trap again, little realizing that he is being put through the same hoop. He marries her, but Jean is still bent on revenge for being dumped the first time. On their honeymoon night, as a train speeds through the night, she tells him she wants to confess some of her past indiscretions. He says that the thing that distinguishes a man from a beast is the willingness to understand and forgive. The bride then launches into a revelation of ex-lovers and affairs . . . and the recital goes on and on

With Charles Coburn, Barbara Stanwyck and William Demarest.

With Eugene Pallette, Janet Beecher, Barbara Stanwyck and Eric Blore.

cious as a woman who knows it all—sly, alluring, smolderingly sexy and with a mind like a computer. Pitted against her, a man like Charles Pike has as much chance as an umbrella under Niagara. Fonda had always liked comedy but it took Sturges to fathom the actor's real ability in this difficult area of performance. This particular role called for a considerable amount of physical comedy, with Fonda taking several extended falls and having things tipped on him, things like

Rehearsing with writer-director Preston Sturges.

through the night. By morning Charles has decided on a divorce from Lady Eve.

Some time later, on another ocean liner, Jean again trips Charles as he passes. Again he falls into Jean's arms but this time he is glad to see her and sorry about past misunderstandings. After his treatment by the English lady he is eager to be united with Jean but so confused he says, "I don't want to understand. I don't want to know. Whatever it is, keep it to yourself. All I know is I adore you. I'll never leave you again. We'll work it out somehow."

As a satire on the man-woman wars *The Lady Eve* stands in a class of its own. Like all Sturges pictures it is populated with a cast of wild characters, most of whom have a quip or two about the human condition. Stanwyck is deli-

plates of food. He mastered it all and maintained stoic composure, so much so that critic Andrew Sarris dubbed him the funniest deadpan comedian since Buster Keaton. He may not have been quite that but his is a beautifully balanced portrait of a man rendered pitifully and hilariously vulnerable by the forces brought against him.

★★★★★★★★★★★★★★★★★★★★★★
WILD GEESE CALLING

1941

A 20th Century-Fox Film, produced by Harry Joe Brown, directed by John Brahm, written by Horace McCoy, based on a novel by Stewart Edward White, photographed by Lucien Ballard, music by Alfred Newman, 77 minutes.

CAST:

John Murdock, *Henry Fonda;* Sally, *Joan Bennett;* Blackie, *Warren William;* Clarabelle, *Ona Munson;* Kelly, *Barton MacLane;* Len, *Russell Simpson;* Mazie, *Iris Adrian;* Jack, *James Morton;* Manager, *Paul Sutton;* Jennie, *Mary Field;* Delaney, *Stanley Andrews;* Swede, *Jody Gilbert.*

With Iris Adrian and Warren William.

With Joan Bennett.

After the elation of working for Preston Sturges, Henry Fonda was disappointed to return to Fox and find that the best Darryl Zanuck had lined up for him was *Wild Geese Calling*, calling for him to return to the wilds as yet another

103

With Ona Munson.

With Warren William.

rural type. In this outing he is a lumberjack with a wanderlust, who quits his job and ends up in the lusty Seattle of 1895. John Murdock there hopes to locate his adventurous friend Blackie Bedford (Warren William), a man short on scruples but a lot of fun. While looking, John meets Sally (Joan Bennett), a pretty dancer in a waterfront saloon. The two fall in love but Sally does not dare tell John that she was Blackie's girl before their meeting, and they get married.

Blackie is also being sought by a tough character known as Pirate Kelly (Barton MacLane), who has found out that Blackie won a hotel in Alaska from him by using loaded dice. When John finds Blackie, the three agree to take off for Alaska, with Blackie keeping his mouth shut about having known Sally before. John saves Blackie from Kelly but he decides not to go in with his friend in running the decrepid hotel and returns to being a lumberjack. He and Sally set up home in a crude cabin and she is befriended by a good-hearted prostitute, Clarabelle (Ona Munson). Seeing Pirate Kelly in town, Sally goes to warn Blackie, who makes a pitch for her. He kisses her just as John enters the room.

John refuses to believe Sally's explanation and stays with her only when he learns that she is pregnant. When she enters the throes of childbirth he goes to town in a desperate search for a doctor. While there he is spotted by Kelly, who fires and wounds him, but Blackie turns up and kills Kelly. He and Clarabelle take over a sailboat and make their way in a storm to John's cabin. There Clarabelle helps Sally bring her baby into the world and Blackie explains that he forced himself on Sally against her wishes. All is forgiven and, now a family man, John is ready to settle down and no longer respond to the call of the wild geese.

Wild Geese Calling is second-grade melodrama and it could do nothing but accelerate Fonda's growing resentment at Darryl Zanuck's apparent lack of interest in finding him first-rate material.

YOU BELONG TO ME

1941

A Columbia Film, produced and directed by Wesley Ruggles, written by Claude Binyon, based on a story by Dalton Trumbo, photographed by Joseph Walker, music by Frederick Hollander, 94 minutes.

CAST:

Helen Hunt, *Barbara Stanwyck*; Peter Kirk, *Henry Fonda*; Billings, *Edgar Buchanan*; Vandemer, *Roger Clark*; Emma, *Ruth Donnelly*; Moody, *Melville Cooper*; Joseph, *Ralph Peters*; Ella, *Maude Eburne*; Minnie, *Renie Rialto*; Eva, *Ellen Lowe*; Doris, *Mary Treen*; Robert Andrews, *Gordon Jones*; Desk Clerk, *Fritz Feld*; Barrows, *Paul Harvey*; Smithers, *Harold Waldridge*.

The success of *The Lady Eve* made a re-teaming of Henry Fonda and Barbara Stanwyck a wise market move but sadly it was not Preston Sturges who brought them together again. Unfortunately, Sturges never thought of anything else for them. Instead it was Wesley Ruggles at Columbia who came up with the amusing but far from brilliant *You Belong to Me*. Once again Fonda is a millionaire, but this time he is the pursuer and not the pursued.

Peter Kirk (Fonda) is a playboy who spots Helen Hunt (Stanwyck) while skiing and in whizzing after her ends up head first in a snowdrift. She is impressed until she finds out he is a member of the idle rich, and since she is a dedicated physician she has no time for his kind. But Peter is also the kind who does not take no for an answer, and due to his steady persistence they get married. Now the real problems begin. Peter has all kinds of time to enjoy his luxurious life. Helen has hardly any time at all and on their first night at home Peter is disgusted to find their

bliss shattered by endless telephone calls for her services.

As the days progress his frustration leads to boredom as he hangs around her office while she tends her very full schedule of examinations and operations. To make matters worse, she seems to specialize in attractive men. Helen comes up with an idea—why doesn't Peter get himself a job. Since he has no qualifications at all, the millionaire ends up as a sales clerk in a department store at $22.50 a week.

Helen is proud of Peter's decision to work—at least it keeps his jealousies out of her office—but things go badly for him at work when the employees, who regard him as a "no good

With Barbara Stanwyck.

With Barbara Stanwyck, Melville Cooper,
Ralph Peters, Mary Treen, Renie Riano, Ellen
Lowe and Maude Eburne

millionaire," complain to the management about his having a job that some needy person could fill. He responds, "Why should a few million dollars keep me from having a chance like everybody else?" Eventually it occurs to him to give up his fortune. He buys a hospital and Helen is appointed chief of staff.

You Belong to Me has its comedic moments but in the hands of less capable actors than Fonda and Stanwyck it would likely have fared badly. Hollywood in 1941 was apparently not aware that the Depression was over and that the public was no longer quite so amused by movies poking fun at the wealthy and the notion that money stands in the way of happiness. It also was not a good vehicle for Fonda because the role was too silly, with little sympathy for his so-called plight as an idle husband of a busy wife. Still, his sense of comedy enabled him to get a few laughs out of peering through the keyhole of his wife's office and bursting in on her administrations to robust male clients.

With Barbara Stanwyck and Gordon Jones.

☆THE MALE ANIMAL

1942

A Warner Bros. Film, produced by Hal B. Wallis, directed by Elliott Nugent, written by Julius and Philip Epstein and Stephen Morehouse Avery, based on the play by James Thurber and Elliott Nugent, photographed by Arthur Edeson, music by Heinz Roemheld, 101 minutes.

CAST:

Tommy Turner, *Henry Fonda;* Ellen Turner, *Olivia de Havilland;* Patricia Stanley, *Joan Leslie;* Joe Ferguson, *Jack Carson;* Ed Keller, *Eugene Pallette;* Michael Barnes, *Herbert Anderson;* Cleota, *Hattie MacDaniel;* Dr. Damon, *Ivan Simpson;* Wally, *Don DeFore;* Hot Garters Garner, *Jean Ames;* Blanche Lamon, *Minna Phillips;* Myrtle Keller, *Regina Wallace;* Coach Sprague, *Frank Mayo;* Alumnus, *William Davidson;* Nutsy Miller, *Bobby Barnes.*

Henry Fonda could never understand why the films for which Darryl Zanuck loaned him to other studios were almost always better than the ones he made for Zanuck. Clearly, if another studio went to the trouble of arranging for him to play a certain role it was because they held him in sufficient regard to take that kind of trouble. Zanuck was a very shrewd man and perhaps he reasoned that he benefitted from other studios going to the expense of acquiring worthy vehicles for his star. It certainly did Zanuck no harm to have Fonda go over to Warners to make the excellent *The Male Animal.* Whatever success the film enjoyed was bound to shine on any Fox vehicles in which he placed Fonda.

The Male Animal is Fonda at his comically appealing best. The film satirizes the ever-prevalent crisis in American academic life—the chasm between the intellectual element and the brawny athletic strain. It first appeared on Broadway in

With Olivia de Havilland.

107

1940 with Elliott Nugent playing the role of assistant professor Tommy Turner, a role he had co-written with humorist James Thurber. Nugent was hired by Warners to direct the film version and he knew that his name meant nothing to the moviegoers as an actor. He did, however, specify in his contract the right to choose the actor to play the gentle, idealistic teacher. Nugent had only one man in mind and Warners agreed instantly with his choice. Fonda.

With Olivia de Havilland and Eugene Pallette.

Many are the movies about American college life, almost all of them rah-rah-rah tributes to sports departments. *The Male Animal* speaks up for the brain factors and since it was partly the brain child of James Thurber it also gets in a few jibes about the man-woman wars. But it goes beyond ribbing the school athletes and makes a few digs at the ultra-conservative character of past American academic life. Here the school trustees definitely veer to the Right, especially the regent, played with flaring nostrils by the bear-like Eugene Pallette. His joy at seeing Ferguson again is almost sinister in its humor, as these two mountains of Babbitt go into football tackles with childish relish. Carson is superb as Ferguson, a fatuous football celebrity whose mind and body are both on the verge of turning to blubber. Olivia de Havilland is the kind of warm, supportive wife every decent-minded professor deserves to have, especially if he is a bit

of a Don Quixote. Those, like Tommy Turner, who challenge the windmills of the Establishment need all the help they can get.

But *The Male Animal* belongs firmly to Fonda. His Tommy is the true, quiet man of integrity, part genial and part tenacious. The role could have become a little silly in lesser hands. Thanks to him, as Elliott Nugent was the first to point out, the film is an improvement on the stage play.

Tommy Turner is a mild-mannered, slightly absent-minded professor, somewhat inclined to take his attractive wife Ellen (Olivia de Havilland) for granted. But problems creep into his life with the appearance on campus of beefy, former football champ Joe Ferguson (Jack Carson), who turns up to create enthusiasm for the coming Big Game. He loudly renews his friendship with Ellen, his school sweetheart, and offends Tommy with his blustering personality. But even more upsetting to Tommy is an editorial Michael Barnes (Herbert Anderson) has written for the school newspaper, in which he praises Tommy for his intention to read a certain letter to his class. The letter is the last written by anarchist Bartolomeo Vanzetti before his execution, a letter expounding the virtues of tolerance. To make the editorial even worse for Tommy, it suggests that the school board does not value liberal-minded teachers. It creates a furor on campus and the dean (Ivan Simpson) warns Tommy that he will likely lose his position if he reads the letter.

With Jack Carson.

Michael is in love with Ellen's sister Pat (Joan Leslie) but she is smitten with a lusty half back (Don DeFore). Ellen pleads with Tommy not to read the letter, lest it jeopardize his imminent posting to a full professorship. He pleads the First Amendment and says he intends to go through with it. She calls him a pig-headed fool and he rejoins by referring to Joe Ferguson as her paramour. This further promotes her anger and she storms out of the house, informing Tommy she intends to join Ferguson at a party.

Misery finds company when Tommy and Michael get together to commiserate over drinks. The drunker they get the more they proclaim their masculinity. Tommy cries, "No tiger would let his mate be stolen. The human animal won't, either. I'll fight." When Ellen and Ferguson return to the house, the inebriated Tommy challenges the startled champ to a fight but all he succeeds in doing is knocking himself out. Ferguson picks the unconscious Tommy up and carries him upstairs. By now the situation with the Turners is starting to bother the egocentric ex-champ. He likes Ellen but he doesn't want to get stuck with her.

The next day the slightly hung-over Tommy reads the fateful letter to his class but he finds that so many people want to hear it he has to perform in the school auditorium. As he reads the Vanzetti letter the hostile members of the school executive staff start to mellow as they discover it contains no political propaganda. Instead it is touchingly humanistic in its plea for understanding. By the end of the reading some of the members are dabbing the tears in their eyes. The incident makes Tommy a campus hero and Ellen reaffirms her love for him. Actually it was she who slipped the letter in his pocket

With Eugene Pallette, Joan Leslie, Olivia de Havilland and Regina Wallace

because in his confusion he would have gone to the auditorium without it. She and Tommy are carried in triumph around the campus—and Joe Ferguson breathes a sigh of relief. Pat also has a change of heart, discovering that the intellectual Michael is far more interesting and courageous than the muscle-bound halfback.

RINGS ON HER FINGER

1942

A 20th Century-Fox Film, produced by Milton Sperling, directed by Rouben Mamoulian, written by Ken Englund, based on a story by Robert Pirosh and Joseph Schrank, photographed by George Barnes, music by Cyril Mockridge, 86 minutes.

CAST:

John Wheeler, *Henry Fonda;* Susan Miller, *Gene Tierney;* May Worthington, *Spring Byington;* Warren, *Laird Cregar;* Tod Fenwick, *John Sutton;* Kellogg, *Frank Orth;* Colonel Prentice, *Henry Stephenson;* Mrs. Fenwick, *Marjorie Gateson;* Mr. Fenwick, *George Lessey;* Peggy, *Iris*

Adrian; Train Conductor, *Harry Hayden;* Miss Callahan, *Gwendolyn Logan;* Butler, *Eric Wilton;* Newsboy, *Billy Benedict;* Mrs. Clancey, *Sarah Edwards;* Mr. Beasley, *Thurston Hall;* Mrs. Beasley, *Clara Blandick;* Capt. Hurley, *Charles Wilson;* Paul, *Edgar Norton;* Chick, *George Lloyd.*

Rouben Mamoulian directed 16 movies between 1929 and 1957, including such classics as *Dr. Jekyll and Mr. Hyde* (1931), *Love Me Tonight* (1932) and *Queen Christina* (1932). All of them bear his style, his fluidity with camera movements and his imaginative lighting—all ex-

110

With Spring Byington and Gene Tierney.

cept *Rings on Her Finger*, which looks like it could have been directed by any capable helmsman. Mamoulian signed a three-picture contract with Darryl Zanuck in 1940 and happily set to work on *The Mark of Zorro*, followed by *Blood and Sand*, both of which won critical approval. Then to conclude the contract Zanuck handed him *Rings on Her Finger*, presumably because he had nothing better at hand. Mamoulian was far from pleased, but his displeasure nowhere near equalled that of Henry Fonda. He was still being praised for his *The Lady Eve* and he was sure more praise would result from *The Male Animal*, as it did. On returning to Fox he was assigned to *Rings on Her Finger*, which was obviously a script inspired by *The Lady Eve*. Zanuck later admitted he told his writing staff to come up with something similar to the Sturges film for Fonda.

Like *The Lady Eve*, this picture deals with a pair of elegant confidence tricksters, May (Spring Byington) and Warren (Laird Cregar), whose object is to nail a millionaire and live off him. To do this they recruit a pretty shopgirl, Susan (Gene Tierney), whom they intend to use as millionaire bait. They spot what they believe is a good prospect, a handsome and lively young man, John (Fonda), whom they overhear at the beach talking knowledgeably and enthusiastically about boats. They assume he must be wealthy and they set Susan to work. John is actually an impecunious clerk and Susan is far too kind and guileless to cheat him. She falls in love with John, and he with her, and they confess everything to each other. Marriage follows but it does not deflect the tricksters from still trying to use Susan

to nab some wealth. They do all they can to break up the marriage, mostly by offering her a genuine millionaire who is eager to marry her. All their ludicrous plans fail—nothing can break up John and Susan.

Rings on Her Finger is pleasant, amusing, passing entertainment. Fonda and Mamoulian may have known they deserved better but as professionals they did their best with what they had. Fonda has several funny scenes. In a casino he finds that he wins on every slot machine and at every roulette table, not knowing that they all have been rigged for him to win. Assuming that he is a mathematical genius, he beams with joy and yells, "They're at my mercy!" At another point in the film he arrives home after a late, late night of drinking, sits on his bed to take off his shoes and, exhausted, simply falls back and immediately goes to sleep. A few moments later the alarm goes off and he springs back to life, ready to start a new day. These moments, and others, attest to Fonda's deft comedic timing, as well as his pleasing persona with this kind of material.

Rings on Her Finger did as well at the box office as Zanuck expected and the critics praised Fonda's work. But in later years he could only refer to the picture as "part of the crap I made for Zanuck." In her autobiography *Self Portrait* (Wyden Books, 1979), Gene Tierney recalled, "In *Rings on Her Finger*, I was reunited with Henry Fonda, who detested the script and suffered throughout the film. That was the beginning of his unrest with Hollywood. 'This huge money they pay you,' he said to me one day, 'it just isn't worth it.' "

With Henry Stephenson, Gene Tierney, Spring Byington and Laird Cregar.

113

☆☆☆☆☆☆☆☆☆☆☆☆☆

THE MAGNIFICENT DOPE

With Lynn Bari.

With Don Ameche.

1942

A 20th Century-Fox Film, produced by William Perlberg, directed by Walter Lang, written by George Seaton, based on a story by Joseph Schrank, photographed by Peverell Marley, music by Emil Newman, 83 minutes.

CAST:

Tad Page, *Henry Fonda;* Claire, *Lynn Bari;* Dawson, *Don Ameche;* Horace Hunter, *Edward Everett Horton;* Barker, *George Barbier;* Messenger, *Frank Orth;* Secretary, *Roseanne Murphy;* Jennie, *Marietta Canty;* Charlie, *Hal K. Dawson;* Mrs. Hunter, *Josephine Whittell;* Salesman, *Arthur Loft;* Peters, *Paul Stanton;* Mitchell, *Harry Hayden;* Sadie, *Kitty McHugh;* Gowdy, *Hobart Cavanaugh.*

Having to follow *Rings on Her Finger* with *The Magnificent Dope* must have caused Henry Fonda to almost choke with disgust. If he had disliked the former he could hardly be expected to like this one, which required him to extend his genial rustic characterization in films like *The Farmer Takes a Wife* and *Chad Hanna* to bumpkin proportions. As a Vermont boy who glories in being unsuccessful, Fonda's *Dope* says, "I haven't any respect for a man who was born lazy; it took me a long time to get where I am." It is doubtful if Fonda ever spoke a line more alien to his nature than that one.

At its best *The Magnificent Dope* pokes fun at the business of merchandising personality, the success schools such as Dale Carnegie ran—How to Win Friends and Influence People. Dwight Dawson (Don Ameche) runs a dubious business of this kind and things are not going well for him. His secretary, also his girl, Claire (Lynn Bari) suggests a radio contest to find the biggest failure in the country and give him the Dawson course, as well as a $500 prize. The winner is Tad Page

With Lynn Bari.

(Fonda), who spends his summer renting boats in Vermont and sits around all winter waiting for the summer. The trouble with Tad is that he is such a charming bucolic that his own philosophy of relaxed unambitiousness is more persuasive than Dawson's aggressive program. Tad falls in love with Claire but is too shy to tell her, so he seeks advice from her on how to win a certain girl back home. He uses the advice and Claire gradually comes to return his love.

The slick Dawson becomes aware of this love but rather than show jealousy he decides to use it to his advantage and have Tad become successful to please Claire. This works well enough for Tad to get a job as an insurance agent and because of his low-key manner he sells a major policy to a rich man. The man has been refused policies in the past because of his high blood pressure but with Tad's relaxing personality his pressure drops so much he easily passes the medical. The big policy commission gives Tad the money he needs to buy a fire engine for his small home town, which is what he has always wanted. In the meantime Claire finds out that Dawson has been aware of Tad's love for her and used it, which only increases her love for Tad and the resolve to return with him to his home town. But Dawson isn't licked—he now turns his aggressive personality course into a relaxed personality course, a la Tad, and picks up lots of customers.

With its spoofing of the get-ahead-at-any-cost school of American philosophy and the amusing routine of a country yokel making fools of the Big City fellows, *The Magnificent Dope* pleased the moviegoers of 1942. It just didn't please Henry Fonda having to be in it.

With George Barbier.

TALES OF MANHATTAN

At Grauman's Chinese Theatre in Hollywood, with Sid Grauman and Fonda's Tales of Manhattan *co-stars Charles Boyer, Rita Hayworth, Charles Laughton and Edward G. Robinson.*

1942

A 20th Century-Fox Film, produced by Boris Morros and S. P. Eagle, directed by Julien Duvivier, written by Ben Hecht, Ferenc Molnar, Donald Ogden Stewart, Samuel Hoffenstein, Alan Campbell, Ladislas Fodor, Laszlo Vadnai, Laslo Gorog, Lamar Trotti and Henry Blankford, photographed by Joseph Walker, music by Sol Kaplan, 118 minutes.

CAST:

Paul Orman, *Charles Boyer*; Ethel Halloway, *Rita Hayworth*; John Halloway, *Thomas Mitchell*; Diane, *Ginger Rogers*; George, *Henry Fonda*; Harry, *Cesar Romero*; Charles Smith, *Charles Laughton*; Elsa Smith, *Elsa Lanchester*; Arturo Bellini, *Victor Francen*; Larry Browne, *Edward G. Robinson*; Williams, *George Sanders*; Father Joe, *James Gleason*; Luke, *Paul Robeson*; Esther, *Ethel Waters*.

Every now and then in Hollywood's Golden Age, the studios would call on their whole roster of stars to appear in ambitious movies made up of a collection of stories or sequences. These compendium movies seldom did any better at the box office than those of conventional structure but they are of some interest to film historians because of the talents involved. Henry Fonda's first exposure to a film of this kind was *Tales of Manhattan*, which producers Boris Morros and S. P. Eagle (later Sam Spiegel) brought to Darryl Zanuck. They had been able to interest the distinguished French director, Julien Duvivier, possibly because it was based on a story by Ferenc Molnar. Then they hired nine other writers to flesh out the vignettes.

The focal point of *Tales of Manhattan* is a set of tails, a man's formal dress suit which has a curse on it. Its first owner is an actor (Charles Boyer), who is shot by the husband (Thomas Mitchell) of the lady (Rita Hayworth) with whom he has been having an affair. The actor's valet gives it to the butler of a playboy (Cesar Romero), who is about to marry a society lady (Ginger Rogers), who finds a compromising love letter in the pocket of the suit in which he intends to marry. He then claims the suit is actually that of his best man (Fonda) and that the valet's suit is his. But the cursed suit has done its work—the playboy loses his prospective bride and she turns her love to the best man, who has loved her all along.

The suit is purchased from a second-hand dealer by the wife (Elsa Lanchester) of an impoverished composer (Charles Laughton), who has finally been offered a chance to conduct his symphony at Carnegie Hall. The suit is far too small for him and the coat rips up the back as he conducts, causing him humiliation with the laughing audience. The situation is saved by the resident maestro (Victor Francen), who takes off his own jacket as a gesture of respect. After the concert the suit is donated to a mission, where it is given to a drunken derelict (Edward G. Robinson) so that he may attend a class reunion of his former ivy league friends, where he

With Ginger Rogers and Cesar Romero.

humiliates himself by stealing a wallet. The suit is later stolen by a thief who makes his departure in a small airplane, but the suit catches fire and he flings it out. It contains a great deal of stolen money, which drops like welcome snow over a black farming community, principally on the home of a happy sharecropper (Paul Robeson). The suit ends its life as the attire of a scarecrow.

Like most films of its kind, the parts of *Tales of Manhattan* don't add up to a really satisfying whole. The sequence involving Fonda seemed to please the critics more than some of the others, especially those scenes played with Ginger Rogers. Hers was the confident figure, his the rather shy one, she the lady who switches her romantic intentions and he the fellow who bashfully wins the prize—her.

THE BIG STREET

1942

An RKO Radio Film, produced by Damon Runyon, directed by Irving Reis, written by Leonard Spigelgass, based on the story *The Little Pinks* by Damon Runyon, photographed by Russell Metty, music by Roy Webb, 88 minutes.

CAST:

Little Pinks, *Henry Fonda*; Gloria, *Lucille Ball*; Case Ables, *Barton MacLane*; Nicely Nicely Johnson, *Eugene Pallette*; Violette, *Agnes Moorehead*; Horse Thief, *Sam Levene*; Professor, *Ray Collins*; Mrs. Venus, *Marion Martin*; Decateur Reed, *William Orr*; Colonel Venus, *George Cleveland*; Ruby, *Louise Beavers*; Lou Adolia, *Juan Varro*; Gentleman George, *Millard Mitchell*; Lonie, *Hans Conreid*; Mrs. Lefkowitz, *Vera Gordon*; Doctor, *Harry Shannon*; McWhirter, *John Miljan*; M.C., *Don Barclay*; Judge Bamberger, *Julius Tannen*.

The pattern continued—routine pictures at Fox and interesting pictures on loan-out. In 1942 the fabled New York storyteller Damon Runyon made his debut as a movie producer and decided on his own story *The Little Pinks* as the vehicle to start. Runyon asked RKO to get Henry Fonda for the role of his title character, a meek and mild busboy known as Little Pinks, and surprised Hollywood by asking for Lucille Ball as the substantial female lead. Ball was at that time a minor movie star, well liked but not highly regarded as an actress. But Runyon sensed that

With Lucille Ball.

she was what his picture needed and he was right.

The Big Street is all Runyon and a mile wide. The guys and dolls are all denizens of Broadway and its environs, and the story focuses on a beautiful but vain and arrogant redhead called Gloria (Ball), who is the moll of a big-shot hoodlum, Case Ables (Barton MacLane). She fancies herself a great entertainer, a view heartily shared by Little Pinks, a timid waiter at Mindy's, who calls her "Your Highness" and idolizes her. He saves her Pekingese dog from a traffic accident and she deigns to be nice to Little Pinks in return, which only increases his devotion. One day Gloria gets a little too arrogant and tells Case

she is thinking of closing her account with him and getting a better job elsewhere. His reaction is to slap her across the face so severely that she falls backwards down a flight of stairs, which cripples her. From now on Gloria is confined to a wheelchair, which does nothing to improve her snappy tongue and snide nature.

Gloria whines that she has to get out of New York and go to Miami, where she feels she can snag herself a wealthy husband. Little Pinks makes it possible—he hitchhikes with her to Florida, pushing her a lot of the way in her wheelchair. Her plans go awry and Little Pinks again comes to her aid by rounding up all the ex-Broadwayites in the area, all the minor chiselers and hoods, and arranging a big party for Gloria in the Miami nightclub owned by Case. Little Pinks wants everybody to come and pay homage to his "highness," and by various means he pulls it off. Gloria basks in this glory, and with whatever strength she has left in her legs she manages to get up for a dance with Little Pinks, who practically carries her around the floor. The effort is too much for her and she dies in his arms, but at least she has gone out like the grand lady she always wanted to be.

The rarefied atmosphere of Runyoniana was a little too specialized for the mass movie audience—this was long before *Guys and Dolls* made his kind of New Yorkese widely familiar— and *The Big Street* did only moderately well at the box office. In Hollywood it did very well for Lucille Ball, who had the best part of her career up till then, possibly ever, and the critics were especially impressed with Fonda's playing of the tenderly devoted Little Pinks, a man with a heart of gold. Perhaps only Runyon could invent such a touchingly naive, sweet character, and in choosing Fonda he knew he had an actor who could pull it off.

With director Irving Reis and Lucille Ball.

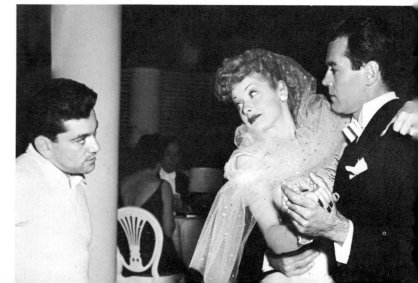

THE IMMORTAL SERGEANT

With Melville Cooper and David Thursby.

1943

A 20th Century-Fox Film, produced by Lamar Trotti, directed by John Stahl, written by Lamar Trotti, based on the novel by John Brophy, photographed by Arthur Miller, music by David Buttolph, 91 minutes.

CAST:

Colin Spence, *Henry Fonda*; Valentine, *Maureen O'Hara*; Sergeant Kelly, *Thomas Mitchell*; Cassity, *Allyn Joslyn*; Benedict, *Reginald Gardiner*; Pilcher, *Melville Cooper*; Symes, *Bramwell Fletcher*; Cottrell, *Morton Lowry*; Bren Carrier Driver, *David Thursby*; Truck Driver, *Guy Kingsford.*

If Henry Fonda disliked most of his Fox films made for Darryl Zanuck, he really hated *The Immortal Sergeant*, which he sneered at for years after as the picture in which Zanuck had him winning the Second World War all by himself. Fonda had completed *The Ox-Bow Incident*,

which Zanuck was hesitant to release because of what he rightly considered its dubious marketability, and he had left the studio in order to report for real wartime service with the U.S. Navy. But Zanuck had friends in high places in Washington and used his contacts to have Fonda sent back to the studio for what he claimed was a film in the national interest. *The Immortal Sergeant* was hardly that. To make the pill harder to swallow, Fonda found he was not playing the title role—that went to Thomas Mitchell—but a British Army corporal, and a Canadian in order to explain the accent.

A British patrol lost in the Libyan desert is led by stalwart old Sergeant Kelly (Mitchell). His

corporal, Colin Spence (Fonda) is a mild-mannered fellow, who dreams about the girl, Valentine (Maureen O'Hara), he left behind in England. Colin was a newspaper reporter and would-be novelist but he never had the courage to tell Valentine he loved her or to compete with his confident rival (Reginald Gardiner). One night the weary British patrol attacks an Italian armored car and wipes it out. But several members of the patrol are killed and the sergeant is badly wounded.

With Maureen O'Hara and Reginald Gardiner.

Knowing that he will be a drawback to the patrol, the sergeant shoots himself, although first giving Colin a talk about courage and duty. Colin is now in command of the survivors and finds he has the qualities of leadership. With only three men left he leads a raid on an oasis held by Germans and wins it. They set fire to the German supplies, which draws the attention of a British army unit, who arrive to find only three men alive, one of whom is the wounded Colin, now

With Thomas Mitchell.

122

unconscious. When he awakes he finds himself in a hospital in Cairo and recommended for a medal. Now a man with proven courage he sends Valentine a telegram, telling her that an engagement ring is on the way. Some months later he and Valentine are married, and Colin gives a prayer for the sergeant who helped him find his courage and abilities.

About the only claim that Zanuck could make for *The Immortal Sergeant* being in the wartime interest was that it became the first Hollywood picture to deal with the British army's campaigns in North Africa. Apart from the fact that the British did this kind of picture better themselves, the result was merely run-of-the-mill. The accent was on action rather than the subtle character study contained in John Brophy's novel. But Fonda was not about to discuss the film, then or ever. The day after he completed his obligations he left town to re-join the navy. He took some satisfaction in *The Ox-Bow Incident* being released afterwards. If it turned out to be his last film, that would be the one he would like the critics and the public to note.

With Allyn Joslyn and Thomas Mitchell.

THE OX-BOW INCIDENT

1943

A 20th Century-Fox Film, produced by Lamar Trotti, directed by William Wellman, written by Lamar Trotti, based on the novel by Walter Van Tilburg Clark, photographed by Arthur Miller, music by Cyril Mockridge, 75 minutes.

CAST:

Gil Carter, *Henry Fonda*; Martin, *Dana Andrews*; Rose Mapen, *Mary Beth Hughes*; Mexican, *Anthony Quinn*; Gerald, *William Eythe*; Art Croft, *Henry Morgan*; Ma Grier, *Jane Darwell*; Judge Tyler, *Matt Briggs*; Davies, *Harry Davenport*; Major Tetley, *Frank Conroy*; Farnley, *Marc Lawrence*; Darby, *Victor Killian*; Monty Smith, *Paul Hurst*; Poncho, *Chris-Pin Martin*; Joyce, *Ted North*; Mr. Swanson, *George Meeker*; Mrs. Swanson, *Almira Sessions*; Mrs. Larch, *Margaret Hamilton*; Mapes, *Dick Rich*; Old Man, *Francis Ford*.

Henry Fonda spoke with affectionate regard about few of his films. *The Ox-Bow Incident* was one he was really proud of. It came into production only because he and director William Wellman so admired Lamar Trotti's script that they badgered Darryl Zanuck into making it. Zanuck had cause to hesitate. In 1943 the accent was on escapist entertainment for wartime audiences. Westerns were popular, provided they had plenty of action, riding, fighting and scenery. *The Ox-Bow Incident* had virtually none of the usual ingredients. Instead it revealed the darker, meaner side of the Old West and focused upon lynching. Zanuck struck a deal with Fonda and Wellman—if they would be willing to work on certain more obviously commercial films he had lined up, then he would let them make *The Ox-Bow Incident*. They agreed.

This is a western cast along the lines of a Greek tragedy and with an uncompromising look at American lawlessness. It begins as two ordinary, roughneck cowboys, Gil (Fonda) and Art (Henry Morgan) ride into the town of Bridger's Wells, Nevada, one day in 1885. They have been out on the range a long time and they need some relaxation, which takes the form—there *is* no other

form—of going to a saloon and drinking. The frustrated Gil gets into a fight and almost kills a man, and Art breaks a bottle over Gil's head to stop him from getting into any more trouble. Gil comes to at about the time a young fellow arrives in the saloon to say that a rancher named Kinkaid has been found murdered and his cattle gone. An angry mob gathers and they decide to form a posse, with a lot of talk about hanging. An old storekeeper, Davies (Harry Davenport) tries in vain to restrain them and a

With Victor Killian, Marc Lawrence, and Henry Morgan.

With Henry Morgan.

vainglorious ex-Confederate officer (Frank Conroy) offers to lead them. The officer's pacifist son Gerald (William Eythe) promises to kill himself if his father makes him part of the lynch mob.

The large group, hungry for blood, ride out of town but Gil and Art soon realize that it is a savage kind of justice and that whomever they catch should be brought back to town for trial. They are almost alone in this view and when the mob comes across three men sitting around their camp fire at night, they charge them with murder and rustling, and tie them up. The leader is a young man named Martin (Dana Andrews) and working for him are a Mexican (Anthony

Quinn) and an old man (Francis Ford). Despite their protestations that their cattle were purchased from the murdered man, Martin and his men are condemned to the rope. Since Martin has no bill of sale he is obviously guilty. The Confederate officer, now completely in charge, makes a concession to Davies' and Gil's compassionate talk and agrees to postpone the hanging until dawn, so that the men can pray and so Martin can write a letter to his wife.

With the coming of the dawn the three men are hanged and the lynch mob take satisfaction in what they have done. On the way back to town they come across the sheriff, who explains that there has been no murder and no rustling. The mob moves on, bewildered and ashamed. Back in his home the Confederate officer shoots himself after being derided by his son. In the saloon, where most of the men are trying to drown their guilt in drink, Gil, who has promised Martin he will deliver the letter to his wife, pulls the letter from his pocket and reads it aloud. The guilt and the shame cause the men to contribute to a fund for the widow and her children. They raise five hundred dollars, which Gil and Art take with them as they leave.

The Ox-Bow Incident has an emotional wallop that does not diminish with time. It is marred a little by the obvious use of studio backdrops in the extended night scenes at the lynch site, but the acting more than compensates for it. It is a searing indictment of mob violence and an

With Anthony Quinn, Francis Ford, Dana Andrews, Frank Conroy and Jane Darwell.

With Harry Davenport, Matt Briggs, Henry Morgan and Ted North.

honest depiction of crude frontier values, leavened here and there with some figures of decency and compassion. Fonda's Gil is one of them, and made the more believable because he is just an ordinary cowpoke, as addicted to booze and brawling as most of his kind, but he can still see the difference between right and wrong. Fonda had every reason to be proud of the film and his work in it. However, as Zanuck predicted, it did poorly at the box office and took quite some time to recover its modest budget. But *The Ox-Bow Incident* is a classic piece of American cinema.

126

★★★★★★★★★★★★★★★
MY DARLING CLEMENTINE

1946

A 20th Century-Fox Film, produced by Samuel G. Engel, directed by John Ford, written by Samuel G. Engel and Winston Miller, based on the novel *Wyatt Earp, Frontier Marshall* by Stuart Lake, photographed by Joseph P. MacDonald, music by Cyril J. Mockridge, 97 minutes.

CAST:

Wyatt Earp, *Henry Fonda*; Chihuahua, *Linda Darnell*; Doc Holliday, *Victor Mature*; Old Man Clanton, *Walter Brennan*; Virgil Earp, *Tim Holt*;

With Victor Mature.

Morgan Earp, *Ward Bond*; Clementine Carter, *Cathy Downs*; Granville Thorndyke, *Alan Mowbray*; Billy Clanton, *John Ireland*; Ike Clanton, *Grant Withers*; Mayor, *Roy Roberts*; Kate Nelson, *Jane Darwell*; John Simpson, *Russell Simpson*; Old Soldier, *Francis Ford*; Bartender, *J. Farrell McDonald*; James Earp, *Don Garner*; Barber, *Ben Hall*; Hotel Clerk, *Arthur Walsh*; Coach driver, *Jack Pennick*; Sam Clanton, *Mickey Simpson*; Phin Clanton, *Fred Libby*.

Like most stars who had served in the war, Henry Fonda wondered if it was possible to pick up where he had left off. Neither he nor the others had to worry for long. All were welcomed home and put into pictures with the same star billing they had had before. Fonda was par-

127

ticularly lucky because John Ford wanted him for *My Darling Clementine*, which was to be made at Fox, where Fonda was still under contract. He could hardly have wished for a better

With Jane Darwell and Roy Roberts.

vehicle in which to resume his movie career. *Clementine* is a classic western and likely to be shown as long as people are interested in this genre.

John Ford's reputation as a master of the western stems mainly from the latter years of his career. He had made many minor silent westerns in his early years as a director, with a major one, *The Iron Horse*, in 1924. But 15 years would pass before he made *Stagecoach*, which registered him as a man with some affinity for the West, and another seven years elapsed before *Clementine*. After that the majority of his films dealt with the legends and images of western Americana. Sentiment tended to undermine his work as he aged, but *Clementine* is darkly hued and realistic, with sentiment well contained. Like so many of his films it is based on family life, in this case the tale of a good family pitted against a bad family. But even the bad family is a close, united group.

Clementine begins with Wyatt Earp (Fonda) and his brothers Morgan (Ward Bond), Virgil (Tim Holt) and Jim (Don Garner) driving their

herd of cattle across Arizona. Wyatt notices a pair of men observing them and rides to meet them—Old Man Clanton (Walter Brennan) and his son Ike (Grant Withers), who make a bid for the cattle, which Wyatt declines. That evening the three older brothers leave Jim to look after the cattle and the campsite while they take a look at nearby Tombstone. They find it to be a pretty wild, lawless town and Wyatt is offered the job of marshal after he subdues a dangerous gunman. He refuses but when he and his brothers return to find Jim murdered and the cattle stolen, Wyatt then becomes the marshal of Tombstone. His main problem turns out to be a feared gambler named Doc Holliday (Mature), who seems to have the town at his mercy, but the two men find mutual respect for one another.

Doc is a cultured, consumptive man, bitter about his past as a doctor and seemingly bent on self-destruction. His dancehall girlfriend, Chihuahua (Linda Darnell), dotes on him and turns jealous when Doc's ex-fiancée from the East, Clementine Carter (Cathy Downs), arrives in town, having spent much time trying to locate him. Doc tries to send her away, claiming that the life he now leads would be ruinous for her. When Clementine meets the shy Wyatt he is smitten with her and takes her to a dance celebrating the foundation of the new church. Things turn serious when Wyatt notices Chihuahua wearing

With Cathy Downs and Victor Mature.

a medallion that belonged to Jim. She confesses that it was given to her by Billy Clanton (John Ireland), who then shoots Chihuahua. Billy is wounded by Virgil, who pursues him to the Clanton home where the Old Man kills him. Doc Holliday resumes some of his former medical stature when he operates on Chihuahua and seemingly saves her life. But she dies a few hours later and Doc then sides with the Earps in their

With Walter Brennan.

Doing the porch post ballet—a little bit of business invented on the spot by director John Ford.

battle with the Clantons at the OK Corral. All the Clantons die in the gunfight and so does Doc. Clementine decides to accept a job as a schoolteacher in the now increasingly civilized town, and Wyatt takes his shy pleasure in telling her that although he and Morgan have to leave town to attend to their cattle business, he will likely be back.

My Darling Clementine is pure western fantasy, as Ford clearly knew in tackling it. It is a myth met head-on with no attempt to tell the facts of Earp and Holliday and Tombstone. This is obvious in Ford's decision to film the story in Monument Valley, with its dramatically stark scenery, rather than in the southern part of Arizona, where Tombstone is actually situated. That the Earps were not quite as heroic as they

seem here is common knowledge, and presenting Doc Holliday as an ex-Bostonian surgeon is at great variance with the truth. But none of this really matters. *Clementine* is a story of values, especially the loyalty of the family unit and the range of good and evil qualities in men. Somewhat ironically the moody, dark spirit of the picture, artfully photographed by the great Joseph MacDonald, makes the fable appear realistic. Such was the genius of Ford.

Clementine was a perfect film in which to reestablish Fonda with the public. His Wyatt Earp is essentially quiet, laconic, homespun and basically moral, the image that he had largely set before the war. Four years after his last film Fonda now seemed that much more mature—a little baggier under the eyes and a few lines in the face, all of which made the image even more credible. Four years of naval service had done nothing to harm his abilities as an actor; on the contrary, it had sharpened them. Both as an actor and a man he was wiser, to say nothing of being even more determined. He had always wanted to hack his own way through the jungles of Hollywood and show business. With this successful return to the screen Fonda was launched on another plateau of his life, and he would indeed make his own way.

☆☆☆☆☆☆☆☆☆☆☆☆☆

THE LONG NIGHT

1947

An RKO Radio Film, produced by Robert and Raymond Hakim, directed by Anatole Litvak, written by John Wexley, based on the screenplay *Le Jour se Leve* by Jacques Viot, photographed by Sol Polito, music by Dimitri Tiomkin, 101 minutes.

CAST:

Joe Adams, *Henry Fonda*; Jo Ann, *Barbara Bel Geddes*; Maximilian, *Vincent Price*; Charlene, *Ann Dvorak*; Sheriff, *Howard Freeman*; Chief

With Barbara Bel Geddes.

With Ann Dvorak.

of Police, *Moroni Olsen*; Frank, *Elisha Cook, Jr.*; Janitor's Wife, *Queenie Smith*; Bill, *David Clarke*; Policeman, *Charles McGraw*; Peggy, *Patty King*; Freddie, *Robert Davis*; Janitor, *Will Wright*; Hudson, *Ray Teal*; Sergeant, *Pat Flaherty*.

Like most movie stars returning after the war Henry Fonda was looking for more mature material. In his case he was particularly intent on breaking his previous image, largely due to

With Ann Dvorak.

the Fox pictures, as a genial innocent or romantic rustic or spoiled playboy. As far as he was concerned that kind of celluloid world was gone forever. To this end he was interested when Anatole Litvak discussed with him his idea for a re-make of the fine French film *Le Jour se Leve*, which had been a big hit with Jean Gabin in 1939. The Gabin film had been a morality tale about a doomed French criminal and Litvak was convinced he could make an American version. Fonda was intrigued.

Joe Adams (Fonda) is a soldier just returned from wartime service, who returns to his small Pennsylvania town and has trouble adjusting to dull civilian life. He takes a job as a sandblaster and meets a pretty girl, Jo Ann (Barbara Bel Geddes) and soon falls in love with her. Both are orphans and sympathetic to each other's background. Complications arise when he learns

that she had been seeing a suave magician, Maximilian (Vincent Price). Joe seeks out the magician's assistant, Charlene (Ann Dvorak), who warns him that Maximilian is a charming seducer. Maximilian visits Joe and claims to be Jo Ann's father and that he wishes Joe to stay away from her.

The lovers cannot stay away from each other, partly because Jo Ann is scared by the unctuous Maximilian, who pays Joe another visit, this time to kill him, but not before gloating about his conquest of Jo Ann. The men struggle and Joe kills the magician with his own pistol. Afraid and confused, Joe refuses to give up to the police and they lay siege to his shabby, boarding house room. Jo Ann pleads with him to give up, but he cannot. The ex-soldier puts up a fight that goes on all night long—until his inevitable death.

The Long Night found little favor with the

With Vincent Price.

talkative and the mood theatrical. In *The New York Times* Bosley Crowther pointed out that "Henry Fonda, while moody and pathetic as the holed-up fugitive, is not the wrath-tortured killer that Mr. Gabin was in the role." The general public may not have understood the reference—all they knew was that *The Long Night* was long and dull. Unfortunately, so would be Fonda's next choice.

public and a drubbing from a concensus of the critics, all of whom enjoyed comparing it disfavorably with its French original. Anatole Litvak, a cultured European, ended up with a film stylistically more European than American, with a great deal of subdued lighting and slow pacing. The critics thought the script overly

★★★★★★★★★★★★★★★★
THE FUGITIVE

1947

An RKO Radio–Argosy Film, produced by John Ford and Merian C. Cooper, directed by John Ford, written by Dudley Nichols, based on the novel *The Power and the Glory* by Graham Greene, photographed by Gabriel Figueroa, music by Richard Hagemen, 104 minutes.

CAST:

The Fugitive, *Henry Fonda;* Mexican Woman, *Dolores Del Rio;* Police Lieutenant, *Pedro Armendariz;* El Gringo, *Ward Bond;* Chief of Police, *Leo Carrillo;* Police Spy, *J. Carroll Naish;* Police Sergeant, *Robert Armstrong;* Doctor, *John Qualen;* Governor's Cousin, *Fortunio Bonanova;* Organ Player, *Chris Pin Martin;* Hostage, *Miguel Inclan;* Singer, *Fernando Fernandez.*

Of all John Ford's major films, *The Fugitive* was the least successful. Aside from being a devout Catholic, Ford was also a very stubborn man and he was determined to do his version of a passion play and set it in Mexico. He and his company spent six weeks shooting in picturesque places like Cuernavaca, Taxco and Cholula, with studio sequences shot in Mexico City. Ford hired the fine cinematographer Gabriele Figueroa and his work makes *The Fugitive* a visual experience, with magnificently lit black-and-white sets and well composed exteriors. But it does not make

With Dolores Del Rio.

it a dramatically exciting picture or help Henry Fonda seem believable in what must have been one of the most difficult roles in his career. No matter how great the talent and the makeup, it is hard to accept him as a Latin American priest.

The priest is the central figure in this Biblical parable, as he is hunted by the military police in an unnamed country where a revolution has outlawed the clergy. The families of the village in which the priest hides all love and honor him, including a beautiful woman (Dolores Del Rio) who bears the child of the police lieutenant (Pedro Armendariz). The priest baptizes her il-

With J. Carroll Naish.

legitimate child and she helps him escape to a neighboring country where the clergy are not persecuted. Before leaving he gives comfort to a wounded American criminal (Ward Bond), who also aids in the escape. The two have a bond of understanding because they are both fugitives, although representing the extremes of good and bad.

In his new residence the priest is sought out by a half-breed (J. Carroll Naish), who tells him the American is dying and seeks absolution. The priest returns but finds the dying American has not asked for religious solace, and that the half-breed is in the employ of the police lieutenant. The half-breed begs for forgiveness, which he gets, and the lieutenant now finds himself in the position of having to execute the man who baptized his child. The villagers pray for their spiritual leader as he goes to his death, and as he dies a new priest is slipped into the village to take his place.

The critics admired *The Fugitive* but the public showed little interest, which did not stop John Ford from claiming it as his favorite picture or from telling Fonda that he thought his performance one of the greatest in the history of films. There is much to admire in *The Fugitive;* indeed, it is a cinematic work of art and it has a haunting atmosphere. But it suffers from being overly reverential. Dudley Nichols, probably at Ford's behest, cleaned up the Graham Greene novel on which it is based, turning the whiskey drinking priest, also living with a woman, into a paragon. Fonda played that paragon with admirable intensity, but at this point in his career what he needed was a good commercial movie.

DAISY KENYON

With Joan Crawford, Ruth Warrick, Peggy Ann Garner, Walter Winchell and Dana Andrews.

1947

A 20th Century-Fox Film, produced and directed by Otto Preminger, written by David Hertz, based on the novel by Elizabeth Janeway, photographed by Leon Shamroy, music by David Raksin, 99 minutes.

CAST:

Daisy Kenyon, *Joan Crawford;* Dan O'Mara, *Dana Andrews;* Peter, *Henry Fonda;* Lucille O'Mara, *Ruth Warrick;* Mary Angelus, *Martha Stewart;* Rosamund, *Peggy Ann Garner;* Marie, *Connie Marshall;* Coverly, *Nicholas Joy;* Attorney, *Art Baker;* Attorney, *Robert Karnes;* Mervyn, *John Davidson;* Marsha, *Victoria Horne;* Judge, *Charles Meredith.*

To those who may have looked askance at Henry Fonda taking third billing in a Joan Crawford soap opera, the answer was simple. *Daisy Kenyon* marked the end of Fonda's long-term commitment to 20th Century-Fox and he would have appeared in almost anything they might have offered him. It was a typical Crawford picture, with yet another of her portrayals of a woman successful in business but unhappy in love.

Daisy is a New York fashion designer in love with a dynamic lawyer, Dan O'Mara (Dana Andrews), who happens to be married to a bitchy wife (Ruth Warrick) and has two children. The passionate affair is a strain on Daisy but one day

With Dana Andrews.

With Joan Crawford.

Daisy arrives home and finds the two men waiting for her with a simple proposition. Which one does she really love?

Daisy Kenyon draws to its breathless close with the distraught heroine realizing that her love for Dan is of the past and that it is her understanding husband whom she loves. By 1947 Crawford had this kind of picture patented, and almost any two competent actors could have played the lover

she meets an army sergeant, Peter Lapham (Fonda), just home from the war and eager to resume his career as a boat designer. He falls in love with Daisy and offers her marriage. After some deliberation she accepts this calm and gentle fellow, and goes to live with him in his Cape Cod cottage. Dan has never stopped loving Daisy and one day his wife overhears a telephone conversation between the two of them. She angrily breaks in to announce that she wants a divorce, plus custody of the children.

Dan's children complicate the matter by claiming they want to live with him. After much ill feeling, which makes the confused Daisy very unhappy, the wife gives in and agrees to the custody going to Dan. Peter is quietly aware of this and decides on a calm, psychological tack.

and the husband. For Fonda the film was a walk-through, although a few critics pointed out that this nice husband of his was possibly a little too passive and sympathetic than any man under the circumstances had a right to be.

Fonda could hardly care less what the critics said. His contract with 20th Century-Fox had come to an end. The seven years were up. He would always look back on this period with a little disgust, but in actual fact he had not done too badly. Four of those seven years were spent away at war and he had appeared in only 11 Fox pictures under that hated contract. Two of those films, *The Ox-Bow Incident* and *My Darling Clementine,* are classics and the rest are acceptable passing entertainment. There are many film actors who have fared a lot worse.

136

ON OUR MERRY WAY

1948

A United Artists release of a Benedict Borgeaus Production, directed by King Vidor and Leslie Fenton, written by Laurence Stalling and Lou Beslow, based on stories by John O'Hara and Arch Obeler, photographed by John Seitz, Ernest Laszlo and Gordon Avil, music by Heinz Roemheld, 107 minutes.

CAST:

Martha Pease, *Paulette Goddard;* Slim, *James Stewart;* Lank, *Henry Fonda;* Al, *Fred MacMurray;* Oliver Pease, *Burgess Meredith;* Floyd, *William Demarest;* Eli Hobbs, *Hugh Herbert;* Maxim, *Edward Ciannelli;* Mr. Sadd, *Charles D. Brown;* Lola, *Dorothy Ford;* Housekeeper, *Nana Bryant;* Cynthia, *Betty Caldwell;* Mr. Atwood, *John Qualen.*

It finally occurred to somebody to team Henry Fonda with his old friend, and star of equal rank, James Stewart, but unfortunately in only one-third of a film. *On Our Merry Way* was filmed under the title *A Miracle Can Happen*, but the producers changed it, probably sensing that the original title might prove a challenge to the critics, moving them to such barbs as, "a miracle can happen if this picture is successful at the box office." Like so many movies that are made up of sequences and studded with stars, this one failed to measure up to what must have seemed like a great potential on the planning boards.

The thematic thread of the film is the question, "What great influence has a little child had upon your life?" The question is drummed up by Martha Pease (Paulette Goddard), who gives it to her husband Oliver (Burgess Meredith), a newspaper want-ad clerk who wants to be a writer. He decides to play roving reporter in order to write a column and the first people to whom he puts the question are a pair of footloose,

down-on-their-luck jazz musicians, pianist Slim (Stewart) and cornetist Lank (Fonda). He next puts it to a pair of Hollywood extras, Gloria (Dorothy Lamour) and Ashton (Victor Moore). Finally to a couple of drifters, Al (Fred MacMurray) and Floyd (William Demarest), who are at the mercy of a little boy who plays practical jokes on them. Each answer produces a story.

The critics all thought that the best episode of *On Our Merry Way* was the first one, with Fonda and Stewart as the musicians who try to fix an amateur music contest in a California beach resort because they are in dire need of money. They try to arrange it so that the son of the mayor will win. The child they say most influenced their lives is a "babe," a six-foot tall beauty (Dorothy Ford) who plays saxophone and

With James Stewart and Burgess Meredith.

wins their band away from them on a bet.

Perhaps it would have been better if the first segment had been made into the whole picture. Everyone seemed to like Fonda and Stewart as the hip but hapless jazzmen, and Andrew Sarris in *The Village Voice* wrote, "Fonda enlivened the otherwise dispensable *On Our Merry Way* with a side-splitting impersonation of a jazz trumpeter on a rocking rowboat, and don't ask me why or how he got there, blowing himself into a volcanic eruption of *mal-de-mer.*" Perhaps the reason this segment is the best is that it was written especially for Fonda and Stewart by the esteemed

With James Stewart and Dorothy Ford.

John O'Hara. John Huston was involved in directing the first part of it but had to leave, and George Stevens took over the rest. But neither Huston nor Stevens wanted their names mentioned in the credit titles. When such men make such decisions, the vibes for the product are usually negative.

138

☆☆☆☆☆☆☆☆☆☆☆☆☆☆
FORT APACHE

With John Wayne, George O'Brien and Ward Bond.

1948

An RKO Radio release of an Argosy Film, produced by John Ford and Merian C. Cooper, directed by John Ford, written by Frank S. Nugent, based on the story *Massacre* by James Warner Bellah, photographed by Archie Stout, music by Richard Hageman, 127 minutes.

CAST:

Capt. Kirby York, *John Wayne;* Lt. Col. Owen Thursday, *Henry Fonda;* Philadelphia Thursday, *Shirley Temple;* Lt. Michael O'Rourke, *John Agar;* Sergeant Major O'Rourke, *Ward Bond;* Capt. Sam Collingwood, *George O'Brien;* Sergeant Mulcahy, *Victor McLaglen;* Sergeant Beaufort, *Pedro Armendariz;* Mrs. Collingwood, *Anna Lee;* Mrs. O'Rourke, *Irene Rich;* Dr. Wilkens, *Guy Kibbee;* Silas Meacham, *Grant Mitchell;* Cochise, *Miguel Inclan;* Sergeant Schattuck, *Jack Pennick;* Mrs. Gates, *Mae Marsh;* Sergeant Quincannon, *Dick Foran;* Newspaperman, *Frank Ferguson;* Bartender, *Francis Ford.*

John Ford made three westerns about the U.S. Cavalry that stand like a separate chapter in the genre. First came *Fort Apache* in 1948, then *She Wore a Yellow Ribbon* a year later and *Rio Grande* the year after. The second is generally favored as the most enjoyable but the first is more accurate in its depiction of army life and the least sentimental of the three. Indeed, *Fort Apache* has a gritty quality, and being photographed in black-and-white it seems closer to the textbooks of military history. For Henry Fonda it was another opportunity to broaden his screen image. In *Fort Apache* he is a martinet, a ramrod of a soldier—no affability, no folksy charm. Again he was grateful to Ford, for thinking of him in a part for which possibly no other director would have cast him.

Lt. Col. Owen Thursday (Fonda) is a dedicated military man, a meticulous, by-the-book soldier. In the Civil War he held wartime rank as a general but afterwards was demoted, like all other wartime appointments, to his former rank. Thursday is an easterner and he looks upon his posting to Fort Apache, Arizona, as an assignment to the wilderness, and he resents it. A widower, he arrives at the fort in the company of his pretty daughter Philadelphia (Shirley Temple), who has a much happier nature than her father. She is made welcome by the wives of the post and she soon meets handsome young Lt. Michael O'Rourke (John Agar), who has just arrived after graduating from West Point and who is the son of the veteran Sergeant Major (Ward Bond).

With George O'Brien and Ward Bond.

With Shirley Temple, Ward Bond and Irich Rich.

Thursday discourages the romance between his daughter and the young lieutenant for class reasons but he is alone in these sentiments. Most of the officers and NCO's at the post are veteran soldiers but Thursday resents their casual western ways and dress and institutes greater discipline. The most respected officer in the company is Captain Kirby York (John Wayne), who has been fighting Apaches long enough to respect them for their courage and their skill in battle. He tries to impart this knowledge to Thursday, who dismisses it. To him the Indians are simply ignorant savages. It is York who negotiates with the Indian chieftain Cochise, because he is an officer who has earned the respect of the Indians. Thursday sees the Indians only as a means of winning a battle and receiving enough military praise to earn him a more civilized posting.

Thursday has his opportunity when Cochise leads his followers across the Mexican border in protest to the cheating of Indian agents. He sends York to meet with Cochise and persuade him to return, but when the Indians reappear on American soil they are met with a large force under Thursday's direct command. If Thursday can bring the Indians back to their reservations he knows Washington will be pleased. He agrees to meet with Cochise but allows no terms, only complete submission. York protests but Thursday accuses him of cowardice and orders him to remove himself from the action. Thursday now engages the Indians in battle but is completely outmaneuvered. He dies in combat, as do all his men. Only the disengaged York and a small group survive.

Some time later, with York now in command of the fort, he entertains a group of newspapermen, who want to know about Thursday and his last battle. York speaks well of his bravery against impossible odds, and thereby launches, for the good of the service, the myth of Colonel Thursday and his last stand. The blunder becomes a page of military glory.

Fort Apache was based upon James Warner Bellah's story *Massacre*, which was obviously inspired by what happened to Lt. Col. George Armstrong Custer at the Battle of the Little Big Horn. Bellah knew and loved the history of the army in the West, and so did Ford. The film is full of detail of those times, possibly moreso than any other film. It shows family life, the roles of the wives at the fort and their social affairs, their dances, and the rigors of frontier army life.

John Wayne is the star of *Fort Apache*, the hero figure, the survivor, but it was typical of

Fonda the actor that he would seize the chance to play an unpopular figure, a troubled and unbending man—something he had never done before. Be that as it may, Fonda was not pleased with the way his postwar film career had drifted. He had made six films, the first, *My Darling Clementine*, was excellent but the others were not. And he was not about to wait for the reaction to *Fort Apache.* By the time the film opened in March of 1948 he had already been on Broadway for a month as the star of *Mister Roberts*. A new chapter in his life had begun.

With Shirley Temple.

JIGSAW

With Betty Harper and Franchot Tone.

1949

A United Artists release of a Tower Film, produced by Edward J. Danziger and Harry Lee Danziger, directed by Fletcher Markle, written by Fletcher Markle and Vincent McConnor, photographed by Don Malkames, music by Robert W. Stringer, 70 minutes.

CAST:

Holward Malloy, *Franchot Tone*; Barbara Whitfield, *Jean Wallace*; Charles Riggs, *Myron McCormick*; Angelo Agostini, *Marc Lawrence*; Mrs. Hartley, *Winifred Lenihan*; Caroline Riggs, *Betty Harper*; Sigmund Kosterlich, *Hedley Rainnie*; Walker, *Walter Vaughn*; Knuckles, *George Breen*; Tommy Quigley, *Robert Gist*; Mrs. Borg, *Helena Songergaard*; and unbilled guest appearances by Henry Fonda, Marlene Dietrich, John Garfield, Marsha Hunt, Burgess Meredith, Leonard Lyons and Kent Smith.

While appearing on Broadway as *Mr. Roberts*, Henry Fonda was asked by his friend Franchot Tone to do a bit part in *Jigsaw*, a modestly budgeted crime movie shot entirely in New York. Tone and his producers had raised the money themselves and no doubt felt that sprinkling a few famous faces throughout the picture would help its marketability, although the film met with little success. Tone played a District Attorney who, while investigating a murder, stumbles across an organized group of racial and religious bigots. One sequence takes place in the Blue Angel night club and the waiter serving Tone and Betty Harper turns out to be Fonda.

MISTER ROBERTS

1955

A Warner Brothers–Orange Film, produced by Leland Hayward, directed by John Ford and Mervyn Leroy, written by Frank Nugent and Joshua Logan, based on the play by Logan and Thomas Heggen, and the novel by Heggen, photographed in Warnercolor and CinemaScope by Winston C. Hoch, music by Franz Waxman, 123 minutes.

CAST:

Lt. (jg) Doug Roberts, *Henry Fonda;* The Captain, *James Cagney;* Ensign Pulver, *Jack Lemmon;* Doc, *William Powell;* CPO Dowdy, *Ward Bond;* Lt. Ann Girard, *Betsy Palmer;* Mannion, *Phil Carey;* Reber, *Nick Adams;* Stefanowski, *Harey Carey, Jr.;* Dolan, *Ken Curtis;* Gerhart, *Frank Aletter;* Lidstrom, *Fritz Ford;* Mason, *Buck Kartalian;* Lt. Billings, *William Henry;* Olson, *William Hudson;* Schlemmer, *Stubby Kruger;* Cookie, *Harry Tenbrook;* Rodriguez, *Perry Lopez;* Insigna, *Robert Roark;* Bookser, *Pat Wayne;* Wiley, *Tige Andrews.*

With William Powell and Jack Lemmon.

It was inevitable that *Mister Roberts* would eventually be made into a film, but it was not inevitable that Henry Fonda would star in it, despite his great identification with the material. By 1955 he had been off the screen for seven years, and they were seven years in which the film business had changed enormously. Between 1948 and 1955 the studios had been divested by

143

law of their theatre chains and television had changed the moviegoing habits of the public. Tastes had changed and many once popular movie stars had sagged in popularity. Fonda was now 50, which was more than 20 years older than Lt. (j.g.) Douglas Roberts was supposed to be in the play. In the theatre, age is easy to disguise. The film camera is different, and Fonda was not expecting to get the part.

When Warner Bros. purchased the screen rights to *Mister Roberts* they offered the lead part to William Holden, who refused it on moral grounds. He felt that the role belonged to Fonda and nobody else. Warners then offered it to Marlon Brando who accepted. However, by this time they had signed John Ford as director and Ford wanted only one actor for the lead. He would not even discuss the use of anyone other than Fonda, and since Ford's name meant

Warners understandably wanted the stage play opened up for the screen and to this end sought naval cooperation to use an actual vessel, the 250-ton cargo ship *U.S.S. Hewell* at the naval base at Midway in the South Pacific. The company then moved to Hawaii, near the naval base at Kaneoke Bay, for further exterior shots; all the interior work was done later at the Warner studio in Burbank. Warners also wanted a broader kind of comedy than in the stage version and in hiring Ford they expected the kind of service camaraderie that marked his cavalry westerns. This was at variance with the spirit of the play as written by Thomas Heggen and Joshua Logan, which dealt more with the despair of sailors stuck in a remote, inactive location rather than with fun and good comradeship. This viewpoint caused problems.

The reunion of Fonda and Ford on such a

With James Cagney.

something at the box office, Warners gave in. This triumph of logic over commerce, unusual in Hollywood, launched Fonda on the rebirth of his film career and his thanks were due to a man he greatly respected.

marvelous project as *Mister Roberts* should have been joyous. It proved to be anything but. Now almost 60, Ford's irascibility had increased along with his drinking and a decline in his health. Formally he had limited his drinking to the

144

evenings—now he was also drinking during the day. Fonda became increasingly unhappy with the kind of direction he was getting, and one evening went to Ford to have it out. After listening for a few minutes Ford sprang from his chair and knocked Fonda down. Fonda, who never brawled, picked himself up and left. Ford tried to apologize and during the next few days was almost embarrassingly considerate in his directing, something he had never been before with any actor. The strained feelings in the company were soon relieved when Ford collapsed with a gall bladder condition and was hospitalized. Jack Warner then asked his friend Mervyn LeRoy to take over the direction. The finished product bore the names of both directors, each of whom claimed more than half of the footage as his, but Joshua Logan came in at the end to re-direct a couple of crucial scenes.

As almost every critic pointed out, *Mister Roberts is* Henry Fonda, and vice versa. For an actor who had excelled in the part for three years—more than a thousand times on Broadway and five or six hundred times in the road productions—it could hardly have been otherwise. In the play and the film Roberts is the fulcrum upon which all else is balanced.

The setting is the South Pacific in the later part of the Second World War and the action takes place aboard a cargo vessel, the *U.S.S. Reluctant*, except that there isn't any action. The ship operates in the backwaters of war and its captain (James Cagney) is an uneducated, pompous bore whose only mark of compassion is the care he gives the palm tree he keeps on the deck. When, in one of their constant battles, Roberts yells, "I realize in wartime they have to scrape

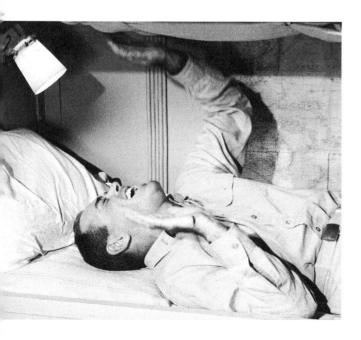

the bottom of the barrel, but where did they dig up you?" he hits the situation clearly on the head. The palm tree becomes a symbol of the crew's despair as they dream about home, women and other pleasures. Roberts, always on their side, is the buffer between them and the captain.

Knowing that the war is passing him by, Roberts places endless requests with the captain for transfer, but they are all denied. The incompetent captain is not about to give up his best man. Roberts does his best to keep the crew's restlessness at a minimum—their behavior has become like that of children—and he gives pep talks to Ensign Pulver (Jack Lemmon), a glib wheeler-dealer who talks a lot about what he will do to the captain but never does anything much, and in turn gets pep talks from Doc (William Powell).

The captain punishes the resentful crew by denying them liberty but makes a deal with Roberts, promising liberty if Roberts will stop making his requests for transfer, and if he will keep the deal a secret. The crew get their liberty, they get to meet the nurses they have been ogling by binoculars for months and they get roaring drunk. Later they come to resent Roberts' passive manner toward the captain and assume he is bucking for promotion. But Roberts finally explodes at the captain's petty tyranny and flings the hated palm tree overboard. He regains the respect of the crew, who band together in a scheme to get Roberts his transfer. As he departs they give him a medal they have made—the

145

Order of the Palm Leaf. Not long after his departure they receive notification that he has been killed.

Mister Roberts lived up to the hopes of its producers and became a box office smash but Fonda was never completely happy with the film, feeling that it had been tampered with and missed some of the poignancy of the original. To him the original was almost sacred. Be that as it may, it is difficult to look at the film and realize it is a work of fiction. Roberts seems very real, as does the setting. His ironic death, in accident and not in action, is well in keeping with the reality of war, and he symbolizes the men who fought monotony as heroically as those in combat. Fonda crafted that portrait to the last brush stroke. *Mister Roberts* was Oscar-nominated as a best film of 1955 but lost to *Marty*. Jack Lemmon's amusingly frantic Pulver won him an Oscar as best supporting actor, but Fonda was not even nominated. More disappointing to him was the sad way it had ended his association with John Ford, closing the book on one of the most important pairings of actor and director in film history. However, much as Fonda believed the film was less than it should have been, it did one important thing—it brought Henry Fonda back to the movies.

WAR AND PEACE

With Audrey Hepburn.

1956
A Paramount–Ponti–De Laurentiis Film, produced by Dino De Laurentiis, directed by King Vidor, written by Bridget Boland, King Vidor, Robert Westerby, Mario Camerini, Ennio De Concini and Ivo Perilli, based on the book by Leo Tolstoy, photographed in Technicolor and VistaVision by Jack Cardiff, music by Nino Rota, 208 minutes.

CAST:
Natasha Rostov, *Audrey Hepburn*; Pierre Bezukhov, *Henry Fonda*; Andrey Bolkonsky, *Mel Ferrer*; Anatole Kuragine, *Vittorio Gassman*; Helene Kuragine, *Anita Ekberg*; General Kutuzov, *Oscar Homolka*; Napoleon, *Herbert Lom*; Platon, *John Mills*; Dolokhov, *Helmut Dantine*; Lise, *Milly Vitale*; Sonja, *May Britt*.

With the success of the movie version of *Mr. Roberts*, whatever doubts Henry Fonda may have had about resuming his film career were swept away. He was not alone in thinking he had been off the screen too long, especially at a time when Hollywood and its market had changed enormously. The veteran movie stars no longer had the impact of former years. But with Fonda there would always be a place in the film world. He was not simply a movie star, he was a valuable actor.

The first producer who came running after him following the release of *Mr. Roberts* was the flamboyant Italian Dino De Laurentiis, who was

With May Britt, Audrey Hepburn and Barry Jones.

about to start an expensive and expansive version of Tolstoy's great novel *War and Peace*. Fonda was astonished to know that De Laurentiis wanted him for the role of Pierre, the gentle and confused seeker of truth who is an interpretative thread through the story. Fonda did not like to play roles other than American and he also felt that his physical being and his manner were not at all in line with the character created by Tolstoy. But apparently no one can withstand the persuasiveness of De Laurentiis, and in the summer of 1955 Fonda found himself in Rome, swept up in a mammoth piece of movie making.

Running a little over three hours, King Vidor's version of *War and Peace* is a kind of *Reader's Digest* version of Tolstoy, but within its limitations it is a superb and comprehensive treatment. It tells the epic story through a handful of major characters. As Napoleon prepares to invade Russia, Pierre Bezukhov (Fonda), an aristocratic liberal, visits his friend Count Rostov (Barry Jones) and his lovely young daughter Natasha (Audrey Hepburn), with whom he falls in love but to whom he diffidently hesitates to propose

because he is illegitimate. With the death of his father, Pierre inherits a fortune and falls under the influence of the beautiful but unscrupulous Helene (Anita Ekberg), whom he marries. His close friend, Prince Andrey Bolkonsky (Mel Ferrer), achieves success as a soldier under General Kutuzov (Oscar Homolka) but returns wounded, a condition made worse by the death of his wife in childbirth. With his own marriage ended by the adultery of his wife, Pierre introduces the grieving Andrey to Natasha, and the pair fall in love.

With Barry Jones, Audrey Hepburn and Mel Ferrer.

Andrey and Natasha plan to marry but before they can do so Andrey is sent into battle against the invading French, with the pacifistic Pierre going along as an observer. He is horrified by the carnage at the battle of Borodino and it breeds in him a resolve to assassinate Napoleon. He returns to Moscow to aid his friends in their evacuation, and is taken prisoner after his unsuccessful attempt to kill Napoleon. As a prisoner he observes much grief and agony, an experience which greatly matures him. Pierre sees at first hand the misery of the French defeat in winter, with soldiers dying by the droves along the way.

At the battle of Berezina the Russian Army delivers the final, paralyzing blows to Napoleon's weary forces. Pierre manages to escape his captors and returns to Moscow, together with hordes of soldiers and civilians intent on rebuilding their country in the wake of victory. Count Andrey has died of his wounds and now Pierre is finally mature enough to court the waiting and willing Natasha.

Any short synopsis of Tolstoy's monumental book is bound to be absurdly inadequate, but King Vidor's version has much to admire. The production values, especially the battle scenes shot in Yugoslavia, are magnificent and the acting is on mostly a good level. Fonda was able to

With Mel Ferrer.

With John Mills.

communicate the confusion of the nice but lumbering Pierre, a man caught up in an angry swirl of history and groping for answers, trying to find out "what happiness is—what value there is in suffering—why men go to war." His adventures lead him to understand at least partly the mysteries of life, humanity, love and loyalty.

War and Peace took longer to make than any film in which Henry Fonda appeared. He knew it would be a long job but he did not reckon on the difficulties of making a film in Italy, where production methods are different and where, he discovered to his dismay, the film had been started without complete funding, and with continual bickering among its backers and producers. He became irritated with the long stay

in Italy and moreso with the difference between his interpretation of Pierre and that of De Laurentiis. "I knew I was physically all wrong for Pierre, but I decided that, with the right spectacles, some strategically placed padding and my hair combed forward, I could pass. Then it seems they didn't want a Pierre who looked like Pierre. One who looked like Rock Hudson is closer to what they had in mind. They went into a nervous shock when they saw my original make-up. The padding went immediately—over my anguished protests. And from that point on, it was a constant struggle between the producer and me as to whether or not I'd wear the spectacles. I won about half the time—usually when he was nowhere near the set."

War and Peace pleased the public but most critics seemed to enjoy taking intellectual pot-shots at it. Fonda came off better than most of the cast. The reviewer for *Time* said, "Henry Fonda's leaness at first seems all wrong for the massive, moon-faced, soul-tortured Pierre. But Fonda builds beautifully into his part, using a physical clumsiness as a counterpoise to his soaring spirit, making his rages seem the more terrible since they flash out from passivity. . . . Fonda acts to the very limit of his considerable powers, and sometimes gives the impression of being the only man in the huge cast who has read the book."

THE WRONG MAN

1957

A Warner Bros. Film, produced and directed by Alfred Hitchcock, written by Maxwell Anderson and Angus MacPhail, photographed by Robert Burks, music by Bernard Herrmann, 105 minutes.

CAST:

Manny Balestrero, *Henry Fonda*; Rose, *Vera Miles*; O'Connor, *Anthony Quayle*; Lt. Bowers, *Harold J. Stone*; Manny's Mother, *Esther Min-* ciotti; Detective Matthews, *Charles Cooper*; Gene Conforti, *Nehemiah Persoff*; Constance Willis, *Laurinda Barrett*; Betty Todd, *Norma Connolly*; Ann James, *Doreen Lang*; Mrs. O'Connor, *Frances Reid*; Olga Conforti, *Lola D'Annunzio*; Gregory, *Robert Essen*; Robert, *Kippy Campbell*; Judge Groat, *Dayton Lummis*; Tomasini, *John Heldabrand*; Danielli, *Richard Robbins*; Detective Holman, *John Vivyan*; McKaba, *Will Hare*; Dr. Banay, *Werner Klemperer*.

With Sherman Billingsley.

Now that his film career had gained its second wings Henry Fonda was determined to make only movies which offered him range as an actor. The idea of working with Alfred Hitchcock was obviously beneficial, but unfortunately it would be in a film different from that master's usual brand and one which would end up being more admired than popular. Indeed, *The Wrong Man* stands almost like the wrong picture in the Hitchcock gallery.

Hitchcock had become intrigued with a news story he had read in the newspapers and he

been identified by a number of witnesses, employees of the insurance company, who claimed that he was the man who held them up and robbed the company at gunpoint, taking the sum of $271. He was subsequently booked and fingerprinted, jailed and faced with harrowing publicity. Balestrero managed to raise a five thousand dollar bail but justice took its time and his wife cracked under the strain, having to be placed in an institution. His trial was considered invalid and while waiting for a retrial the real thief was caught and confessed.

thought it had sad, strange and haunting qualities. It was about a man named Manny Balestrero, a New York musician who made $85 a week playing the bass at a Manhattan night spot, the posh Stork Club. During the afternoon of January 13th, 1953, Balestrero visited the offices of a Long Island insurance company in order to get a loan on his policy because his wife was ill and they were badly in need of money. The following day he was arrested by the police, having

Hitchcock wanted to make a film that would reveal the pain of false identification and he asked his scenarists, Maxwell Anderson and Angus MacPhail, to write the script following the exact details of the Balestrero case. The trouble with *The Wrong Man* is that it is too literal. In trying to be honest, Hitchcock compromised his great talent of suspense and pacing. The result was a film more depressing than it should have been, but with a performance from Fonda that

With Vera Miles, Robert Essen,
and Kippy Campbell.

disturbingly accented the anguish of a plain, ordinary man being put through misery. Fonda
had, of course, been through this route a couple
of times before in *You Only Live Once* and *Let
Us Live*. Now, as an older man and in a film less
obviously dramatic than the others, the anguish
seemed even more painful.

The film can hardly be faulted for accuracy.
Hitchcock used the same locations as in the actual events: the Stork Club, the streets of East
Brooklyn and even the courtroom where the trial
had taken place. Fonda always said that he appreciated the experience of working with Hitchcock even though the film was not among his
best. He admired Hitchcock's preparation, his
"blueprint" method of making films, and how
he always knew precisely what he wanted. His
direction was sparse because he hired the actors
he knew could provide what he needed. He set
them in place and expected them to give him
what he wanted. But in the case of *The Wrong
Man*, perhaps a touch more passion, a little more
fire would have made an impressive film even
moreso.

With Nehemiah Persoff and Vera Miles.

152

THE TIN STAR

1957

A Paramount Film, produced by William Perlberg and George Seaton, directed by Anthony Mann, written by Dudley Nichols, based on a story by Barney Slater and Joel Kane, photographed in VistaVision by Loyal Griggs, music by Elmer Bernstein, 93 minutes.

CAST:

Morg Hickman, *Henry Fonda*; Ben Owens, *Anthony Perkins*; Nona Mayfield, *Betsy Palmer*; Kip, *Michel Ray*; Bart Bogardus, *Neville Brand*; Doc McCord, *John McIntyre*; Millie Parker, *Mary Webster*; Zeke McGaffrey, *Peter Baldwin*; Ed McGaffrey, *Lee Van Cleef*; Buck Henderson, *Richard Shannon*; Judge Thatcher, *James Bell*; Harvey King, *Howard Petrie*; Clem Hall, *Russell Simpson*.

Ten years had passed since *Fort Apache* and it was time to get Henry Fonda back into the cinematic Wild West. He would not, of course, agree to be in a western just for the sake of it. The script had to be interesting and when he was told it was by his old friend Dudley Nichols, he knew it would be strong on character, and when he learned the director would be Anthony Mann, then he knew it was worth his while. Mann had directed Fonda's friend Jimmy Stewart in a succession of superb westerns—*Winchester '73* (1950), *Bend of the River* (1952), *The Naked Spur* (1952), *The Far Country* (1954), and *The Man from Laramie* (1955). Recommendation enough.

In *The Tin Star* Fonda is a bounty hunter named Morg Hickman and when first seen he is riding into a peaceful town with a dead body roped across the back of his pack horse. He has come to pick up the bounty money and he is greeted coolly by the citizenry, who don't think much of men who make their living in this fashion. He proceeds to the sheriff's office where he finds the position held by a callow young man, Ben Owens (Anthony Perkins). Morg also finds that the dead man has a distant relative in town, Bart Bogardus (Neville Brand), a menacing bully

With Anthony Perkins.

of a man who makes it known Hickman had best leave. The cool bounty hunter wants no trouble. Riding out of town he gives a lift to a young lad, whose young widow mother, Nona Mayfield (Betsy Palmer), offers Hickman lodging for the night. The next day trouble starts when Bogardus kills an Indian in town and resists arrest by the young sheriff.

When Ben approaches Bogardus in the street, Bogardus conceals a gun behind his hat but Hickman is standing nearby and shoots the gun from Bogardus's hand. It turns out that Hickman had been a sheriff, but became a bounty hunter when disillusioned with public morality; now the eager young sheriff asks for guidance. The main thrust of Hickman's advice is, "Study men—not guns." When the town doctor (John McIntyre) is killed, the suspicion falls on a pair of wild brothers, Ed (Lee Van Cleef) and Zeke McGaffrey (Peter Baldwin). The sheriff organizes a posse, but it is the blood hungry Bogardus who leads them. The sheriff proceeds by himself and tracks the brothers to a cave in the mountains, but again it is Hickman who comes to his aid and brings about the capture.

Back in town Bogardus whips up anger with a drunken mob and leads them to the jail for a lynching. Hickman advises the sheriff to move against them with a double-barrelled shotgun.

leaves, declining the pleas of the sheriff to stay and take the job. Hickman, who had found his own peace, which includes the young widow and her son, tells the young man he has the courage and the respect to hold the job.

Like all good westerns, *The Tin Star* is a morality tale, with a lot of talk about a man facing up to responsibility by himself and not expecting help from others, and the fact that in the learning process the teacher also learns. The film is modestly scaled and contains far less action

With Anthony Perkins.

With Anthony Perkins and Howard Petrie.

The mob moves back and the sheriff calls Bogardus's bluff. The bully retreats but turns with his guns blazing. The sheriff is quicker. The town goes back to its peaceful ways and Hickman

than the Mann-Stewart westerns. This obviously was a factor in Fonda accepting the role. He was never a very physical actor and now at the age of 52 his lack of enthusiasm for horses and riding was even less.

In *The Tin Star* his bounty hunter is a man embittered by past experience and now doing a job simply because it's work he knows how to do, not because he likes it. He is a loner—and Fonda knew how to convey the spiritual isolation of such a man. As Bosley Crowther said in reviewing the picture, "All you have to do is look at his eyes." Fonda was probably the only actor who could ever play a bounty hunter and make the man seem graceful.

☆☆☆☆☆☆☆☆☆☆☆☆

12
ANGRY MEN

1957

A United Artists Film, produced by Henry Fonda and Reginald Rose, directed by Sidney Lumet, written by Reginald Rose, photographed by Boris Kaufman, 95 minutes.

CAST:

Juror No. 8, *Henry Fonda;* Juror No. 3, *Lee J. Cobb;* Juror No. 10, *Ed Begley;* Juror No. 4, *E. G. Marshall;* Juror No. 1, *Martin Balsam;* Juror No. 2, *John Fiedler;* Juror No. 5, *Jack Klugman;* Juror No. 6, *Edward Binns;* Juror No. 7, *Jack Warden;* Juror No. 9, *Joseph Sweeney;* Juror No. 11, *George Voskovec;* Juror No. 12, *Robert Webber;* Judge, *Rudy Bond;* Guard, *James A. Kelly;* Court Clerk, *Bill Nelson;* Defendant, *John Savoca.*

"Henry Fonda has a most reassuring face. Something about the set of the jaw, the leaness of the cheeks, the moodiness of the eyes, inspires respect and confidence. The parts he has played in films and on the stage have made him close to an American symbol of the unbiased, uncorrupted man, and he is just about perfect for the role of Juror #8 in Reginald Rose's *12 Angry Men.*" So said Hollis Alpert at the start of his *Saturday Review* review of this exceptional movie. When asked which of his films he held in the kindest regard, Fonda always mentioned *The Grapes of Wrath, The Ox-Bow Incident* and this one, but it is possible *12 Angry Men* was at the top of his list because it was the one film on which he worked as a producer. Fonda admired Rose's television play and tried to get several studios interested in making it as a film but none thought it sufficiently commercial. He then formed a partnership with Rose and they raised the money to make it themselves. Rose had once served on a New York jury and his *12 Angry Men* is a dramatization of how disturbing an experience he found it.

The 95-minute running time of the film is also the time period of its action. It begins as a trial ends during a hot and humid summer afternoon

155

With Lee J. Cobb.

in Manhattan's Court of General Sessions. The tired judge (Rudy Bond) tells the tired jury that justice is now in their hands. What is also in their hands is the life of a scared boy (John Savoca), charged with knifing his father to death. The twelve men retreat to the jury room and soon arrive at a decision—11 for conviction and one for acquital, Juror #8. The jurors are a cross-section of ordinary New Yorkers. One is a man (Jack Warden) who simply wants to wrap it up as fast as possible so that he can attend a ballgame. Another is a calculating businessman (E. G. Marshall). Others are a sour, prejudiced old man (Ed Begley), an advertising executive (Robert Webber) whose idea of truth is couched in terms of slogans, and a man (Martin Balsam) who will vote with the majority in order to be popular. Only one of them is dangerous—a bully by nature (Lee J. Cobb), who runs a messenger service and punches people rather than argue with them. Only one is the dogged voice of reason, Juror #8, an architect who senses a reasonable doubt in the testimony and feels he must explore

With Jack Klugman, Edward Binns, Ed Begley and E. G. Marshall.

it. They take another vote, this time with four deciding on acquittal. They argue for another quarter of an hour and vote again, this time with nine for acquittal. In the heat and humidity they thrash the issue back and forth, and at the end of an hour and a half there are 12 votes for acquittal.

12 Angry Men is a fascinating but uncomfortably close examination of the workings of constitutional law and the fact that a life can be in the decisions of 12 people who are themselves full of faults, failings and doubts. The film makes it graphically clear that the people who enforce the law are all too human, and that there are calm, decent people like Juror #8 who are willing to weigh the evidence and look for innocence rather than rush toward the verdict of guilt.

The film won unanimous critical approval. Eleanor Roosevelt saw it and said she thought Fonda was magnificent, "but the whole cast is made up of excellent actors. As a character study, this is a fascinating movie, but more than that, it points up the fact which too many of us have not taken seriously, of what it means to serve on a jury when a man's life is at stake. In addition, it makes vivid what 'reasonable doubt' means when a murder trial jury makes up its mind on circumstantial evidence."

12 Angry Men was the first film directed by then 32-year-old Sidney Lumet, a stage director whom Fonda selected for this job. Despite not having worked with film before, Lumet keeps the

action moving within the limited confines of the jury room. In this he had the help of the veteran cameraman Boris Kaufman. The most important factor in making the film was the selection of the 12 angry men. They were all top grade actors, experienced with the stage as well as film, and their work here is an excellent example of ensemble acting. To get the effect he wanted Lumet rehearsed his cast for two weeks—the usual procedure with a play but not with film. He plotted every camera movement with Kaufman and he was thereby able to get an acting flow that gave life and excitement to what was essentially a claustrophobic set.

Despite the accolades, *12 Angry Men* did poorly at the box office. It was given conventional bookings instead of the specialized bookings such a film needs. It brought Henry Fonda an Academy Award nomination as a co-producer but not as an actor. Sidney Lumet and Reginald Rose were also nominated for Oscars. None of them won. Filmed in 20 days at a cost of $340,000, it never brought a profit to its producers. In fact, it never brought enough to pay Fonda his deferred salary. That fact never bothered him. Instead he took pride in the film's constant bookings in schools and study groups, and that with time it gained recognition as an American classic.

With director Sidney Lumet.

STAGE STRUCK

1958
An RKO–Buena Vista Film, produced by Stuart Miller, directed by Sidney Lumet, written by Ruth and Augustus Goetz, based on the play *Morning Glory* by Zoe Akins, photographed in Technicolor by Franz F. Planer and Maurice Hartzband, music by Alex North, 95 minutes.

CAST:
Lewis Easton, *Henry Fonda*; Eva Lovelace, *Susan Strasberg*; Rita Vernon, *Joan Greenwood*; Robert Harley Hedges, *Herbert Marshall*; Joe

Sheridan, *Christopher Plummer*; Constantine, *Daniel Ocko*; Benny, *Pat Harrington*; Victor, *Frank Campanella*; Adrian, *John Fiedler*; Gwen Hall, *Patricia Englund*; Frank, *Jack Weston*; Elizabeth, *Sally Gracie*; Regina, *Nina Hansen*.

With Susan Strasberg.

With Christopher Plummer and Joan Greenwood.

Stage Struck offered Henry Fonda little as an actor but it allowed him to stay in New York and make a movie about the theatre, and he was all in favor of that. It also helped Sidney Lumet, making his second film as a director, and 20-year-old Susan Strasberg, a friend of the family. Strasberg had played a small part in *Picnic* (1955), but this was her debut in a starring role. It was a remake of *Morning Glory* (1933), which had brought Katharine Hepburn her first Oscar.

With Susan Strasberg.

port of the fatherly Hedges she gets through the first night with flying colors. The critics and the public applaud, and the three men who love her instinctively know that Eva's love and life will be with the theatre and not with them.

One critic described *Stage Struck* as *42nd Street* without the music. The moviegoers in 1958 were not very impressed, possibly because by this time films about show biz had become old hat, and also because Strasberg was no Hepburn. For Fonda the film was a breeze, playing a compassionate producer with quiet authority. For lovers of New York City the beautiful Technicolor photography of Franz Planer is a poignant reminder of safer times in The Big Apple, with exciting shots of bistros in Greenwich Village and penthouses along Park Avenue, and myriad points between. The film's major interest, however, is for those interested in the theatre. *Stage Struck* is full of sequences showing backstage operation

Unfortunately *Stage Struck* did nothing nearly as much for young Strasberg.

Eva Lovelace (Strasberg) is an actress intent upon Broadway success, and Lewis Easton (Fonda) is a famed stage producer who believes she can make it, especially since he is in love with her. Also impressed with her are a veteran actor, Robert Harley Hedges (Herbert Marshall), and playwright Joe Sheridan (Christopher Plummer). At a party with them she drinks too much and nervously but impressively recites the balcony scene from *Romeo and Juliet* and then falls asleep in a guest room. Awakening after everybody else has gone, she confesses her love for Easton and in the following days they enjoy a romantic interlude. But he finally tells her it isn't wise to go on because it will do her career no good. She must succeed on her merits.

Eva then comes under the romantic guidance of Sheridan. He has become very unhappy with his temperamental leading lady, Rita Vernon (Joan Greenwood), and he coaches Eva in her role. Rita walks out and Sheridan persuades Easton that Eva can do the job. With the sup-

With Susan Strasberg and Herbert Marshall.

of the theatres, the offices, the dressing rooms and the attendant life. It had been a nice indulgence for Fonda, but it had not done much for his film career.

159

WARLOCK

With Dorothy Malone and Anthony Quinn.

1959

A 20th Century-Fox Film, produced and directed by Edward Dmytryk, written by Robert Alan Aurthur, based on the novel by Oakley Hall, photographed in CinemaScope and DeLuxe Color by Joe MacDonald, music by Leigh Harline, 122 minutes.

CAST:

Johnny Gannon, *Richard Widmark;* Clay Baisdell, *Henry Fonda;* Tom Morgan, *Anthony Quinn;* Lilly Dollar, *Dorothy Malone;* Jessie Marlowe, *Dolores Michaels;* Judge Holloway, *Wallace Ford;* Abe McQuown, *Tom Drake;* Bacon, *Richard Arlen;* Curley Burne, *DeForest Kelley;* Skinner, *Regis Toomey;* Richardson, *Vaughn Taylor;* Dr. Wagner, *Don Beddoe;* Mr. Petrix, *Whit Bissell;* Shaw, *J. Anthony Hughes;* Calhoun, *Donald Barry;* Billy Gannon, *Frank Gorshin.*

With Anthony Quinn.

With the disappointing public reaction to his New York movies *12 Angry Men* and *Stage Struck*, Henry Fonda's agents were eager to get him back to Hollywood and something more commercial—like a western. *Warlock* was a good choice. It was also an unusual one because the drama was darkly toned and the relationships complex. Despite a title that suggested witchcraft—it refers to the name of the town in which the action takes place—*Warlock* actually sug-gested that by the early 1880's aging gunmen like the one played by Fonda had become something of a displaced generation. His Clay Baisdell, a lawman with a probable criminal past, is a rather melancholy figure.

Baisdell is hired by the town council of War-lock because cowboys from the nearby ranches cause too much damage, and occasional killings, when they ride into town for fun. Part of Bais-dell's understanding with the town is that his club-footed companion Tom Morgan (Anthony Quinn) will run a gambling hall and saloon and that Baisdell will get part of the profits. They agree. The vice will be controlled. One of the cowboys, Johnny Gannon (Richard Widmark) is disgusted by the way his pals have been abusing the town and signs on as Baisdell's deputy. When Baisdell's girlfriend Lilly Dollar arrives in town she takes a shine to Johnny, but Baisdell doesn't mind because he has become smitten with a young lady, Jessie (Dolores Michaels), who opposed his appointment but gradually comes under his quiet, moody spell.

Peace gradually falls over Warlock and with it a feeling by the citizens that their marshal is a bit of a menace to have around. Tom Morgan points this out to him and urges that the two of them move on. It comes as a shock to Baisdell when he finds out that Tom is a murderer. Tom gets drunk and starts to shoot up the town and it becomes Baisdell's job to stop him. Tom knows that the only way to end their outmoded lifestyle and their strange friendship is for Baisdell to kill

him, and he does. Baisdell packs his bags and leaves Warlock. Maybe Jessie will follow.

With good production values and a running time of two hours, *Warlock* is an impressive western, and a peculiar one in that the relationship between the Fonda and Quinn characters is enigmatic, even with a suggestion of homosexuality. The marshal has come to feel uncomfortable about carrying his deformed friend around with him, and the friend fatalistically knows they

With Dolores Michaels and Richard Widmark.

have come to the end of the line. The marshal would like to settle down because his kind of West is gone. That concept was not new even in 1959, but it is Fonda's sad air of chivalry and disillusion that makes the role interesting, like watching a man looking for dignity under desperate conditions. *Warlock* sneaks in some unconventional elements in what seems like a conventional framework, perhaps too much so for its own good. In his westerns Fonda always had a faraway look in his eyes. In this one it is an even more distant and slightly troubled gaze.

163

☆☆☆☆☆☆☆☆☆☆☆☆☆☆☆☆☆☆☆☆☆

THE MAN WHO UNDERSTOOD WOMEN

1959

A 20th Century-Fox Film, produced and directed by Nunnally Johnson, written by Nunnally Johnson, based on the novel *Colors of the Day* by Romain Gary, photographed in Technicolor by Milton Krasner, music by Robert Emmett Dolan, 135 minutes.

With Leslie Caron.

CAST:

Ann Garantier, *Leslie Caron;* Willie Bauche, *Henry Fonda;* Marco Ranieri, *Cesare Danova;* Preacher, *Myron McCormick;* Le Marne, *Marcel Dalio;* G. K., *Conrad Nagel;* The Baron, *Edwin Jerome;* Soprano, *Bern Hoffman;* Kress, *Harry Ellerbe;* Milstead, *Frank Cady;* Doctor, *Ben Astar.*

Henry Fonda had been a friend of Nunnally Johnson's since the two had worked together on *Jesse James* in 1939. Twenty years later the urbane writer-producer asked Fonda to star in *The Man Who Understood Women*, which Johnson had scripted from Romain Gary's novel and which Johnson would also direct. Perhaps it would have been better if Fonda declined, but it must have been impossible for him to say no to such an affable and respected man as Johnson. But in making this spoof on Hollywood and its strange people Johnson was too close to the subject to have judgment, and the film is too confused and diffused to make any final satiric point.

Willie Bauche (Fonda) is an aging Hollywood wunderkind, along the lines of Orson Welles and

Charlie Chaplin, who falls in love with a lovely young actress, Ann Garantier (Leslie Caron), and after marrying her determines to turn her into another Garbo. He writes, directs and acts in a film with her but seems more interested in the result of her screen image than her real one. She feels neglected. But the film is a success, which is what Willie needs because, although his films have won Oscars, they have lost money, and his studio boss (Conrad Nagel) is tired of Willie.

In Nice, Ann meets a handsome French aviator (Cesare Danova) and falls for his charm, because he is a man who understands women. Willie tries to seek out the lovers' rendezvous and hires a gunman to rub out the opposition. But the gunman is persuaded by a romantic old Baron (Edwin Jerome) that lovers should not be separated, they should live or die as a couple.

Knowing that Ann is in danger, Willie frantically tries to find her. She and the aviator in the meantime have decided to end their affair, and as they talk about it the gunman approaches. But the gunman is killed by the Baron, who has had a change of heart, and Willie in his wild search falls down a Riviera hillside and is badly injured. He finally comes to in the hospital and the happy young wife tells him how funny he looks in his bandages. Says Willie, "Yep, here I lie in the Valley of the Shadow of Death and all I get is yuks."

With Cesare Danova and Leslie Caron.

The Man Who Understood Women didn't get many yuks, except in Hollywood where people in the know could pick up on Johnson's barbs about the nature of film folk. The film is at its best in the first half, set in Hollywood and packed with pointed observations about the industry, but in the second half it becomes a comedic romp and rather absurd. Nunnally Johnson was one

With Leslie Caron.

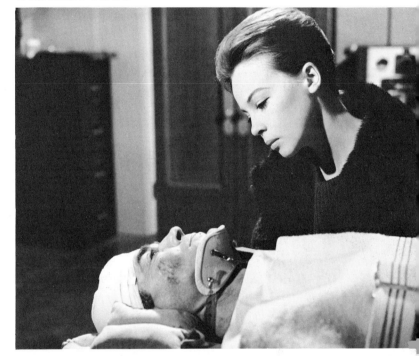

of the most talented men in Hollywood history but he here bit off more than he could chew. In *Films in Review*, editor Henry Hart commented, "Fonda does well in his none-too-consistent role, especially in the early, and best, sequences, in which he mocks the Hollywood rat race he has become part of. When he says of himself, 'beneath this gaudy haberdashery beats the heart of a simple Methodist,' one hears, or thinks he hears, Nunnally Johnson speaking of himself." Perhaps Fonda's own feelings about the film may be assumed from his not choosing to make another film for three years.

☆☆☆☆☆☆☆☆☆☆
ADVISE AND CONSENT

1962

A Columbia Film, produced and directed by Otto Preminger, written by Wendell Mayes, based on the novel by Allen Drury, photographed in Technicolor and Panavision by Sam Leavitt, music by Jerry Fielding, 139 minutes.

CAST:

Robert Leffingwell, *Henry Fonda;* Senator Seabright Cooley, *Charles Laughton;* Senator Brigham Anderson, *Don Murray;* Senator Bob Munson, *Walter Pidgeon;* Senator Lafe Smith, *Peter Lawford;* Dolly Harrison, *Gene Tierney;* The President, *Franchot Tone;* Vice President, *Lew Ayres;* Herbert Gelman, *Burgess Meredith;* Johnny Leffingwell, *Eddie Hodges;* Senator Stanley Dante, *Paul Ford;* Senator Van Ackerman, *George Gizzard;* Ellen Anderson, *Inga Swenson;* Hardiman Fletcher, *Paul McGrath;* Senate Minority Leader, *Will Geer;* Senator Bessie Adams, *Betty White;* Senator Tom August, *Malcolm Atterbury;* Senator Paul Hendershot, *William Quinn;* Senator Kanaho, *Tiki Santos;* Senator Velez, *Raoul De Leon;* British Ambassador, *Tom Helmore.*

With Paul McGrath.

After a screen absence of three years Henry Fonda needed a worthwhile picture to bring him back and Otto Preminger's announced big budget treatment of Allen Drury's successful political novel, *Advise and Consent,* seemed like a good bet. It used a cast of well-known veteran actors and it was filmed amid the proper settings in Washington. In dealing with Washington, Hollywood had in the past mostly used the capital either for inspirational or humorous pictures. Preminger thought the time right to make one that would show the nations political life with some of its complexity showing.

Advise and Consent reveals some of the underside of political life, things like scandals, concessions, loyalty probes and character assassinations.

With Don Murray.

With Eddie Hodges.

Since one of the main characters, Robert Leffingwell, seemed somewhat patterned after Adlai Stevenson, a man Fonda greatly admired, he was eager to play the part.

Drury's large novel had to be scaled down, even for this two hour and 19 minute version. The plot in brief: the obstinate president (Franchot Tone), despite his being a dying man, asks the Senate to advise and consent to the appointment of the brilliant but controversial Robert Leffingwell as Secretary of State. This meets with some stiff opposition, particularly from southern Senator Seabright Cooley (Charles Laughton), who has long held a personal grudge. He digs up a mentally unbalanced clerk (Burgess Meredith) who testifies that Leffingwell was once a member of a Communist group.

Leffingwell admits in private to the president that this is true but that it was brief and insignificant; to the Senate, with the president's approval, he denies the charge. The committee chairman, Senator Brigham Anderson (Don Murray) is advised that Leffingwell's denial under oath is perjury and he demands a withdrawal of nomination. When the president refuses, Anderson feels that the matter should be brought out for the good of the country. Before he can make that move Anderson finds himself in trouble, as an ambitious young Senator, Van Ackerman (George Gizzard), threatens to blackmail him with the exposure of a homosexual incident long ago. Unable to face this shame or to confess it to his wife, Anderson commits suicide. Not long after this sad incident the Senate votes on Leffingwell's nomination. It ends in a deadlock, with the favor tending toward the mild-mannered vice-president (Lew Ayres). Word then arrives that the president has died. Now advanced to the highest position in the land, the vice-president assumes courage and strength, and declines to vote. He says, "I'd prefer to name my own Secretary of State."

Although technically impeccable, *Advise and Consent* impressed neither the critics nor the public as anything other than a splashy, sensationalized version of political life in Washington. Democrat Fonda failed to win much comment with his Stevensonian figure, perhaps because the role was awash in a sea of theatrical dinghies. However, Fonda's plausible political image did not go unnoticed in Hollywood. He would be called back into "office" in other pictures.

☆☆☆☆☆☆☆☆☆

THE LONGEST DAY

1962

A 20th Century-Fox Film, produced by Darryl F. Zanuck, directed by Andrew Marton, Ken Annakin and Bernhard Wicki, written by Cornelius Ryan, based on his book, photographed by Jean Bourgoin, Henri Persin and Walter Wottitz, music by Maurice Jarre, 180 minutes.

CAST:
Colonel Vandervoort, *John Wayne;* General Cota, *Robert Mitchum;* General Roosevelt, *Henry Fonda;* General Gavin, *Robert Ryan;* Commander, *Rod Steiger;* Schultz, *Richard Beymer;* General Haines, *Mel Ferrer;* Sergeant Fuller, *Jeffrey Hunter;* Private Martini, *Sal Mineo;* Private Morris, *Roddy McDowall;* Lieutenant Sheen, *Stuart Whitman;* Colonel Newton, *Eddie Albert;* General Barton, *Edmond O'Brien;* Private Steele, *Red Buttons;* Lieutenant Wilson, *Tom Tryon;* General Bedell Smith, *Alexander Knox;* Captain Frank, *Ray Danton;* General Eisenhower, *Henry Grace;* Captain Harding, *Steve Forrest.*

When he had launched himself into the incredibly complex job of producing *The Longest Day*, Darryl F. Zanuck sent a desperate note to

Lord Louis Mountbatten, "I believe I have a tougher job than Ike had on D-Day—at least he had the equipment. I have to find it, rebuild it, and transport it to Normandy." It is greatly to Generalissimo Zanuck's credit that he did indeed find the equipment, the backing, the permission, the cooperation and the manpower to make this excellent visualization of Cornelius Ryan's masterful account of the Allied landings on the French coast on June 6th, 1944. To anyone involved in the film it would thereafter be known as Z-Day. Zanuck's first command decision was to hire the man who wrote the book to write the screenplay, and to be his supervisor. Together they scouted and used the exact locations of the landings and sought help from all the governments involved. The resulting three-hour film is about as comprehensive an accounting of that particular piece of history as it is possible to make, despite its being dotted with familiar faces.

Henry Fonda had never cared much for Zanuck on the personal level but he was not going to let that stop him from accepting a cameo role in the film. Zanuck offered him a choice of three parts and the one Fonda considered the most interesting was that of Brigadier General Theodore Roosevelt, the son of President Teddy Roosevelt. The general was 57 years old at the time of D-Day and had to use a cane because of an old leg injury, but he was not likely to let those facts deter him. Fonda liked that sort of man.

Roosevelt was in command of the 4th Division and he insisted, despite the objections of his superiors, in personally leading his men in the first wave to hit Utah Beach. When Roosevelt-Fonda, with cool gaze and steady voice, gathers his men around him on that beach and says, "We're starting the war from right here," no one could possibly doubt him.

HOW THE WEST WAS WON

Henry Fonda; Julie Rawlings, *Carolyn Jones*; Zebulon Prescott, *Karl Malden*; Cleve Van Valen, *Gregory Peck*; Zeb Rawlings, *George Peppard*; Roger Morgan, *Robert Preston*; Lilith Prescott, *Debbie Reynolds*; Linus Rawlings, *James Stewart*; Charlie Gant, *Eli Wallach*; General Sherman, *John Wayne*; Mike King, *Richard Widmark*.

The gigantic Cinerama production *How the West Was Won* was bound to be a hit and Henry Fonda was one of the many stars who accepted offers to populate it. His and those of the other stars were more than cameos, they were well-crafted character parts in a story that spanned

With George Peppard.

1963
An MGM–Cinerama Film, produced by Bernard Smith, directed by Henry Hathaway, John Ford and George Marshall, written by James R. Webb, based on the Life Magazine series, photographed by William H. Daniels, Milton Krasner, Charles Lang, Jr. and Joseph La Shelle, music by Alfred Newman, 155 minutes.

CAST:
Narrator, *Spencer Tracy*; Eve Prescott, *Carroll Baker*; Marshall, *Lee J. Cobb*; Jethro Stuart,

169

Taking snaps of two South Dakota Sioux Indians — William Shakes Spear and Chief Ben Black Elk.

most of the nineteenth century. Karl Malden and Agnes Moorehead are the leading characters, as a married couple attracted to the prospect of free land in the West in the 1830's. They are drowned in a river accident but their children survive. One of them, Eva (Carroll Baker) marries a fur trapper, Linus Rawlings (James Stewart) and they settle on a farm. Comes the Civil War and one of their sons, Zeb (George Peppard) joins the Union Army. He stays in the army after the war and as a cavalry officer he is sent to Colorado to help guard the pioneering railroad against the Indians, whose land they are crossing.

It is while serving in this adventure that Zeb meets a well-weathered old buffalo hunter named Jethro Stuart (Fonda). Stuart's job is to keep the railroaders supplied with meat but he doesn't care much for the way they disregard the Indians and he clashes with construction boss Mike King (Richard Widmark), who refuses advice about Indian rights. Jethro has lived among the Indians long enough to respect them and be respected in turn. Zeb asks Jethro to arrange a meeting with the Indian chief, at which the soldier promises that the railroad will stay within the route laid out in the treaty. But King sees a short cut and takes it, thereby endangering the Indian's meat supply, the buffalo herds. In

retaliation they drive an enormous herd through the railroad camp and wreck it. Zeb and Jethro know that it is only a temporary setback—there is no stopping the railroad. Zeb resigns from the army with the idea of moving further west and starting his own family, which he does, and he asks Jethro to come with him. Jethro declines. He has built himself a home in the mountains, with his Indian friends around him, and he is happy to stay there and not be a part of this so-called civilization.

How the West Was Won did the kind of business its producers had expected, and deservedly so. In its original Cinerama presentation (later reduced for more conventional projections) it was visually magnificent. It also told its long and episodic story well and it is easy to see why so many stars agreed to be involved. Fonda's sequence was directed by the veteran George Marshall, although some of it was cut, as were other segments in order to bring the huge picture down to three hours, for road show bookings with intermission. Fonda played Jethro with flair, sporting long hair and big moustache but, more importantly, conveying the dignity and earthy wisdom of such a man. The kind of man who didn't so much win the West as tried to save it.

170

★ ★ ★ ★ ★ ★ ★ ★ ★ ★ ★

SPENCER'S MOUNTAIN

1963
A Warner Bros. Film, produced and directed by Delmer Daves, written by Delmer Daves, based on the novel by Earl Hamner, Jr., photographed in Warnercolor by Charles Lawson, music by Max Steiner, 118 minutes.

CAST:
Clay Spencer, *Henry Fonda;* Olivia Spencer, *Maureen O'Hara;* Clayboy, *James MacArthur;*

With Maureen O'Hara.

Grandpa, *Donald Crisp;* Preacher Goodman, *Wally Cox;* Claris Coleman, *Mimsy Farmer;* Miss Parker, *Virginia Gregg;* Grandma, *Lillian Bronson;* Dr. Campbell, *Whit Bissell;* Colonel Cole-

Clay Spencer is a quarry worker, whose ambition is to build a home in the mountains for his family. Other than that he enjoys life, drinking whiskey, playing poker and, as his nine children attest, making love to his resourceful wife. One thing Clay doesn't like is the church: "They don't allow drinkin' or smokin', card playin', pool shootin', dancin', cussin', or huggin', kissin' and lovin', and I'm for all of them things." This doesn't stop him making friends with the new preacher, the timid Mr. Goodman (Wally Cox). Living with the family is Grandpa (Donald Crisp), who came out as a pioneer and gave each of his sons a piece of his land, and the spirit that it is Spencer country.

The parents save all they can in order to build their dream home but their eldest son, Clayboy (James MacArthur), turns out to have quite a brain, according to his teacher (Virginia Gregg), who advises that the boy should go to college. In order to send him off to higher education Clay ends up selling his land to raise the money. In the meantime Clayboy meets a pretty girl (Mimsy

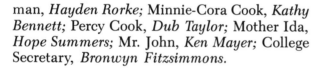

With Mimsy Farmer, James MacArthur and Maureen O'Hara.

man, *Hayden Rorke;* Minnie-Cora Cook, *Kathy Bennett;* Percy Cook, *Dub Taylor;* Mother Ida, *Hope Summers;* Mr. John, *Ken Mayer;* College Secretary, *Bronwyn Fitzsimmons.*

Henry Fonda had been with the same agents since his arrival in Hollywood, but in 1963 he decided to change to new representation. The first thing they arranged for him was *Spencer's Mountain,* explaining that if he wanted to continue to appear on the stage and still maintain name value he would have to be more commercial in his movie life. This film is commercial, a big, folksy-family picture set amid the scenic splendors of Wyoming (in the Grand Teton Mountains around Jackson's Hole) and giving Fonda the role of a lusty workman with nine children, and the gorgeous Maureen O'Hara as his wife. Producer-director-writer Delmer Daves had been very successful with his recent folksy-family films like *A Summer Place* and *Parrish,* and *Spencer's Mountain* continued his winning streak.

With James MacArthur and Maureen O'Hara.

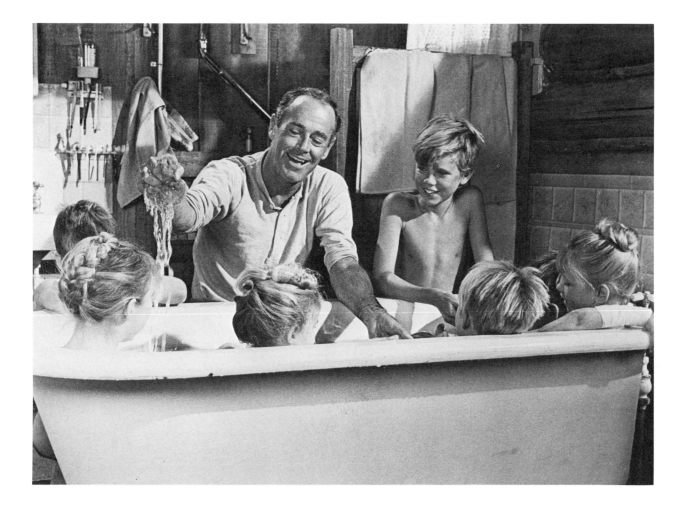

Farmer) and learns a lot about love and/or sex, and Grandpa dies when he walks into the path of a tree felled by Clay. In the end the family stands and waves goodbye to Clayboy as he leaves for college.

Spencer's Mountain was a box office winner, what with its country charm, feisty family life, beautiful photography, Max Steiner score, and a fairly raunchy attitude toward teen-age sex. In later years Fonda shuddered whenever anyone mentioned the film. In his estimation, "It damned near set film making back 25 years." *Variety* shared the general low critical regard but added, "Fonda, in particular, can take what easily could have been an ordinary hayseed and invest such a role with depth, purposefulness and dignity." Be that as it may, Fonda never forgot, or forgave his agents, that in making this film he lost out on an opportunity to try for Edward Albee's new play *Who's Afraid of Virginia Woolf?*

☆☆☆☆☆☆☆☆☆☆☆☆☆☆☆☆☆
THE BEST MAN

1964

A United Artists Film, produced by Stuart Miller and Lawrence Turman, directed by Franklin Shaffner, written by Gore Vidal, based on his play, photographed by Haskell Wexler, music by Mort Lindsey, 102 minutes.

CAST:

William Russell, *Henry Fonda*; Joe Cantwell, *Cliff Robertson*; Mabel Cantwell, *Edie Adams*; Alice Russell, *Margaret Leighton*; Sheldon Bascombe, *Shelley Berman*; Art Hockstader, *Lee Tracy*; Mrs. Gamadge, *Ann Sothern*; Don Cant-

well, *Gene Raymond*; Dick Jensen, *Kevin Mc-Carthy*; T. T. Claypole, *John Henry Faulk*; Oscar Anderson, *Richard Arlen*; Mrs. Claypole, *Penny Singleton*; Speechwriter, *George Kirgo*; Tom, *George Furth*; and Mahalia Jackson, Howard K. Smith and Dick Stout as themselves.

The Best Man brought Henry Fonda back to politics, and with a promotion. From nominee for Secretary of State in *Advise and Consent* to nominee for president in this scathing Gore Vidal version of life on the highest political levels, where the infighting and tactics seem more vicious and frightening than in any game of martial arts. Vidal's play had been a hit on Broadway in the election year of 1960. Producers Stuart Miller and Lawrence Turman waited until the next election year to do the film version, and visually boosted it with actual campaign footage from 1960. The result was impressive. *The Best Man* is possibly the best film made about American politics, although it failed to make a great impression upon the public. The sad truth seems to be that the public interest in politics is somewhat less than its interest in other forms of sport.

The film fairly explodes onto the screen with its coverage of a convention in Los Angeles, using the Sports Arena for the frantic crowd scenes and the Ambassador Hotel for the more personal but no less dramatic look behind the razzle dazzle. The contenders for their party's nomination are William Russell (Fonda), a man of high

With Cliff Robertson.

With Lee Tracy.

ideals, and Joe Cantwell (Cliff Robertson), a senator with only a hazy concept of idealism. To help him gain the sympathy of women voters, Russell's wife Alice (Margaret Leighton) agrees to postpone their divorce and lend apparent support to his cause. Cantwell's wife Mabel (Edie Adams) is a glamorous but shallow woman who will do just about anything to win.

Both contenders need the backing of the president (Lee Tracy), a man in ailing health but an otherwise tough old politician. Cantwell holds a file on Russell which proves emotional instability in his past life, and he threatens to use it. But Russell's manager comes up with a witness (Shelley Berman) who can attest to Cantwell's homosexual activities during his army days. Russell is reluctant to use this information but the president urges him to fight smear with smear. Then the president is stricken with a heart attack and dies before he can voice favor for

175

With Margaret Leighton.

either candidate. On the convention floor Russell makes a surprise turn in his tactics and announces that instead of running himself he will place his support behind another candidate, a "dark horse." If nothing else it assures the dropping of the smears and makes it that much more difficult for Cantwell to gain office.

These are the bare plot bones of *The Best Man*, a film that seethes with political subtlety and venom. In dealing with dirty politics it pulls no punches. The howling hubbub of the convention is the background but the real drama is the quiet, no-holds-barred dialogue between the contenders and the people around them. The producers wisely hired Gore Vidal to write the screenplay, thereby losing none of the sting of his stage original. Lee Tracy, who had played the president in the Broadway version, was called to repeat his highly praised performance for the film, and the critics were impressed with Cliff Robertson's chilly portrayal of the unscrupulous Cantwell. Some people inferred that this was a role inspired by Richard Nixon. However, there was no doubt that Fonda's Russell was inspired by his friend Adlai Stevenson. Stevenson was regarded as a

With Kevin McCarthy, Cliff Robertson, Gene Raymond and Margaret Leighton.

philosophic, quietly humorous and wise man. In Fonda he could hardly have had a better screen persona. There was a rueful quality about both men.

176

FAIL SAFE

1964

A Columbia Film, produced by Max E. Youngstein, directed by Sidney Lumet, written by Walter Bernstein, based on the novel by Eugene Burdick and Harvey Wheeler, photographed by Gerald Hirschfeld, 111 minutes.

CAST:

The President, *Henry Fonda;* General Black, *Dan O'Herlihy;* Groeteschele, *Walter Matthau;* General Bogan, *Frank Overton;* Colonel Grady, *Edward Binns;* Colonel Cascio, *Fritz Weaver;* Buck, *Larry Hagman;* Secretary Swenson, *William Hansen;* General Stark, *Russell Hardie;* Knapp, *Russell Collins;* Raskob, *Sorrell Booke;* Ilsa Wolfe, *Nancy Berg;* Thomas, *John Connell;* Sullivan, *Frank Simpson;* Betty Black, *Hildy Parks;* Mrs. Grady, *Janet Ward;* Sergeant Collins, *Dom DeLuise;* Foster, *Dana Elcar;* Mr. Cascio, *Stuart Germain;* Mrs. Cascio, *Louise Larabee.*

The year 1964 was Henry Fonda's political year. Having failed to win the presidency in *The Best Man,* he was rewarded soon after with the position in *Fail Safe,* although on terms no politician ever wants to face—the decision to press the button. When the novel about nuclear warfare was purchased by Columbia there was some talk about Washington frowning on its being made into a film that would not be in the public interest. However, Columbia had a more immediate problem on its hands with Stanley Kubrick, who did not want *Fail Safe* looming as competition for his *Dr. Strangelove,* which dealt with the same area although in a blackly satiric manner. Since Columbia were also the distributors of Kubrick's film they placated him by releasing his first. The great success of the Kubrick picture turned out to be to the detriment of *Fail Safe,* which was, unlike *Dr. Strangelove,* drained

of every vestige of humor. The public had little interest in a dead serious treatment of the possibility of accidentally starting a nuclear war.

The chilling theme of the film is not so much a discussion of national defense policy as a consideration of the machines which man has

created for his defense, and how those machines can take on a life of their own. Or as one scientist glumly remarks, "the computers have their own logic." True, but they also have no responsibility and they are built in the likeness of nobody.

The action of *Fail Safe* takes place at Strategic Air Command in Omaha, the War Room of the Pentagon and the bomb shelter under the White House, where the president remains alone, except for the company of his Russian translator (Larry Hagman). A squadron of SAC bombers, through the transmission of a set of faulty instructions, are headed toward Moscow and they are ordered back. But due to mechanical failure one plane flies on. Nothing the scientists can do has any effect. The president gets on the telephone to the Kremlin and explains the situation to the Russian premier. Nothing can be done to prevent Moscow from being destroyed, and in compensation for the ghastly error and to prevent war with Russia, the president orders New York to be similarly obliterated.

Fail Safe makes these horrifying possibilities painfully real, and Fonda performs masterfully

With Larry Hagman.

as the decent minded president faced with the ultimate calamity. The film does not make villains of the military; indeed, they are the ones who strive mightily to head off the conflict. The truly frightening men in *Fail Safe* are the scientists, particularly the one played by Walter Matthau, a coldly reasonable man who calmly speaks of destruction on an indescribable scale.

Sidney Lumet added to his laurels with his direction of this film and once again he had to direct Fonda within narrow physical confines, even smaller than the jury room of *12 Angry Men.* All of Fonda's scenes take place in the air raid shelter, and the loneliness of the tiny room makes his conversations with the Russian premier even more bleak and poignant. He is one man with the fate of mankind in his hands. Life and death are reduced to blips on his electronic map, and it is his job to persuade the Russians that the atomic attack is unintentional.

In reviewing *Fail Safe, Time* pointed out that the conversation becomes harrowing, "Walled up in a white cell somewhere under Washington, president Fonda speaks steadily and carefully in a voice that is intense but curiously flat, as though every word were crushed by a burden of significance too great to bear. And as the voice drones on and on, pleading and reasoning and pleading, the figure of the actor slowly swells and charges with tension and importance, the presence of the man becomes the person of mankind and his voice the voice of the species pleading for its life. The whole of history seems consummated in an instant; Armageddon rages in a telephone booth."

With director Sidney Lumet (with viewfinder).

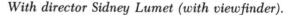

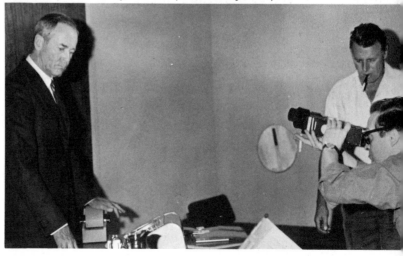

SEX AND THE SINGLE GIRL

1964

A Warner Bros. Film, produced by William T. Orr, directed by Richard Quine, written by Joseph Heller and David R. Schwartz, based

With Lauren Bacall.

on the book by Helen Gurley Brown, photographed in Warnercolor by Charles Lang, Jr. music by Neal Hefti, 110 minutes.

CAST:
Bob Weston, *Tony Curtis;* Dr. Helen Brown, *Natalie Wood;* Frank, *Henry Fonda;* Sylvia, *Lauren Bacall;* Rudy, *Mel Ferrer;* Gretchen, *Fran*

Jeffries; Susan, *Leslie Parrish;* The Chief, *Edward Everett Horton;* Motorcycle Cop, *Larry Storch;* Cabbie, *Stubby Kaye;* Dr. Anderson, *Otto Kruger;* Randall, *Howard St. John;* Holmes, *Max Showalter;* Sylvester, *William Lanteau;* and Count Basie as himself.

After *The Best Man* and *Fail Safe, Sex and the Single Girl* was like following champagne with a soft drink. Henry Fonda had several times turned down his agents' advice that he should do the film because he needed a good comedy at this point. The offer increased in financial volume and when he heard that one of his favorite authors, Joseph Heller (*Catch 22*), would be involved in the scripting, Fonda gave in. He afterwards regretted it because the final script resembled Helen Gurley Brown's novel in name

With Lauren Bacall.

Weston threatens to kill himself unless Helen returns his love, and finally when he reforms she confesses her love. In the meantime he has to compete with Rudy (Mel Ferrer), a psychiatrist who also loves Helen.

In the end the five principal characters leave for Los Angeles airport to escape from each other but in the wild ride along the freeway they play musical cabs, in and out of traffic jams, and end up in each others arms, except for Rudy, who loses Helen to Weston. Battling Frank and Sylvia realize that they can't live without each other.

Sex and the Single Girl has a lot of gloss and glib chatter but as critic Judith Crist said in *The New York Herald Tribune*, it "is enough to put one off sex, single girls and movies for the season." Other critics pointed out that in movies of this kind it is usually the veteran players who come off best since they can at least fall back on their expertise. Fonda's only comment whenever the film was mentioned was a snort of disgust.

With Tony Curtis.

only and put him back in something as lightweight as *The Magnificent Dope.* Just how much Heller had to do with it is hard to say, since he and his co-writer David Schwartz were already working on material that had been adapted from the Brown book by somebody else, but it was supposed to be a satire on scandal magazines, psychiatry and marriage.

Bob Weston (Tony Curtis) is the editor of a magazine he proudly boasts of as being the filthiest scandal sheet in the nation. He plans to do an article on sex research psychologist Dr. Helen Gurley Brown (Natalie Wood) and expose her as a frustrated woman. To do this he poses as his friend Frank (Fonda), a businessman who lives next door with his sharply tongued wife Sylvia (Lauren Bacall). Their marriage is noted for its battles. Weston tells Helen he needs her advice on his marital problems and since she finds him both attractive and interesting she agrees. All kinds of mix-ups follow, in which

THE ROUNDERS

1965

An MGM Film, produced by Richard E. Lyons, directed by Burt Kennedy, written by Burt Kennedy, based on the novel by Max Evans, photographed in Technicolor by Paul E. Vogel, music by Jeff Alexander, 85 minutes.

CAST:

Ben Jones, *Glenn Ford;* Howdy Lewis, *Henry Fonda;* Mary, *Sue Anne Langdon;* Sister, *Hope Holliday;* Jim Ed Love, *Chill Wills;* Vince Moore, *Edgar Buchanan;* Agathe Moore, *Kathleen Freeman;* Meg Moore, *Joan Freeman;* Bull,

With Glenn Ford.

Denver Pyle; Tanner, *Barton MacLane*; Arlee, *Doodles Weaver*; Mrs. Norson, *Allegra Varron*.

At last, a good comedy, but one that the 1965 management of MGM did not know how to handle. They released *The Rounders* as part of a double bill with a claptrap picture designed for the teenage market, *Get Yourself a College Girl*. Most critics hastened to applaud *The Rounders*, but the reviews were too late to save the booking situation. MGM apparently felt there was little market for a movie about a pair of middle-aged bronco busters in the contemporary West. It might be remembered that MGM also did not know how to handle *Ride the High Country*, also produced by Richard E. Lyons, and seemed puzzled when it became a cult item. Not that *The Rounders* is quite up to the level of *High Country*, but it belongs in the same neighborhood. It took Henry Fonda back to being a sim-

ple cowboy, a la his Gil Carter in *The Ox-Bow Incident*, but under much happier circumstances. Here there is no lynching, no banks or trains to be robbed, no shooting, no posses, no outlaws. Perhaps that's what confused the fellows at MGM.

With Hope Holiday, Sue Ann Langdon and Glenn Ford.

This is the story of Ben Jones (Glenn Ford) and Howdy Lewis (Fonda), who travel around together as bronco busters during the round-up seasons in northern Arizona and New Mexico, always trying to save up enough money to quit and maybe move to Tahiti and open a bar. But Ben and Howdy are, like most of their kind, given to drinking and gambling, and always have to go back to work. Most of their work is done for a cheapskate of a rancher named Jim Ed Love (Chill Wills), who pays them seven dollars per horse they break, take it or leave it. In the winter they agree to work for Love rounding up stray cattle and horses, and staying in a ramshackle hut.

As part of the deal, Love insists on the boys accepting a roan which he has not been able to break. All winter they try to break the roan but it always throws them. They sell the spirited horse to Vince Moore (Edgar Buchanan), who makes corn liquor out of mash. The roan develops a liking for the mash and the displeased Moore takes him back to his previous owners. After being paid off by their boss, Ben and

Howdy decide that the best thing to do with the roan is enter him in the rodeo as a horse that cannot be ridden. They expect to make a lot of money.

The roan performs as expected and throws its riders for a loop but also sustains an injury to itself in so doing. Lying unconscious in a stable, the roan appears doomed and the boys have to face the fact they must shoot it, but before they summon up enough courage the horse recovers—presumably a victim of too much liquor mash—and kicks the stable to pieces. Ben and Howdy shell out their money to the stable owner and resign themselves to going back to work for mean old Jim Ed Love.

The Rounders is a genial comedy, knowingly scripted and directed by western expert Burt Kennedy and giving a generous view of modern western life. The use of locations around Sedona, Arizona, is a definite bonus. But the real values are its two veteran stars, both of whom had by this time spent a lot of time in cinema saddles and well knew the kind of men they were playing. A right good pair.

With Glenn Ford, Joan Freeman, Denver Pyle, Allegra Varron, Kathleen Freeman and Edgar Buchanan.

IN HARM'S WAY

With John Wayne and Burgess Meredith.

1965

A Paramount release of a Sigma Film, produced and directed by Otto Preminger, written by Wendell Mayes, based on the novel by James Bassett, photographed by Loyal Griggs, music by Jerry Goldsmith, 165 minutes.

CAST:

Capt. Rockwell Torrey, *John Wayne;* Commander Paul Eddington, *Kirk Douglas;* Lt. Maggie Haynes, *Patricia Neal;* Lt. William McConnel, *Tom Tryon;* Bev McConnel, *Paula Prentiss;* Ensign Jeremiah Torrey, *Brandon De Wilde;* Ensign Annalee Dorne, *Jill Hayworth;* Admiral Broderick, *Dana Andrews;* Clayton Canfil, *Stanley Holloway;* Commander Powell, *Burgess Meredith;* CINCPAC I Admiral, *Franchot Tone;* Commander Neal Owynn, *Patrick O'Neal;* Lt. Commander Burke, *Carroll O'Connor;* CPO Culpepper, *Slim Pickens;* Ensign Griggs, *James Mitchum;* Col. Gregory, *George*

Kennedy; Quartermaster Quoddy, *Bruce Cabot*; Liz Eddington, *Barbara Bouchet*; Capt. Tuthill, *Tod Andrews*; Lt. Cline, *Larry Hagman*; and *Henry Fonda* as CINCPAC II Admiral.

In Harm's Way placed Henry Fonda back in the U.S. Navy for the first time since *Mr. Roberts*, and with a tremendous promotion. Here he is a four-star admiral in command of the Pacific fleet. Would Lieutenant Roberts have reached such rank had he survived and had he stayed in the navy? It's hardly likely. Roberts was strictly a wartime officer, with none of the tenacity and dedication it takes to reach high rank. Fonda's own years in the navy had exposed him to both kinds of men and it is a further mark of his skill that he could be equally believable as either.

Otto Preminger's gargantuan movie is purely entertainment and not a documentary. John Wayne is a captain who fails on his first mission after the attack on Pearl Harbor but later gloriously redeems himself, and Kirk Douglas is a commander who turns bitter after his wife is killed in the Pearl Harbor fiasco and leads a boozy, cynical existence. But he, too, redeems himself when he commandeers an airplane, flies over the Japanese fleet and reports their position before being shot down. In addition to these two main characters, Preminger peopled his large canvas with all manner of naval types.

Fonda's role in *In Harm's Way* is a cameo but a very effective one. His admiral looks and behaves like the real thing. In reviewing the film for *The New York Times*, the late Bosley Crowther commented, "Fonda makes this admiral a firm, crisp, decisive type. He seems more interested in naval operations than in promoting a personality. This is refreshing and convincing in a film that is virtually awash with flimsy and flamboyant fellows with all the tricks of the trade of Hollywood."

BATTLE OF THE BULGE

1965

A Warner Bros.–Cinerama Film, produced by Milton Sperling and Philip Yordan, directed by Ken Annakin, written by the producers and John Melson, photographed in Technicolor and Ultra Panavision by Jack Hildyard, music by Benjamin Frankel, 167 minutes.

CAST:

Lt. Col. Kiley, *Henry Fonda*; Col. Hessler, *Robert Shaw*; General Grey, *Robert Ryan*; Col. Pritchard, *Dana Andrews*; Sergeant Duquesne, *George Montgomery*; Schumacher, *Ty Hardin*; Louise, *Pier Angeli*; Elena, *Barbara Werle*; Major Wolenski, *Charles Bronson*; General Kohler,

Werner Peters; Conrad, *Hans Christian Blech;* Lt. Weaver, *James MacArthur;* Guffy, *Telly Savalas.*

With a change of title *Battle of the Bulge* could be about almost any battle in which the American and German armies faced each other in the Second World War. Filmed in Spain amid terrain unlike the Ardennes, the accent here is on cinema and not history. For Henry Fonda it

With Robert Ryan.

was yet another of the commercial movies his agents insisted he should do now and then to keep his name before the mass movie audience. The pay was good, the work fairly easy and he treated himself to a European tour afterwards. He would have to close his ears to historians who found the film offensive in its casual regard for military facts. The immense German breakthrough around Bastogne, the last and costly campaign of the Germans to halt the American advance at the end of 1944, is here used as a backdrop for stories of personal military effort and heroism on both sides. Inasmuch as the film was a Cinerama production, it was obviously filmed with the visual canvas in mind.

The plot is slim, despite the film's almost three hours of running time. The protagonists are a brilliant German colonel of tank warfare, Hessler (Robert Shaw), an American Major General, Grey (Robert Ryan), his intelligence chief, Col. Pritchard (Dana Andrews), and the chief's assistant, Lt. Col. Kiley (Fonda), a policeman in civilian life. Kiley makes himself unpopular with the brass by dogging them with his hunch that the Germans are preparing a massive offensive. His policeman's nose tells him this, yet his superiors consider the notion ridiculous. Kiley's ferreting around makes him all the more sure— and in short order he proves to be absolutely correct. The Americans are shattered with the German advance and particularly confused when the enemy employ troops dressed in U.S. uniforms and complete with U.S. accents.

The film thereafter is a blow-by-blow account of the elaborate conflict, with much footage devoted to fire, explosions and tank encounters. The climax, with tanks of both sides engaging in combat on a vast, flat plain is historically false since no terrain of that kind was in the actual battle. But the Cinerama people did not invest all these millions of dollars in order to give a lecture. Dramatically, Robert Shaw, playing Hessler with blond heroic dedication, comes off better than the other actors, since time is devoted to his compassion for the green young recruits

With Charles Bronson.

under his command, his conflict with indecisive superiors and his sympathy for his battle-weary aide (Hans Christian Blech). On the American side Fonda comes off best because he once again gave a clichéd part some credibility by being restrained and gentle. Fonda always knew how to use his eyes. When he looks around the battlefields of this movie he at least conveys a soldier's amazement at the horror of it all, and not an actor's anticipation of his next cue.

THE DIRTY GAME

CAST:
Kourlov, *Henry Fonda;* General Bruce, *Robert Ryan;* Perego, *Vittorio Gassman;* Nanette, *Annie Girardot;* Laland, *Bourvil;* Dupont, *Robert Hossein;* Berlin C. M., *Peter Van Eyck;* Natalia, *Marcia Grazia Buccela.*

With Robert Ryan.

1966
An American International–Landau–Unger Film, produced by Richard Hellman, directed by Terrence Young, Christian-Jacque and Carlo Lizzani, written by Jo Eisinger, photographed by Pierre Petit, Richard Angst and Enrico Menczer, music by Robert Mellin, 91 minutes.

After completing *Battle of the Bulge,* Henry Fonda stayed in Europe to participate in what must have seemed on the planning boards a taut, sophisticated spy picture but which turned out to be fairly conventional stuff. Aptly titled *The Dirty Game*—by 1966 audiences were well aware that there was no longer anything noble in be-

190

With Peter Van Eyck.

ing a spy and that it was a nasty business no matter what side—it tells a three-part tale, with Fonda in the last part as an American agent who makes a necessary departure from East Germany and hastens to West Berlin, where his part of the film was shot.

In the first sequence an American agent (Vittorio Gassman) in Rome masquerades as a kidnapper so that he will be hired by the enemy. His assignment, to kidnap a scientist who has invented a new jet fuel, works to the favor of his own side. The second sequence takes place in Africa, on the coast of the Gulf of Aden, where two American submarines lie in danger of being attacked. The matter is resolved in an underwater encounter by skin diver agents of both sides.

In the concluding episode of *The Dirty Game*, an agent named Kourlov (Fonda) crashes through to the safety of a West Berlin hotel room, but sits there knowing that enemy agents will catch up with him and end his life. They do.

Fonda's episode is the best because it conveys more of the grim, gritty reality of the desperate spy business—the other episodes tend toward James Bondism. The film is held together by one character, an American general (Robert Ryan) who relates the stories while reminiscing about his adventures. As the CIA agent who returns to the West after 17 years in East Germany, Fonda is the very picture of a tired and anxious man. The part called for almost no dialogue on his part and so his voice was not a factor in the nationality of the man. As always, Fonda is what he is supposed to be. However, *The Dirty Game* did poorly in U.S. distribution and ended up as a television package, and rarely seen even as that.

191

A BIG HAND FOR THE LITTLE LADY

1966

A Warner Bros. Film, produced and directed by Fielder Cook, written by Sidney Carroll, based on his teleplay *Big Deal in Laredo*, photographed in Warnercolor by Lee Garmes, music by David Raksin, 95 minutes.

Sam Rhine, *James Kenny;* Toby, *Allen Collins;* Pete, *Jim Boles;* Jackie, *Gerald Michenaud;* Mrs. Drummond, *Virginia Gregg;* Old Man, *Chester Conklin;* Owney Price, *Ned Glass;* Mrs. Craig, *Mae Clarke.*

With Jason Robards and Charles Bickford.

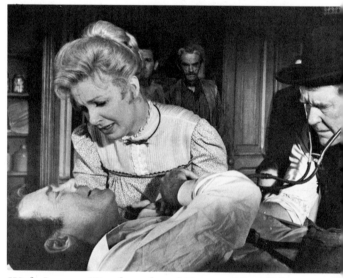

With Joanne Woodward and Burgess Meredith.

CAST:

Meredith, *Henry Fonda;* Mary, *Joanne Woodward;* Henry Drummond, *Jason Robards;* Ballinger, *Paul Ford;* Benson Tropp, *Charles Bickford;* Doc Scully, *Burgess Meredith;* Otto Habershaw, *Kevin McCarthy;* Dennis Wilcox, *Robert Middleton;* Jesse Buford, *John Qualen;*

Back in Hollywood after his filming in Europe, Henry Fonda would now find himself in a string of westerns, all of them of gritty nature and none requiring him to do much riding or brawling, neither of which he ever liked. *A Big Hand for the Little Lady* is the best of them. A western only because of its setting, it is a comedy with

With Gerald Michenaud and Joanne Woodward.

an O. Henry ending, presenting Fonda as a family man with a passion for gambling—or so it seems. Sidney Carroll did the screenplay from his own well-received television play *Big Deal in Laredo,* and it might have been better to have used that title for the film.

The film begins as a group of prominent men in the Laredo of 1896 gather for their annual poker game, a game so meaningful to them that they drop whatever business they have in order to partake. Rancher Henry Drummond (Jason Robards) makes an early departure from his daughter's wedding, attorney Otto Habershaw (Kevin McCarthy) quickly wraps up a trial, and both men rush to be on time for their dead-serious contest with cards with several other wealthy citizens. As they gather around a table in the backroom of a hotel, a mild-mannered man named Meredith (Fonda) arrives at the hotel with his wife Mary (Joanne Woodward) and their son Jackie (Gerald Michenaud). Their story is that they are poor people who have finally saved up $500 to put down on a piece of land. But Meredith is a compulsive gambler and he begs to be let into the game. He struggles manfully but the family nest egg looks to be lost. Wracked with worry, Meredith suffers a heart attack.

Explaining that they desperately need the money, the stricken Meredith asks that his wife be allowed to take over the hand. Claiming she knows nothing about poker, the men grudgingly allow her in. She takes over Meredith's hand, which happens to be a very good one, and on the strength of it she is able to borrow a thousand dollars from banker Ballinger (Paul Ford), who says other money will be forthcoming if she

193

With Joanne Woodward.

tension so necessary for this picture, shot mostly in the confines of one room. They prove that no matter how vast and visual the screen may become, the final effectiveness in film storytelling will always be with the skill of the actors. *Big Hand* is an outstanding Fonda vehicle. In reviewing the film for *Life*, Richard Schickel said, ". . . Henry Fonda's characterization of the shamblin', gamblin' man is a joy, a deeply comic portrayal of the self-abasement and whining desperation of a man caught up in an ignominious passion. In this, his 60th movie, he transcends his customary image without sacrificing that

With Jason Robards, Joanne Woodward and Charles Bickford.

does well. Mary does indeed do well. One by one the veteran gamblers drop out of the game, all of them expressing their admiration for such a plucky lady, so strong in holding her family together. It turns out that Mary and Meredith are expert card sharks and that the game was a beautifully executed scheme in cahoots with the banker to fleece the wealthy participants.

The pleasure of *Big Hand for the Little Lady* is the ensemble acting. Producer-director Fielder Cook picked a superb group to play his gamblers, all of them consummate players, whose timing and facial expressions create the humor and the

graceful ease that is his hallmark." Unfortunately, *A Big Hand for the Little Lady* impressed the critics more than it did the public. Still, for anyone with an interest in acting, it is a film to seek out and study.

194

★★★★★★★★★★★★★★★
WELCOME TO
HARD TIMES

1967

An MGM Film, produced by Max E. Youngstein and David Karr, directed by Burt Kennedy, written by Burt Kennedy, based on the novel by E. L. Doctorow, photographed in Technicolor by Harry Stradling, Jr., music by Harry Sukman, 103 minutes.

CAST:

Will Blue, *Henry Fonda;* Molly Riordan, *Janice Rule;* Man from Bodie, *Aldo Ray;* Zar, *Keenan Wynn;* Adah, *Janis Paige;* Isaac Maple, *John Anderson;* Jenks, *Warren Oates;* Jessie, *Fay Spain;* Brown, *Edgar Buchanan;* Alfie, *Denver Pyle;* Jimmy Fee, *Michael Shea;* Mae, *Arlene*

With Janice Rule.

Golonka; Avery, *Lon Chaney, Jr.;* John Bear, *Royal Dano;* Jack Millay, *Alan Baxter;* Mr. Fee, *Paul Birch;* Bert Albany, *Dan Ferrone;* Major Munn, *Paul Fix;* Hanson, *Elisha Cook.*

Welcome to Hard Times is one of those peculiar films—a flop with points of interest. Its initial problem was a title that did little but confuse. It refers to a grimy little western town called Hard Times and was not an invitation to a depression. Writer-director Burt Kennedy, a man with a passion for westerns, wanted to make one that was full of gritty reality and to this end he was able to enlist Henry Fonda, whose only interest in making westerns was that they were not routine. He had enjoyed working with Kennedy on *The Rounders* and from reading the script he could envision this one as having some

With Aldo Ray.

196

of the qualities of *The Ox-Bow Incident*. That fine film at least ended with some comment on the redemption of wrongdoers who realize the errors of their ways. *Hard Times* has almost an air of total hopelessness about it.

Hard Times lies in a beautiful valley, but that is about its only virtue. It consists of one muddy street and a string of wooden buildings, with the saloon the main point of gathering and relaxation. Will Blue (Fonda) is the leading citizen and unofficial embodiment of the law, but he is this only by comparison with the rest of the tatty humans who live in this remote hamlet. During one stormy evening a man (Aldo Ray) rides into town and quickly makes his ugly, menacing presence known. He grunts instead of speaks and helps himself to whiskey by smashing the tops off bottles and gulping the contents. He abuses a prostitute, drags her to a room and, after having his way with her, kills her. When a friend comes to her defense, the stranger, now known as the man from Bodie, kills him, too.

Begged by the others for help, the none too courageous Will devises a scheme. He asks his girl friend Mollie (Janice Rule) to engage Bodie's attention so that he can sneak up on him. The plan goes awry and Mollie is beaten and humiliated. Rather than risk his life, Will stands back. As a final gesture of contempt, Bodie sets fire to the town and laughingly rides off. Life improves somewhat when a businessman named Zar (Keenan Wynn) arrives in town with a wagonload of girls. The nearby gold miners come to town to enjoy themselves and business is good all round. Then Bodie comes back. This time Will finds the gumption to outsmart him and gun him down, although he is wounded in the process. And life in Hard Times goes on.

Hard Times is just too hard for its own good. It plays like a Greek tragedy but without much point. Burt Kennedy's direction of some fine actors makes the film visually interesting, but Aldo Ray's villain is so overplayed as to be ludicrous. He does everything but twirl a moustache and roll his eyes. Fonda's Will Blue is believable but the character is that of a weak and mangy man, one who survives out of desperation rather than courage. He lives in a community of moral squalor, and if this is his choice, then he deserves no pity. Perhaps life in the real Wild West was something like this. But it leaves a veteran lover of westerns feeling somewhat wistful about the days of Buck Jones, Tim McCoy and Ken Maynard.

With Fay Spain, Arlene Golonka and Janis Paige.

With Lon Chaney, Jr., Janice Rule and Alan Baxter.

197

FIRECREEK

1968

A Warner Bros. –Seven Arts Film, produced by Philip Leacock, directed by Vincent McEveety, written by Calvin Clements, photographed in Warnercolor by William Clothier, music by Alfred Newman, 104 minutes.

CAST:

Johnny Cobb, *James Stewart;* Larkin, *Henry Fonda;* Evelyn, *Inger Stevens;* Earl, *Gary Lockwood;* Whittier, *Dean Jagger;* Preacher, *Ed Begley;* Mr. Pittman, *Jay C. Flippen;* Norman, *Jack Elam;* Drew, *James Best;* Meli, *Barbara Luna;* Henrietta Cobb, *Jacqueline Scott;* Leah, *Brooke Bundy;* Arthur, *J. Robert Walker;* Willard, *Morgan Woodward;* Hall, *John Qualen;* Dulcie, *Louise Latham;* Mrs. Littlejohn, *Athena Lorde;* Fyte, *Harry 'Slim' Duncan;* Aaron, *Kevin Tate;* Franklin, *Christopher Shea.*

Apart from their work together in a chapter of *On Our Merry Way,* Henry Fonda and James Stewart did not make a film together until *Firecreek* in 1968. By that time both of them had been in Hollywood for 32 years and it is a pity someone had not thought of using the two old friends together in a first-rate vehicle before this. *Firecreek* is somewhat less than first rate, and is an odd choice for the pair because it pits them against each other in a tough, somber western. And it is Fonda's first film as an outright, unmitigated, scruffy villain.

The town of Firecreek is small and peaceful until Larkin (Fonda) and his handful of bandits ride in. A couple of them, Earl (Gary Lockwood) and Drew (James Best), are soon brawling over a pretty Indian girl (Barbara Luna), and Earl is about to drown Drew in a horse trough when Johnny Cobb calls a halt. Cobb (James Stewart) is a local farmer and also the part-time sheriff, drawing a salary of two dollars a month for keeping order in the usually sleepy hamlet. Larkin nurses a wound received in a recent robbery and finds solace with the attractive Evelyn (Inger Stevens) at the boarding house of her father (Jay C. Flippen). She is impressed by Larkin and encourages him to reform. He responds to her romantic interest.

During the first night a dim-witted stable boy (J. Robert Porter) hears a cry from the Indian girl's house and finds Drew molesting her. In the struggle he accidentally kills Drew and Larkin's

With James Stewart

198

With Inger Stevens.

men accuse him of murder. To keep the boy safe, Cobb locks him up, but after Cobb leaves the men break into the jail and lynch the boy. When he returns to town Cobb declares his intention of arresting Larkin and his men. They jeer at this and challenge him. Despite being badly wounded he manages to shoot Larkin's men. Now there are only Cobb and Larkin left, both wounded. Cobb tries to reload his gun but Larkin shoots it out of his hand. Then Larkin takes deliberate aim, but he never fires because a shot rings out that ends his life—Evelyn has shot him. The town returns to being peaceful.

Firecreek did only mild business in the theatres. Perhaps the audiences were tired of grim westerns or perhaps they expected more fun from the combination of Fonda and Stewart. As grim westerns go, it was a well-made item, with splendid use of its locations in Arizona's spectacular Oak Creek Canyon and the red rocky

With Inger Stevens and Jay C. Flippen.

With James Best, Gary Lockwood, Jack Elam, Barbara Luna and James Stewart.

speak a little sarcastically about it being somebody's "bright idea" to cast him as a villain pitted against his old friend, and maybe he shouldn't have done it. "Any man who tries to kill Jim Stewart has to be marked as a man who's plain rotten. You can't get much worse than that."

With James Stewart.

countryside around Sedona. Both stars are entirely believable in their roles—Stewart as a gentle man pushed into furious anger by the bestial behavior of the visitors and Fonda as the cold-hearted outlaw. Whenever he was reminded of the picture, Fonda would shake his head and

YOURS, MINE AND OURS

1968
A United Artists-Desilu-Walden Film, produced by Robert F. Blumofe, directed by Melville Shavelson, written by Melville Shavelson and Mort Lachman, based on a story by Madelyn Davis and Bob Carroll, Jr., photographed in Technicolor by Charles Wheeler, music by Fred Karlin, 111 minutes.

CAST:
Helen North, *Lucille Ball*; Frank Beardsley, *Henry Fonda*; Darrel Harrison, *Van Johnson*; The Doctor, *Tom Bosley*; Frank's date, *Louise Troy*; Motorcyclist, *Ben Murphy*; Colleen North, *Jennifer Leak*; Nicky North, *Kevin Burchett*; Janette North, *Kimberley Beck*; Tommy North, *Mitchell Vogel*; Jean North, *Margot Jane*; Phillip

201

North, *Eric Shea;* Gerald North, *Gregory Atkins;* Teresa North, *Lynnell Atkins;* Mike Beardsley, *Timothy Matthieson;* Rusty Beardsley, *Gilbert Rogers;* Rosemary Beardsley, *Nancy Roth;* Greg Beardsley, *Gary Goetzman;* Louise Beardsley,

With Lucille Ball.

Suzanne Cupito; Veronica Beardsley, *Michele Tobin;* Mary Beardsley, *Maralee Foster;* Germain Beardsley, *Tracy Nelson;* Joan Beardsley, *Stephanie Oliver.*

In addition to *A Big Hand for the Little Lady,* *Welcome to Hard Times* and *Firecreek,* Henry Fonda also made a movie for television, *Stranger on the Run,* in which he played a drunken derelict thrown off a train in a western town. When offered a modern comedy like *Yours, Mine and Ours,* he must have welcomed it like a cool drink in the desert. After all those gritty westerns he was back in a U.S. Navy uniform and playing opposite Lucille Ball. In the 26 years since they had appeared together in *The Big Street,* Lucy had become a major figure in television

production. In making a feature film for her own company, she was in a position to call the shots, and the man she wanted for her leading man was Fred MacMurray. When he proved unavailable, she then turned to Fonda.

On the surface the idea of a widower with ten children meeting and marrying a widow with eight children, and then having another child together, might have seemed preposterous. But the screenplay was based on fact. It is the actual story of Warrant Officer Frank Beardsley and naval nurse Helen North, a California couple who romantically combined forces and households. In the screenplay they bump into each other in a supermarket. Knowing how hard it is for him to cope with his ten kids as a single parent, Frank's friend Darrel (Van Johnson) plays cupid and encourages a romance between the

With Van Johnson and Lucille Ball.

pair. It soon culminates in marriage and the large combined family move into a big house with four bathrooms. Frank tries to run the place along disciplined naval lines but finds that resolving young conflicts and jealousies is harder than his regular job in naval aviation. Housekeepers become a problem, with none lasting more than a few days. The bickering and the resentments among the two sets of children come to an end when their parents announce the expectancy of a new baby. Now they all have something in common. Frank's eldest son goes off to war and

pair of veteran players whose zest and skill keep their material afloat. Fonda's Frank might be Mr. Roberts all these years later, the same caring man, and when warm and wise Helen says, when asked for her secret of marital success, "A little love, a little discipline—and a husband who

With Lucille Ball.

Helen's eldest daughter falls in love, and things start to settle down, or at least relatively.

A film like this—with its endless jokes about the problems of rearing children by the score, shopping, laundry, Christmas, domestic foibles, dishwashing, bathroom usage—could have sunk under its own weight. It is to the credit of scripter-director Melville Shavelson that it didn't. But even more credit is due Fonda and Ball, a

doesn't criticize," then the audience relates to a genuine human being. Maurice Rapf in *Life* made a good point: "Fonda and Ball don't have to be seen in bed to convince us they know what to do when they get there. These professionals can convey more about love in a look or a gesture or a mumbled word than a lot of screen newcomers can with ten pages of dialogue or five minutes of hard-breathing amorous acrobatics."

204

MADIGAN

1968
A Universal Film, produced by Frank P. Rosenberg, directed by Don Siegel, written by Henri Simoun and Abraham Polonsky, based on the novel *The Commissioner* by Richard Dougherty, photographed in Technicolor by Russell Metty, music by Don Costa, 101 minutes.

CAST:
Daniel Madigan, *Richard Widmark*; Anthony X. Russell, *Henry Fonda*; Julia Madigan, *Inger Stevens*; Rocco Bonaro, *Harry Guardino*; Charles Kane, *James Whitmore*; Tricia Bentley, *Susan Clark*; Midget Castiglione, *Michael Dunn*; Barney Benesch, *Steve Ihnat*; Hughie, *Don Stroud*; Jonesy, *Sheree North*; Ben Williams, *Warren Stevens*; Dr. Taylor, *Raymond St. Jacques*; Hap Lynch, *Bert Freed*; Mickey Dunn, *Harry Bellaver*; James Price, *Frank Marth*; Earl Griffin, *Lloyd Gough*; Esther Newman, *Virginia Gregg*; Rosita, *Toian Machinga*; Rita Bonara, *Rita Lynn*.

Henry Fonda was never very happy with *Madigan*. It was a well made cops-and-crime story but in changing the title of Richard Dougherty's novel *The Commissioner*, they shifted the focus to the secondary character of Detective Daniel Madigan, played by Richard Widmark. Despite Universal's claim that Fonda's role as the commissioner would receive equal attention, it never did. This was embarrassing because Fonda respected Widmark. One of the reasons Fonda agreed to do the picture was director Don Siegel, with whom he had enjoyed working on *Stranger on the Run*. He and Siegel were at loggerheads with producer Frank Rosenberg all through production, but the balance between the characterizations was never resolved. For all that, *Madigan* was a good film of its kind, the kind that Universal had practically copyrighted

With Richard Widmark and Harry Guardino (right).

With Raymond St. Jacques.

With Susan Clark.

in 1948 when they made *The Naked City*, the first of the almost documentary-like crime movies shot in New York.

Madigan and his colleague Rocco Bonaro (Harry Guardino) track a killer, Barnet Benesch (Steve Ihnat), and find him in an apartment, in bed with a girl. Since the pretty girl is naked, the detectives pay her a little too much attention and Benesch makes his escape, after first relieving them of their guns. The two men are hauled over the coals by Commissioner Russell (Fonda) and docked some pay. Russell has a number of problems facing him, including a black doctor (Raymond St. Jacques), who accuses the police of brutally treating his activist son. In addition, Russell's best friend, Chief Inspector Charles Kane (James Whitmore), is guilty of covering up a bribery in which his son is involved.

On the home front things are also uncomfortable. Madigan, a pragmatic cop who believes in taking advantage of his badge, is nagged by a wife (Inger Stevens) who feels he pays more attention to his work than to her, and suspects that he is still carrying on with an old girl friend (Sheree North).

The commissioner, a by-the-book disciplinarian, is involved in an adulterous affair with a young married lady (Susan Clark), which tends to make him a little edgy at the office. He gives Madigan and Bonaro three days to bring in Benesch or else. Through a lot of hard sleuthing and slogging they manage to catch up with the vicious Benesch, who has in the meantime killed

With James Whitmore and Richard Widmark.

a pair of patrolmen. They finally trap him in an apartment-hotel, but it costs Madigan his life. His wife later tells the commissioner that she considers him a heartless monster for the way he runs his department.

It is easy to see why Fonda would have been interested in playing Commissioner Russell. The two men are similiar. Both are cool, dignified, hard-working professionals. Both are less calm and more complicated than their surface manner would lead people to believe. Fonda under-

stood that kind of man, and his playing of Russell as being austere and deceptively slow must have been drawn from his own experiences in life. It is also easy to see why Fonda should have been disappointed in the way *Madigan* was produced, making it a good cops-and-robbers movie but less of the deep character study he had hoped. But by 1968 Fonda had long learned to expect disappointment in the making of pictures. If he didn't like them he simply put them behind him.

☆☆☆☆☆☆☆☆☆☆☆☆☆☆☆☆☆☆☆☆☆☆☆☆☆☆

THE BOSTON STRANGLER

1969

A 20th Century-Fox Film, produced by Robert Fryer, directed by Richard Fleischer, written by Edward Anhalt, based on the book by Gerold Frank, photographed in DeLuxe color by Richard H. Kline, musical direction by Lionel Newman, 116 minutes.

With George Kennedy.

CAST:

Albert DeSalvo, *Tony Curtis;* John S. Bottomly, *Henry Fonda;* Phillip J. Di Natale, *George Kennedy;* Julian Soshnick, *Mike Kellin;* Terrence Huntley, *Hurd Hatfield;* Frank McAfee, *Murray Hamilton;* John Asgeirsson, *Jeff Corey;* Diane Cluney, *Sally Kellerman;* Edward W. Brooke, *William Marshall;* Peter Hurkos, *George Voskovec;* Mary Bottomly, *Leora Dana;* Irmgard DeSalvo, *Carolyn Conwell;* Dr. Nagy, *Austin Willis;* Cloe, *Jeanne Cooper;* Bobbie Edan, *Lara Lindsay;* Lyonel Brumley, *George Furth;* Ed Willis, *Richard X. Slattery;* Eugene R. Rourke, *William Hickey;* Ellen Ridgeway, *Eve Collyer;* Alice Oakville, *Gwyda Donhowe.*

From playing a dignified New York police commissioner in *Madigan,* Henry Fonda next went to playing an even more dignified old-line Bostonian professor of law in *The Boston Strangler,* and was again involved in solving crime. Based upon Gerold Frank's book about an actual series of crimes, the film had to scale down the complexity of the book, with its myriad details, its following of clues that led nowhere and its probing of the weirder elements of society. Richard Fleischer directed this almost two-hour version with clever usage of split screen and multi-panel techniques, giving the film a somewhat documentary style and getting across all the main points in Frank's study of the more bizarre side of crime. He also gained a fine performance from Tony Curtis, playing against his usual flip image.

The film begins with a coverage of several murders, all of them involving women and all killed by strangulation. The common denominator is the use of a double square knot in the rope. The police are inundated with calls and tips, mostly useless. The Attorney General of Massachusetts (William Marshall) sets up a

208

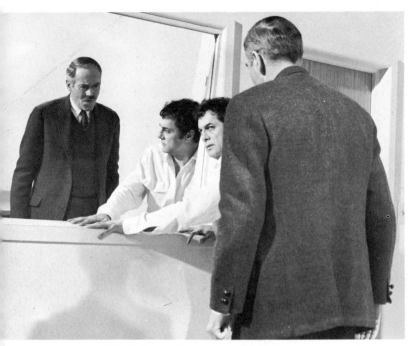

With Tony Curtis.

special bureau of investigation and appoints John S. Bottomly (Fonda) to head it. Bottomly is an expert criminologist, but is reluctant to take the case. Nevertheless, "he challenged me and I was sucked in," he says. Since the continuing strangulations appear to be sexually orientated, Bottomly's investigations confront him with a string of deviates and perverts, some of whom simply want attention. The first seven deaths are those of elderly women; the eighth is a young girl.

In desperation, the police hire the famed ESP expert Peter Hurkos (George Voskovec), but even his intuition fails to find the killer, and the murders now reach ten, the latest also a young woman. The film now switches to the home of Albert DeSalvo (Curtis), an apparently well-balanced, working class man with a wife and daughter. DeSalvo is the killer, and his next victim fights back and bites his hand. He beats her unconscious but she survives. His luck turns worse when he enters an apartment where his

next victim's husband is still home. The man gives chase and with the help of the police DeSalvo is arrested, and because of the bite on his hand he is identified. A judge warns that he is unfit to stand trial and DeSalvo is remanded to a hospital. The doctors refuse to allow Bottomly to cross-question DeSalvo because he is a man with two separate personalities. They ask, "What if he is innocent and you push him over the edge?" The patient Bottomly finally gets their consent when he promises that DeSalvo will never be prosecuted.

Bottomly slowly works on DeSalvo and one night he tells his wife, "I think he's about to crack. I'm enjoying this and I don't like myself for it." DeSalvo later attacks his wife during a hospital visit and tries to strangle her. This concludes the identification of the man who has murdered 13 women in Boston, but because of his mental condition he will spend the rest of his life in a mental institution.

The Boston Strangler treats its material almost clinically and avoids sensationalism. Perhaps the film would have done better at the box office had it been more lurid. For Fonda it was an interesting job because it allowed him to play an educated, civilized man who discovers some things about his own nature that disturb him. At first revolted by the assignment, the cultured Bostonian becomes more fascinated with the bizarre crimes and finally derives some enjoyment in baiting and breaking down the complex, tortured, bewildered DeSalvo. Just as Bottomly

With Mike Kellin and George Kennedy

himself was challenged by his task, so Fonda was challenged by playing this man. It was the kind of challenge he always looked for as an actor but rarely found—especially in Hollywood.

ONCE UPON A TIME IN THE WEST

With Charles Bronson.

1969

A Paramount Film, produced by Fulvio Morsella, directed by Sergio Leone, written by Sergio Leone and Sergio Donati, based on a story by Leone, Bernardo Bertolucci and Dario Argento, photographed in Technicolor by Tonino Delli Colli, music by Ennio Morricone, 165 minutes.

CAST:

Frank, *Henry Fonda*; Jill McBain, *Claudia Cardinale*; Cheyenne, *Jason Robards*; The Man, *Charles Bronson*; Brett McBain, *Frank Wolff*; Morton, *Gabriele Ferzetti*; Sheriff, *Keenan Wynn*; Sam, *Paolo Stoppa*; Wobbles, *Marco Zuanelli*; Barman, *Lionel Stander*; Knuckles, *Jack Elam*; Stony, *Woody Strode*.

Henry Fonda always had a great respect for writers and constantly complained to producers that unless they had a good script they could hardly expect a good picture. Sometimes he had

212

no choice but to proceed with material he really didn't think was worth doing. When he read the script of *Once Upon a Time in the West* he immediately turned it down. It was a translation from the Italian and seemed to him thin and trite. He was aware that producer Sergio Leone had made three tremendously successful westerns with Clint Eastwood—*A Fistful of Dollars, For*

a Few Dollars More, and *The Good, the Bad and the Ugly*—and he was flattered that Leone considered him his favorite American actor, but the script was awful. Leone and his backers kept after Fonda. For advice he turned to his friend Eli Wallach, who had worked for Leone. Wallach's advice was to ignore the script, because to Leone a script was just a set of guidelines. Wallach explained that he was a director who made up his material as he went along, and that

he was a cinematic genius. Fonda decided to risk it.

Fonda could have had his choice of several parts, but he decided to play the principal villain, a part light years removed from anything he had ever done. His villian in this film is a heartless, cold-blooded killer, devoid of mercy. The film opens with this evil man, Frank, and his henchmen advancing on a ranch, where they kill the father, the mother, a son and a daughter. All that remains of the family is an eight-year-old boy, who looks up pleadingly at Frank. Frank draws his pistol and slaughters the boy.

Once Upon a Time in the West takes place in late nineteenth-century Kansas and Frank is one of a number of men hired by the railroad to clear people off the lands in their proposed path. Greed, vengeance and violence throb throughout this long and spawling movie. Frank's big problem is to gain control of a town which is owned by a beautiful lady from New Orleans, Jill McBain (Claudia Cardinale). The railroad must have the town because it stands in the middle of well-watered land. Frank takes on the job of liquidating people because it satisfies his evil nature. He kills Jill's intended groom but finds his job made difficult by a pair of gunmen, Cheyenne (Jason Robards) and The Man With No Name (Charles Bronson). It is this mysterious, quiet man who ends Frank's career. It seems Frank killed his father when The Man was a boy and he has been looking for him all this time. He kills Frank slowly and sticks an harmonica in his mouth, ordering him to play, because that is what Frank did with his father. At the conclusion of *Once Upon a Time in the West,* Jill has full claim to her land and the only male left alive is The Man, who rides into the sunset.

It is difficult to summarize the plot of this film, since it is a highly stylized stream of vignettes. Sergio Leone may have idolized the westerns of John Ford, William Wellman and Howard Hawks but he could not, or chose not to, make one as simply constructed as those masters of the genre did. Most of the film was shot in Spain, like most spaghetti westerns, but in deference to Ford he filmed some sequences in Monument Valley.

The critical reaction was divided. Some thought it overly impressionistic, almost like a fantasy western, and others thought it brilliant, if somewhat too long and involved. The American public did not like it very much whereas the film did marvelously well in a number of European cities. Europeans were perhaps not so

With John Frederick and Michael Harvey.

age. But then, who would think Henry Fonda was 64 anyway? He is a little more weathered, certainly, a little thinner on top, but as slim, as lithe, as active as he was in *The Farmer Takes a Wife* 34 years ago. He probably has many surprises in store for us yet."

bothered by seeing Fonda as a vicious villain. Americans who had grown up with him as a symbol of American decency found the change hard to stomach. In the *Chicago Daily News*, Sam Lesner said, "Fonda is a cobra. It's a performance of chilling malevolence." That drastic departure from the image of Mr. Roberts was too much for his admirers, although Fonda himself claimed to have enjoyed making the picture.

In discussing this departure from image, John Russell Taylor of the *London Times* made this point: "It is altogether possible that during his long and successful career as a star, Fonda the actor has had a slightly raw deal. The penalty, perhaps, of being a star. An actor is paid to do; a star is paid to be . . . No doubt it came as an immense relief to Henry Fonda (as an actor, if not as a man) to shoot down that eight-year-old in cold blood in *Once Upon a Time in the West*, if only because it is the last thing he, of all people, would be expected to do in a film. At 64 one might think it a little late for a change of im-

TOO LATE THE HERO

1970

A Cinerama Film, produced and directed by Robert Aldrich, written by Robert Aldrich and Lucas Heller, based upon a story by Aldrich and Robert Sherman, photographed in Technicolor by Joseph Biroc, music by Gerald Fried, 144 minutes.

CAST:

Tosh Herne, *Michael Caine;* Lieutenant Lawson, *Cliff Robertson;* Thorton, *Ian Bannen;* Col. Thompson, *Harry Andrews;* Capt. Hornsby, *Denholm Elliott;* Campbell, *Ronald Fraser;* McLean, *Lance Percival;* Johnstone, *Percy Herbert;* Captain Nolan, *Henry Fonda;* Major Yamaguchi, *Ken Takakura.*

The Dirty Dozen (1967), dealing with a bunch of roistering soldiers in the European theatre of World War Two, was a spectacular success for director-producer Robert Aldrich. Three years later he turned his attention to the Asian theatre of the same war with *Too Late the Hero,* and fared less well. Again he focused on the variety of men who make up wartime regiments, this lot being British army infantry sent behind the Japanese lines in the New Hebrides in 1942 to blow up a radio site. Sent with them is an American naval lieutenant (Cliff Robertson), who speaks fluent Japanese. When the British officers are killed off, he takes command, which causes a few raw sentiments, especially with a rough cockney private (Michael Caine). By the end of the mission, only the cockney is left alive.

For Henry Fonda *Too Late the Hero* meant just a few days work to do a cameo role, obviously placed for name value in a picture manned almost entirely by British players. And his agents clearly thought the picture would do more business than turned out to be the case. Here Fon-

da is naval Captain Nolan, who devises the mission behind the lines and sends the lieutenant along, but without pointing out how battle-weary the British unit actually is and how little chance there is of surviving. This sequence with

With Cliff Robertson.

Fonda comes before the credit titles of the film; those who make a point of coming in on films after the credit titles will never know why his name is connected with it.

☆☆☆☆☆☆☆☆☆☆☆☆☆☆☆

THERE WAS A CROOKED MAN

1970

A Warner Brothers–Seven Arts Film, produced and directed by Joseph L. Mankiewicz, written by David Newman and Robert Benton, photographed in Technicolor by Harry Stradling, Jr., music by Charles Strouse, 126 minutes.

CAST:

Paris Pittman, Jr., *Kirk Douglas;* Woodward Lopeman, *Henry Fonda;* Dudley Whinner, *Hume Cronyn;* Floyd Moon, *Warren Oates;* The Missouri Kid, *Burgess Meredith;* Cyrus McNutt, *John Randolph;* Mr. Lomax, *Arthur O'Connell;*

With Kirk Douglas.

Warden Le Goff, *Martin Gabel*; Coy Cavendish, *Michael Blodgett*; Madam, *Claudia McNeil*; Tobaccy, *Alan Hale*; Whiskey, *Victor French*; Mrs. Bullard, *Lee Grant*; Ah-Ping, *C. K. Yang*; Edwina, *Pamela Hensley*; Skinner, *Bert Freed*; Jessie Brundige, *Barbara Rhoades*; The Governor, *J. Edward McKinley*.

No film by the witty, urbane Joseph L. Mankiewicz ever takes an ordinary view of its subject matter. With Mankiewicz there are

With Jeanne Cooper.

always twists and stings. The trouble with *There Was a Crooked Man*, which is both a western and a prison picture, is that the view of humankind is so cynical and negative that the viewer is left with no point of view of his own. According to Mankiewicz and his writers in this well-produced but overlong film, all men are crooked, period. Only one character, the sheriff (later warden)

played by Henry Fonda, has any moral fiber and even he turns crooked in the end.

Set mostly in a territorial prison, presumably in Arizona, Warners spent $300,000 building a massive jail at a point in the desert about 45 miles northeast of Indio, California. Designer Edward Carrere did so well that audiences can be excused for assuming it to be the real thing. Like most prison movies, this one concerns the drawing together of a number of characters and placing them in the same cell. The main character is the rather cultured but psychopathic Paris Pittman, Jr. (Kirk Douglas), who steals half a million dollars from a ranch and hides it in a rattlesnake hole. Later spotted in a brothel, Pittman is hauled off to jail. One of his fellow inmates is Floyd Moon (Warren Oates), jailed for shooting Sheriff Woodward Lopeman (Fonda) in the leg while the unarmed lawman apprehended him.

Pittman makes the mistake of bragging about his half million dollar deposit in the desert and among the men who make it known that they are willing to help Pittman break out of jail is the warden (Martin Gabel). However, the warden is killed while trying to stop a brawl among the prisoners and his replacement turns out to be Woodward Lopeman.

With director Joseph L. Mankiewicz.

With Kirk Douglas.

the stench, the frustration and the despair of the prisoners, so much so that the decency exemplified by Fonda's warden is almost a jarring note in this atmosphere of spite and amorality. Kirk Douglas's characterization is consistent throughout, a brightly intelligent, sometimes amusing but basically mean-spirited criminal. The problem with Fonda's role as the warden is

Lopeman is an honest man, humane in his treatment of prisoners and dedicated to the idea of prison reform. He spots the leadership qualities of Pittman and assigns him to supervising the building of a new dining hall. It is during the inauguration of the hall, attended by the state governor and his guests, that Pittman stages a revolt and makes his break.

He reaches his rattlesnake hole, after first having killed off the men with whom he made his escape, shoots all the snakes and pulls out the bundle containing the money. But he does not count on the fact that there is a rattler in the bundle itself. The snake bites him in the neck and Pittman dies, thoroughly disgusted with this trick of fate.

Shortly thereafter the pursuing warden arrives, slings the corpse over a horse and proceeds to the prison. At the gates Lopeman halts and thinks; he looks at the bag with the half million dollars, then sends the horse with the body through the gates as he turns his own horse in the opposite direction and rides away, presumably for Mexico.

Perhaps *There Was a Crooked Man* is too bleak a comment on humankind. It is certainly graphic in depicting prison life of the times, the sweat,

that Mankiewicz sets him up so believably as an honest man, a compassionate, caring man, that his decision to desert his job and take off with the loot seems entirely out of keeping with the character. There must surely be *some* decent men, even in this neck of the woods. *There Was a Crooked Man* is a fine piece of film making but it overplays its mocking hand. The aftertaste is a little too bitter.

THE CHEYENNE SOCIAL CLUB

1970

A National General Film, produced and directed by Gene Kelly, written by James Lee Barrett, photographed in Technicolor and Panavision by William Clothier, music by Walter Scharf, 103 minutes.

CAST:

John O'Hanlan, *James Stewart*; Harley Sullivan, *Henry Fonda*; Jenny, *Shirley Jones*; Opal Ann, *Sue Ann Langdon*; Willouby, *Dabbs Greer*; Pauline, *Elaine Devry*; Barkeep, *Robert Middleton*; Marshall Anderson, *Arch Johnson*; Carrie Virginia, *Jackie Russell*; Annie Jo, *Jackie Joseph*; Sara Jean, *Sharon De Bord*; Nathan Potter, *Richard Collier*; Charlie Bannister, *Charles Tyner*; Alice, *Jean Willes*; Corey Bannister, *Robert J. Wilke*; Peter Dodge, *Carl Reindel*; Dr. Foy, *J. Pat O'Malley*; Dr. Carter, *Jason Wingreen*; Clay Carrol, *John Dehner*.

Two grizzled old cowpokes, Harley Sullivan and John O'Hanlan slowly ride across a vast western landscape. Harley's drawling voice drones on and on and on . . . about his family and his dogs and his doings. John, a long-suffering listener, finally speaks up. "You know where we are now, Harley?" "Not exactly." "We're in the Wyoming Territory and you've been talkin'

With James Stewart.

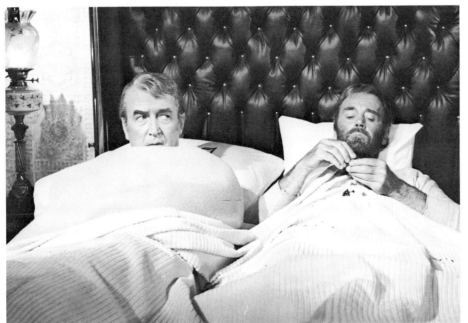

all the way from Texas." Harley looks wounded, "Just been keepin' you company." Replies John, "I appreciate it, Harley, but if you say another word the rest of the day I'm gonna kill you."

This is the opening scene of *The Cheyenne Social Club.* Harley is Fonda and John is James Stewart, and it would have been almost impossible to find a pair of actors who could better play

With James Stewart.

a pair of old friends. Whether as grizzled cowpokes or veteran actors, they appear together in this amusing western with the ease and naturalness that could only come of long acquaintance. Of their work together, *The Cheyenne Social Club* is by far *the* Fonda-Stewart movie. The idea of doing the film was Stewart's. His friend James Lee Barrett, who had scripted a number of Stewart films, thought it would be a good vehicle for the two actors and

showed it to Gene Kelly. A single reading was all he needed to agree, provided Fonda would also agree. Few films have been conceived as easily as this one.

The two old cowboys are making their way to Cheyenne because John's brother has died and left him an inheritance, although he doesn't know what it is. It turns out to be what the townspeople call a social club, but what it is in fact is a nice, comfortable bordello, and just about the center of gravity in Cheyenne. The madam is Jenny (Shirley Jones). She and her staff of a half-dozen pretty girls make the new boss welcome, and Harley becomes a partner in the enterprise, although he doesn't do anything except enjoy the hospitality of the house. Amiable Harley just takes life as it comes. John, on the other hand, is a little more straitlaced and somewhat embarrassed by his new wealth, or rather, by the source of the wealth. He comes to the decision that he will have to change things— maybe turn the place into a saloon. The girls are dismayed, but not nearly as dismayed as the citizenry, who regard John's decision as contemptible.

John changes his mind about changing the club when he realizes what might happen to the girls, who are likely to be destitute. He finds himself thrown into jail for defending himself in

With Shirley Jones and James Stewart.

a barroom brawl and while there he learns that Jenny has been thrashed by an outlaw, Corey Bannister (Robert J. Wilke). To avenge her, John seeks out Bannister and guns him down, which wins him respect in town but also brings on the enmity of the whole Bannister clan of six brothers and sundry hirelings. Harley, away for a while, arrives back in time to help win the battle when the club is attacked by the Bannisters. But this, they learn, is likely to be a continual battle as more of the related bandits turn up. Rather than be involved in perpetual warfare, John signs over the social club to Jenny. He and Harley take their leave and head back over the landscape, with John presumably doomed to spend the rest of his life listening to the incessant chatter of his old pal Harley.

It would have been nice if Fonda and Stewart had appeared together again but they could have done worse than this as a final pairing. *The Cheyenne Social Club* is a genial if slightly raunchy western, handsomely photographed—not in Wyoming but near Santa Fe, New Mexico—and a perfect showcase for two veteran actors who also happened to be true old friends.

☆☆☆☆☆☆☆☆☆☆☆☆

SOMETIMES A GREAT NOTION

1971

A Universal Film, produced by John C. Foreman, directed by Paul Newman, written by John Gay, based on the novel by Ken Kesey, photographed in Technicolor by Richard Moore, music by Henry Mancini, 114 minutes.

CAST:

Hank Stamper, *Paul Newman*; Henry Stamper, *Henry Fonda*; Hank's wife, *Lee Remick*; Lee Stamper, *Michael Sarrazin*; Joe Ben Stamper, *Richard Jaekel*; Joe's wife, *Linda Lawson*; Andy, *Cliff Potts*; John, *Sam Gilman*.

With Paul Newman.

comes home, where his father greets him as a hippie. The only one who understands that Lee doesn't fit in with the rough family is Hank's wife (Lee Remick). The Stampers go ahead with their contract, despite threats of violence from townspeople and incidents of sabotage, such as cables snapping and log piles being scattered.

With Paul Newman, Linda Lawson, Richard Jaeckel and Lee Remick.

Sometimes a Great Notion—a vague title that did nothing to help the film—marks a turning point in Henry Fonda's screen image. This was the first time he appeared as an old man. Previously there had been no reference to his age. In his recent westerns he was obviously an older man, although usually playing younger than his age, but now he was ready to go with the years. Sixty-five at the time of making *Notion*, he actually seems older playing the crotchety head of a family of lumberjacks in Oregon. It is also the first film in which Fonda plays a crude, earthy character. He speaks of the fundamentals of life as "eating, drinking, sleeping and screwing—that's all there is to it." It is a mild shock, considering his image as a man always associated with common American dignity.

The Stampers are a rugged family of loggers in a small Oregon coastal town and they go their own way, no matter what. If they have a contract to fill, they fill it even if the rest of the town is on strike. Henry Stamper (Fonda) tells the union officials to get lost. His two sons, Hank (Paul Newman) and Joe Ben (Richard Jaekel) feel the same way. Henry's youngest son, Lee (Michael Sarrazin), who has been a dropout from family tradition for the past few years, now

Things get worse for the Stampers. A football game in which they participate turns into a brawl and nasty things are said, especially about old Henry, whose wife committed suicide. Later he loses his log truck when it plunges over a cliff. But nothing will stop him and he goes ahead with the floating of his logs down the river to the mill.

223

With Paul Newman and Michael Sarrazin.

Undermanned for the task, things go wrong. Joe Ben is knocked into the river by a log and slowly drowns. Henry loses an arm when a log falls on him and he later dies in the hospital, still an irascible old individualist. Lee joins with his brother to hire a tugboat to finish the job.

Sometimes a Great Notion was Paul Newman's second film as a director and credit is due for his handling of a splendidly visual subject. The picture was made entirely on location in and around the Oregon fishing village of Newport, amid genuine logging communities. Newman's taste, on the other hand, is questionable, particularly in the closing scene of the tugboat moving down the river. He has the severed arm of old Henry lashed to a mast, the middle finger of which is extended in the familiar symbol of contempt. It hardly seems like the proper gesture of vaunted American doggedness and individuality the film espouses to salute. It also seems uncomfortably at odds with the Fonda image. Is his tough, gruff old lumberjack the man Tom Joad might have grown into? Is this patriarch a little noble or a bit senile? The script doesn't make it clear. What *Sometimes a Great Notion* did make clear was that Henry Fonda was getting older and that this perhaps wasn't the best way to make the point.

With Paul Newman.

THE SERPENT

With Yul Brynner.

1973

A Les Films La Boetie—Euro International—Rialto Film, produced and directed by Henri Vernueil, written by Henri Vernueil and Gilles Perrault, based on the novel by Pierre Nordi, photographed in Eastmancolor and Panavision by Claude Renoir, music by Ennio Morricone, 120 minutes.

CAST:

Vlassov, *Yul Brynner;* Davies, *Henry Fonda;* Boyle, *Dirk Bogarde;* Berthon, *Phillippe Noiret;* Tavel, *Michel Bouquet;* Lepke, *Martin Heid;* Expert, *Farley Granger;* Annabel Lee, *Virna Lisi;* Deval, *Guy Trejan;* Kate, *Elga Anderson;* Questioner, *Robert Alda;* Tatiana, *Natlie Nerval.*

Another sophisticated spy picture—and another one that did not find much distribution in America. Perhaps the public had long tired of the callousness of modern espionage, a game in which there seemed to be no genuine loyalties, and preferred the flashy nonsense of James Bond.

With Dirk Bogarde.

With Yul Brynner and Phillippe Noiret.

For *The Serpent*, French producer-director Henri Vernueil strove for a truly international coverage of the complicated business by hiring Yul Brynner as a Russian, Dirk Bogarde as a high-ranking British Secret Service officer, and Henry Fonda as the director of the CIA in Washington. By now audiences could be forgiven for believing that Fonda really belonged in the capital.

Like espionage itself, *The Serpent* is a convoluted tale. The main character is a coldly suave Russian colonel, Vlassov (Yul Brynner), who defects to the West. He is granted political asylum to the U.S. and CIA Chief Davies (Fonda) runs a check on his story. This includes lie detectors, programmed information and various computerized devices. Vlassov reveals the identities of a number of French and West German officials who are in the employ of the Soviets. This causes the collapse of the career of the French Minister of the Interior (Philippe Noiret) and a number of suicides among French and German officials, all of them presumably spies. The suicides turn out to be murders and the suspect is someone identified only as The Serpent, because he leaves behind a cigarette case with a gold dragon on it.

The true villain of the piece is the British Secret Service officer of high rank, Boyle (Dirk Bogarde), who actually works for the Soviets. And Vlassov's defection is really a ruse, designed to eliminate a number of western agents by false accusations and evidence. Such is the subject matter of *The Serpent*, a well-made account of capers among the espionage players, none of whom inspire much confidence or admiration, no matter whose side they appear to be on.

The film is of interest to espionage students since it shows operations in various points in Europe as well as Washington, but for Fonda it was yet another job calling for his cool, steely,

efficient executive image. It could hardly have been much of a challenge.

There is, however, some fun in watching Fonda as the rather good-natured CIA chief deploying all manner of technical devices to gradually break down the confidence of the Russian agent played by the cool Brynner. Slowly it dawns upon the Russian that he has been outfoxed, and in the end he is exchanged for a captured American pilot.

With Phillippe Noiret.

ASH WEDNESDAY

1973

A Paramount Film, produced by Dominick Dunne, directed by Larry Peerce, written by Jean-Claude Tramont, photographed in Technicolor by Ennio Guarnieri, music by Maurice Jarre, 100 minutes.

CAST:
Barbara Sawyer, *Elizabeth Taylor;* Mark Sawyer, *Henry Fonda;* Erich, *Helmut Berger;* David,

Keith Baxter; Dr. Lambert, *Maurice Teynac;* Kate, *Margaret Blye;* German Woman, *Monique Van Vooren;* Bridge Player, *Henning Schlueter;* Mario, *Dino Mele;* Mandy, *Kathy Van Lypps;* Nurse Ilse, *Dina Sassoli;* Paolo, *Carlo Puri.*

Henry Fonda received second billing in *Ash Wednesday,* but it is entirely an Elizabeth Taylor picture in which Fonda is seen only in the last

With Elizabeth Taylor.

With Elizabeth Taylor and wife Shirlee on location.

half hour, although he is heard in telephone conversations during the course of the film. *Ash Wednesday* was sadly in line with most of the Taylor films made in the Seventies—of little success. It is something of a puzzle how an actress of such fame and with perpetual exposure in the newspapers of the world could appear in films of such limited appeal.

Barbara Sawyer (Taylor) is 55, but because of her depression over her long-declining marriage she looks haggard and older than her years. She has wealth and a fine home in Grosse Pointe, Michigan, but her husband Mark (Fonda) pays her little attention as he goes his way as a powerful attorney. She decides to go to Europe and undergo facial operations that will restore her beauty. The period spent in an Italian clinic proves even more successful than she had hoped,

and after recuperation Barbara looks 20 years younger and truly beautiful. She proceeds to a magnificent ski resort in Cortina d'Ampezzo, there to await the arrival of Mark. But he is delayed and to while away the time she takes up with an amusing, chic fashion photographer (Keith Baxter), who has already had several face lifts. He introduces her to the local smart set, one of whom, an elegant Parisian playboy (Helmut Berger), leads her into a love idyll.

Barbara manages to extract herself from the clutches of the playboy in time for the arrival of her husband. Their 30-year-old daughter (Margaret Blye) arrives first and warns her that her father is in love with a younger woman and seeks a divorce. When Mark finally arrives he is surprised and delighted with Barbara's new look and they enjoy some pleasant moments together. But he still wants a divorce. He tells her she can, with her new appearance, start a new life. He urges her to seek such a life, explaining that he, too, is tired of the past, tired of being a tycoon-lawyer. There must be something better for both of them.

Ash Wednesday is truly a Taylor vehicle, allowing her to parade in beautiful clothing created by Edith Head, amid gorgeously photographed Italian winter backgrounds in the Dolomite Mountains. The film is interesting in its coverage of cosmetic surgery, although the detailed photography of the facial operations is somewhat hard to stomach and caused the film to be given a Restricted rating. The surgery was the real thing and performed by the eminent Parisian face lifter Dr. Rodolph Troques, but not of course on Taylor, whose tired, old face at the film's outset was supplied by make-up artist Alberto De Rossi.

Fonda's performance in *Ash Wednesday* is yet another in his gallery of quiet, dignified authority figures, this one being a rather world-weary super-lawyer, sympathetic toward his wife but nonetheless determined to go his own way. It could hardly have been a part that caused him to do much extending of his dramatic knowledge.

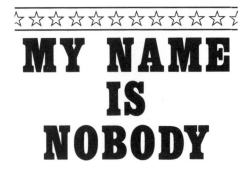

MY NAME IS NOBODY

1974

A Titanus release of a Sergio Leone Film, produced by Fulvio Morsella, directed by Tonino Valerii, written by Ernesto Gastaldi, photographed in Technicolor by Armando Nannuzzi and Guiseppe Ruzzolini, music by Ennio Morricone, 117 minutes.

CAST:

Nobody, *Terence Hill;* Jack Beauregard, *Henry Fonda;* Sullivan, *Jean Martin;* Sheriff, *Piero Lulli;* Red, *Leo Gordon;* Honest John, *R. G. Armstrong;* Westerner, *Neil Summers;* Flase Barber, *Steve Kanaly;* Scope, *Geoffrey Lewis.*

Although written and directed by others, Sergio Leone was clearly the mastermind or the inspiration behind *My Name Is Nobody,* an Italian western partly shot in New Mexico, New Orleans and Spain. Perhaps because of the various locations and sympathies involved, the

230

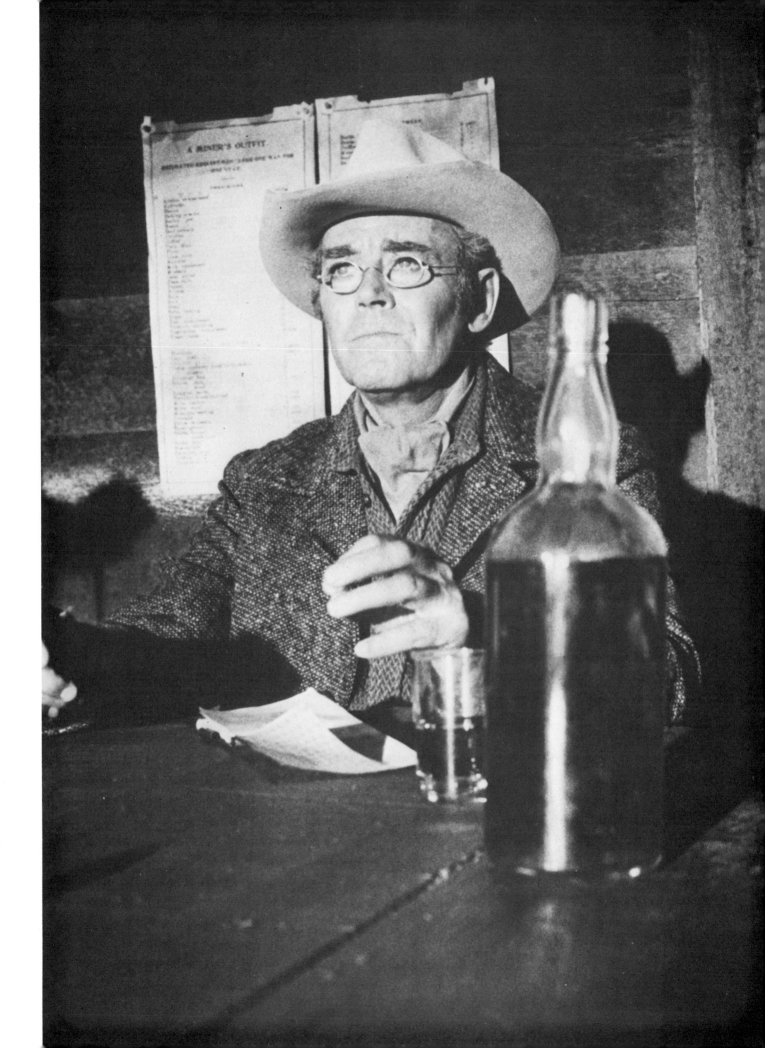

film has the air of a fantasy, rather like Peckinpah through the eyes of Leone. Set in 1899, the film goes a step beyond Peckinpah's *The Wild Bunch* as Leone and his disciples bring on Henry Fonda as an aging, legendary gunman who wipes out a huge wild bunch of outlaws and seemingly

and he craves excitement in the dying days of the West. In the New Mexico village where Jack Beauregard (Fonda) lives, Nobody is hired to kill him by leaving a bomb in a basket in the barber shop. But such is Jack's cool manner and instinct—he knows something must be wrong—that Nobody flings the basket back at the men who hired him. Nobody comes to idolize Jack, whose life has been spent shooting down bandits and feared gunmen.

Jack, on the other hand, is long tired of it all. He not only wants to retire but wants to retire in Europe and comfortably sink into oblivion. He heads for New Orleans and the liner that will take him away from the life that now seems dead and empty. But Nobody dogs him all the way. He thinks Jack owes it to history to go down in a blaze of fire fighting the remaining Wild Bunch. Since there is a little something in it for him, Jack accepts the challenge, but with well-calculated tactics. When he tackles the large band it is at a distance and with well-aimed ri-

pulls down the curtain on the Wild West. The film is of interest in the Fonda film catalog as his final western. He had made 15 westerns since *Jesse James*, some of them major items, and whether he liked it or not he had chalked up some identity with the genre. Fonda had no strong interest in the West, he had no yen to be a rancher and he did not care very much for horses. Yet his very American male image—the cool, steady gaze, the flat drawl and the loping walk—made him perfect for westerns.

The Nobody of the title is a wild young man (Terence Hill) who likes to be known as just that,

fle shots. Knowing that some of them are carrying sacks of dynamite, he aims for them and blows more than a hundred men to smithereens. When last seen Jack Beauregard is sitting at a desk, wearing spectacles, looking like a retired clerk and writing about his life—presumably in Europe.

My Name Is Nobody is thus Henry Fonda's western swan song. A good one, but spoiled by the florid acting of Terence Hill in the title role

With Terrence Hill.

and by some of the dramatic excesses that mar most of the spaghetti westerns. The film is a little too grand and over-sophisticated for its own good. The hodgepodge score by Ennio Morricone, for example, ranges from ragtime to near-rock. How much better had it an elegiac score by a veteran American film composer, or for that matter, how much better had it been made by John Ford. Still, as a picture about a man wrapping up his days in the old West it could hardly have had a better actor than one who was doing precisely that.

THE LAST DAYS OF MUSSOLINI

1974

A Paramount release of an Aquita Cinematografica Film, produced by Enzo Peri, directed by Carlo Lizzani, written by Carlo Lizzani and Fabio Pittorru, photographed in Eastmancolor by Roberto Gerardi, music by Ennio Morricone, 126 minutes.

CAST:

Mussolini, *Rod Steiger;* Clara Patacci, *Lisa Gastoni;* Cardinal Schuster, *Henry Fonda;* Colonel Valerio, *Franco Nero;* Pedro, *Lino Capolicchio.*

For anyone interested in the fate of Benito Mussolini this film presents a graphic account of the final week in his life, when diverse factions were trying to claim him. The Germans were trying to get him out of Italy, the Allies wanted him in order to try him as a war criminal, the provisional Italian government hoped to take him into custody and the National Liberation Committee, the fierce Italian freedom fighters, simply wanted to kill him as soon as he could be found. Unfortunately for Mussolini, they were the ones who got to him first. He had hoped to escape to Switzerland, where he wanted to contact Winston Churchill about his plans to save Europe from a Communist take-over.

Paramount agreed to represent *The Last Days of Mussolini* in the United States, but they could find little interest among the theatre owners. The film deserved better treatment since it is not only a commendable and accurate dramatization of those chaotic times when the Second World War was shuddering to its halt, but it is also a superior and exciting war movie. Much credit is due Rod Steiger for his portrayal of the hunted, disillusioned and confused Il Duce, a man toppled from his former heights of egocentric glory. However, as an item in the Henry Fonda listing it is mostly a curiosity. Fonda plays the Milan Cardinal who desperately tried to negotiate between Mussolini and the various parties who were trying to get to him. It is a cameo role and Fonda plays it with suitable dignity, and yet he seems somehow out of place. He is too recognizably Fonda to fit into this realistic treatment of recent history.

MIDWAY

1976
A Universal Film, produced by Walter Mirisch, directed by Jack Smight, written by Donald S. Sanford, photographed in Technicolor by Harry Stradling, Jr., music by John Williams, 132 minutes.

CAST:
Capt. Matt Garth, *Charlton Heston;* Admiral Chester W. Nimitz, *Henry Fonda;* Capt. Maddox, *James Coburn;* Admiral Spruance, *Glenn Ford;* Commander Rochefort, *Hal Holbrook;* Admiral Yamamoto, *Toshiro Mifune;* Admiral Wm.

With Robert Wagner, Charlton Heston and James Coburn.

F. Halsey, *Robert Mitchum*; Commander Jessop, *Cliff Robertson*; Lt. Commander Blake, *Robert Wagner*; Admiral Jack Fletcher, *Robert Webber*; Admiral Pearson, *Ed Nelson*; Vice Admiral Nagumo, *James Shigeta*; Haruka Sakura, *Christina Kakubo*; Commander Max Leslie, *Monte Markham*; Capt. Browning, *Biff McGuire*; Lt. Commander McClusky, *Christopher George*; Lt. Commander Waldron, *Glenn Corbett*; Capt. Buckmaster, *Gregory Walcott*; Ensign Garth, *Edward Albert*.

Called to the colors again! Not only back in the navy but in the role of Admiral Chester W. Nimitz, one of America's most distinguished sailors in the Second World War. And who better to play him? Who better than a reliable actor who had a chance to see admirals at work in the South Pacific? *Midway*, with the mighty roar of broadsides and bombs reproduced in Sensurround, deals with that crucial battle in June of 1942, when the American navy was able to turn back the Japanese fleet and ensure, among other things, that the enemy forces would never reach the U.S. west coast. The Walter Mirisch epic makes for a good history lesson but bogs down somewhat with fictional episodes about private naval lives, one of which is the trouble a captain (Charlton Heston) has when his ensign son (Edward Albert) wants to marry an Hawaiian girl of Japanese parentage. Getting permission for this union seems as wieldy as requisitioning an aircraft carrier.

Midway is admirable in its technical achievements but it serves as an example of the problems encountered when producers try to make almost documentary-like coverage of vast historical events commercial by beefing them up with subplots. The lines get confused and the values juggled. Henry Fonda's role is not billed as a cameo because he appears a number of times throughout the film—fortunately. His authorative presence is as valuable to this movie as Admiral Nimitz's was in the actual battle. The audience may be confused, but Fonda-Nimitz looks as if he knows where everything is and how everything works.

☆☆☆☆☆☆☆☆☆☆☆☆☆☆☆☆

ROLLERCOASTER

1977

A Universal Film, produced by Jennings Lang, directed by James Goldstone, written by Richard Levinson and William Link, based on a story by Sanford Sheldon, Levinson and Link, suggested by a Tommy Cook story, photographed in Technicolor and Panavision by David M. Walsh, music by Lalo Schifrin, 119 minutes.

CAST:

Harry Calder, *George Segal;* Hoyt, *Richard Widmark;* Young Man, *Timothy Bottoms;* Simon Davenport, *Henry Fonda;* Lt. Keeler, *Harry Guardino;* Fran Calder, *Susan Strasberg;* Tracy Calder, *Helen Hunt;* Helen Calder, *Dorothy Tristan;* Old Caretaker, *Harry Davis;* Tourist, *Monica Lewis.*

Audiences who saw *Rollercoaster* in first-run, suitably equipped theatres had the benefit of experiencing Sensurround, a cunning device that links high-fidelity sound reproduction with low frequency vibrations and helps the viewer to feel more associated with the projected images. Universal had used the device with *Midway* and *Earthquake,* but in *Rollercoaster,* by having cameras mounted on the front of the carriages as they spun up and down and around the rails of giant switchbacks, it was enough to give audiences motion sickness. When seen on television, *Rollercoaster* loses much of that impact; what is left is a well-crafted cat-and-mouse suspense thriller that blends a little of the spirit of Hitchcock with a lot of the kind of disaster expertise perfected by Irwin Allen. But what it has to do with Henry Fonda is very, very little.

Although it runs two hours, *Rollercoaster* can be summed up in a sentence: It's about a devilishly clever, psychopathic young man (Timothy Bottoms), who hopes to get an entertainment park to hand over a million dollars before he blows up its biggest rollercoaster and

sends its riders to their hideously mangled deaths. The film begins with a sample of what he can do, as he wastes a switchback ride and causes slaughter among the customers. From then on it becomes the job of a cool, government safety expert (George Segal) to outwit the brilliant young madman.

As a visual thriller *Rollercoaster* succeeds admirably. The direction is taut and the photography, particularly the use of Magic Mountain, the huge entertainment park near Los Angeles, is breathtaking. But in a study of the work of Henry Fonda it barely rates a mention. Although not billed as a cameo, it is a small and unattractive role, with Fonda playing an ill-tempered bureaucrat, the boss of the safety inspector hero. The most that can be said of his work here is that he was an Old Pro doing his job and getting well paid. And worth every penny.

TENTACLES

1977

A 20th Century-Fox release of an Ovidio Assonitus Film, produced by E. F. Daria, directed by Oliver Hellman, written by Jerome Max, Tito Carpi, Steve Carabatsos and Sonia Malteni, photographed in Technicolor by Roberto D'Ettorre, music by S. W. Cipriani, 102 minutes.

With Cesare Danova.

CAST:

Ned Turner, *John Huston;* Tillie Turner, *Shelley Winters;* Will Gleason, *Bo Hopkins;* Mr. Whitehead, *Henry Fonda;* Vicky Gleason, *Delia Baccardo;* John Corey, *Cesare Danova;* Mike, *Alan Boyd;* Capt. Robards, *Claude Akins;* Judy, *Sherry Buchanan;* Chuck, *Franco Diagene;* Don, *Maro Fiorini;* Mother, *Helena Makela.*

What's a fine actor like Henry Fonda doing in a trashy picture like *Tentacles?* Answer: not very much. Neither for that matter are John Huston and Shelley Winters. All three were obviously hired to lend marquee value to this limp Italian version of *Jaws*, with a giant octopus in place of a huge killer whale. The tentacles in question belong to a monster that terrifies a small Southern Californian coastal town. The fearful beast chews up a number of citizens in graphic and gory fashion before a marine biologist (Bo Hopkins) strikes upon a solution, which is to train a pair of whales to go after the octopus and destroy it. The whales do the job.

Bo Hopkins is the only actor who comes off with any merit in *Tentacles*, since he has the biggest and most interesting role. John Huston seems so bored with his part as a snoopy reporter that he can be forgiven if he ever chooses to deny his association with the film. As for Fonda, he simply has a few brief walk-ons as the head of a marine tunneling company, which is blamed for stirring up the monster and bringing on the grief. In all of these small scenes Fonda appears irritable. He, too, may be forgiven.

238

☆☆☆☆☆☆☆☆☆☆☆☆☆☆

THE GREAT SMOKEY ROADBLOCK

1978

A Mar Vista–Ingo Preminger Film, produced by Allan F. Bodoh, directed and written by John Leone, photographed in color by Ed Brown, Sr., music by Craig Safan, 100 minutes.

CAST:
Elegant John, *Henry Fonda*; Penelope, *Eileen Brennan*; Beebo, *Robert Englund*; Disc Jockey, *John Byner*; Guido, *Austin Pendelton*; Ginny, *Susan Sarandon*; Lulu, *Melanie Mayron*; Alice, *Marya Small*; Glinda, *Leigh French*; Celeste, *Dana House*.

When a completed movie sits on the shelf for a couple of years and undergoes several changes of title in the process, the vibes are not good.

With Eileen Brennan.

240

When Henry Fonda agreed to star in this wacky comedy it was called *The Last of the Cowboys*, but when it was released it came out as *The Great Smokey Roadblock*, although they were also thinking of calling it *Elegant John and His Ladies*. In accepting the film Fonda first made it clear that if it was about cowboys he was in no condition to ride a horse. The producer then explained that the original title referred to the contemporary term for truck drivers—cowboys. With that understood Fonda then spent six weeks on location in northern California filming what would be his last movie with top billing. Unfor-

tunately it would get limited bookings, mostly in drive-ins, and not be seen by many people who appreciated Fonda.

Elegant John (Fonda) is a 65-year-old veteran truck driver who doesn't really want to quit, but if he must, then he wants to make one last perfect, wild cross-country run. The feisty but ailing old scamp is hospitalized for sundry ailments and while there his beloved 18-wheel Kenworth truck is repossessed by a finance company. John breaks out of hospital, steals his truck and heads for the hills of Utah, there to visit his lady love, Penelope (Eileen Brennan), who runs

With Robert Englund and Dub Taylor.

a brothel. Since she, too, is having trouble with the police, they decide upon taking all the girls in the truck and heading out. This will be John's last perfect run.

They are pursued by the police and aided by trucker friends via their CB radio communications. A wild disc jockey (John Byner) also lends his support and the event is covered by television. Other trucks, cars, campers and motorcyclists join John and the mighty cavalcade hurtles along the highways. The girls sell their services to raise money for gas. The police arrange a massive roadblock at a bridge on the Palatchee River, setting their cars three deep. But along comes roar-ing John and smashes through it all, sending police cars flying. The effort, however, is too much for John and he dies in the arms of Penelope, but with a smile on his face as he gloats over having made his last perfect run.

The Great Smokey Roadblock was a rather raunchy picture in which to star the aging Fonda, as well as a physically taxing one, since he had by this time taken to wearing both a pacemaker and a hearing aid. He seemed to enjoy making it and perhaps more people would have enjoyed seeing it had the film received wider distribution. Perhaps it is back on the shelf and awaiting another title.

THE SWARM

1978

A Warner Bros. Film, produced and directed by Irwin Allen, written by Stirling Silliphant, based on the novel by Arthur Herzog, photographed in Panavision and Technicolor by Fred J. Koenekamp, music by Jerry Goldsmith, 116 minutes.

CAST:

Brad Crane, *Michael Caine*; Helena, *Katharine Ross*; General Slater, *Richard Widmark*; Dr. Hubbard, *Richard Chamberlain*; Maureen Schuster, *Olivia de Havilland*; Felix, *Ben Johnson*; Anne MacGregor, *Lee Grant*; Dr. Andrews, *Jose Ferrer*; Rita Bard, *Patty Duke Astin*;

With Katharine Ross.

Jud Hawkins, *Slim Pickens*; Major Baker, *Bradford Dillman*; Clarence, *Fred MacMurray*; Dr. Krim, *Henry Fonda*; General Thompson, *Cameron Mitchell*; Paul Durant, *Christian Juttner*; Dr. Newman, *Morgan Paull*; Dr. Martinez, *Alejandro Rey*; Pete Harris, *Don Barry*; Mrs. Durant, *Doris Cook*; Mr. Durant, *Robert Varney*.

If the gathering together of an impressive number of greatly experienced and famous actors was the main factor in successful film making, then *The Swarm* should have been a certifiable triumph. Sadly it was anything but. Producer-director Irwin Allen populated his picture with a dozen distinguished players, five of whom were Oscar winners, but he failed to come up with dialogue and situations that allowed those players to appear credible. Irwin Allen by this time had won himself a title in Hollywood as a Master of Disaster. He had long realized the public's vicarious delight in watching bizarre adventures (*The Lost World, Voyage to the Bottom of the Sea, Five Weeks in a Balloon,* etc.) and people caught in perilous circumstances, such as sinking ships (*The Poseiden Adventure*) and fires in high buildings (*The Towering Inferno*). With *The Swarm* he aimed to titillate his audiences with the sight of human beings ravaged by clouds of killer bees.

The Swarm is made up of millions of bees from South America. They arrive for no apparent reason in southeast Texas and settle on a military base near Houston. An entomologist (Michael Caine) arrives to supervise the situation. When some people are horribly stung to death, their children take revenge by raiding the bees, which only makes the problem worse. The bees, who seem to have an almost military sense of tactics, attack the town of Marysville and kill several hundred people, including some children. The town is evacuated but many of its citizens die when the train in which they make their escape is invaded by the bees, who cause it to go out of control and crash. The city of Houston is reduced to chaos by the bees and every attempt to halt them proves ineffective. But then the entomologist discovers that the warning signal at the military base puts out a signal that employs the same sound patterns the bees use in their mating call. That signal is then used to lure the bees to a distant point, at which they meet a fiery end.

The Swarm struck neither the critics nor the public as especially frightening or interesting. And certainly nothing that weighed heavily upon the talents of its cast of veteran stars. Henry Fonda was listed in the advertisements at the end of the roster of star names—"and Henry Fonda as Dr. Krim"—a sure sign that a respected name is appearing in a cameo role. His role was that of a distinguished entomologist brought in as a consultant when disaster strikes and who sacrifices his life by testing an antibiotic. If nothing else it must have seemed a good way to get out of this picture.

FEDORA

1978

A Rialto release of a Geria-SFP Production, produced and directed by Billy Wilder, written by Wilder and I. A. L. Diamond, based on the story *Crowned Heads* by Tom Tryon, photographed in Eastmancolor by Gerry Fisher, music by Miklos Rozsa, 110 minutes.

CAST:

Barry, *William Holden;* Fedora, *Marthe Keller;* Vanda, *Jose Ferrer;* Countess, *Hildegard Knef;* Balfaru, *Frances Sternhagen;* Manager, *Mario Adorf;* Count, *Hans Jaray;* Krites, *Gottfried John;* with Michael York as himself and Henry Fonda as himself.

Billy Wilder's *Sunset Boulevard* (1950) is one of the most brilliant, knowing and witty movies ever made about the movie business and its people. With *Fedora* he attempted to plumb the same well, even using the same star, William Holden, as the leading figure. Sadly *Fedora* does not amount to even a shadow of *Sunset Boulevard*. It is a dull and convoluted tale about a 67-year-old movie goddess of Garbo or Dietrich proportions who still looks like a young woman and who lives in seclusion on a Mediterranean island, virtually a captive of a countess (Hildegard Knef) and her staff. A down-on-his-luck Hollywood director (Holden) traces Fedora (Marthe Keller) to try and persuade her to make a comeback, but she commits suicide by throwing herself under a train, a la Anna Karenina. It turns out that the crotchety old countess is actually Fedora and that she has been palming off her daughter, for the sake of vanity, as herself—until the daughter can't stand it any more.

Henry Fonda agreed to play a cameo role for Wilder, and a very easy one at that—as himself, although pretending to be the President of the Academy of Motion Picture Arts and Sciences, whose job it is to present Fedora with an Oscar for her contributions to the cinema. In addition to salary, Fonda spent a week on the Greek Island of Madouri, where his services were required for short periods on three afternoons. The short scene

With Marthe Keller and Rex McGee.

called for him to present the Oscar to Fedora, with her back to the sun, and the sun in his eyes, so that he has trouble clearly seeing the face of the legendary actress. It took a while to get this effect. Unfortunately it did not do much to help save Wilder's strange, incredible movie.

METEOR

1979
An American International Release, produced by
Arnold Orgolini and Theodore Parvin, directed
by Ronald Neame, written by Stanley Mann and
Edmund H. North, photographed in color by
Paul Lohmann, music by Laurence Rosenthal,
103 minutes.

CAST:
Bradley, *Sean Connery*; Tatiana, *Natalie Wood*;
Sherwood, *Karl Malden*; Dubov, *Brain Keith*;
Adion, *Martin Landau*; Sir Michael Hughes,
Trevor Howard; Secretary of Defense, *Richard
Dysart*; Easton, *Joseph Campanella*; The Presi-
dent, *Henry Fonda*.

Since *Meteor* needed a star to play the cameo
role of President of the United States—who better than Henry Fonda? One critic suggested that
since Fonda had appeared in that role so many
times he should think about actually running for
office. But *Meteor* is not so much a film for actors
as for Special Effects wizards. In this one they
devised not only a five-mile-wide asteroid plum-
meting to earth but a tidal wave, an avalanche
and an earthquake. Sean Connery is an American
scientist and Brian Keith is a Russian scientist,
with Natalie Wood doing the translations for
them. Since the disaster heading for the earth
is as menacing to the Soviets as the Americans,
the president gets on the phone to his Russian
counterpart and suggests that they combine their
space program experts and their weaponry in
order to destroy the approaching calamity.

Meteor suffers from the shortcomings that
blight so many movies about disasters and horri-
ble happenings—inferior dialogue and charac-

With Karl Malden.

terizations. The Special Effects are interesting, but the film did not do the box office business its producers had hoped. Among the actors Henry Fonda got off lightly. All he had to do was speak with authority on the phone and step up to the presidential rostrum to impart information. He didn't have to be involved in the making of *Meteor*—or see it.

CITY ON FIRE

1979

An Avco Embassy release of a Sandy Howard-Astral-Bellevue-Pathe Film, produced by Claude Heroux, directed by Alvin Rakoff, written by Jack Hill, David P. Lewis and Celine La Freniere, photographed in color by Rene Verzier, music by William McCauley and Matthew McCauley, 101 minutes.

CAST:
Dr. Frank Whitman, *Barry Newman;* Diane Brockhurst Lautrec, *Susan Clark;* Nurse Andrea Harper, *Shelley Winters;* Mayor William Dudley, *Leslie Nielsen;* Jimbo, *James Franciscus;* Mag-

gie Grayson, *Ava Gardner;* Chief Albert Risley, *Henry Fonda;* John O'Brien, *Mayor Moore;* Herman Stover, *Jonathan Welsh;* Capt. Harrison Risley, *Richard Donat;* Andrew, *Ken James;* Dr. Fox, *Donald Pilson;* Terry James, *Terry Haig;* Councilman Paley, *Cec Linder;* Mrs. Adams, *Hilary LeBow;* Beezer, *Jeff Mappin;* Mr. Clark, *Earl Pennington.*

City of Fire is a bargain basement version of *The Towering Inferno,* although it attempts to cover more ground. A Canadian film made in Montreal, it nevertheless aims at the U.S. market by leading the viewers to think it is some vast American town in peril. It called on the services of a pair of Hollywood-based Canadians—Leslie Nielsen and Susan Clark—and as many famous faces as the budget would allow. Henry Fonda has a small role as a veteran fire chief, whose expertise is called upon just as he is about to retire; Ava Gardner is a boozy television reporter; Barry Nelson is a surgeon; and Shelley Winters waddles around as a dedicated nurse.

It tells the tale of an employee of a huge oil refinery who becomes disgruntled when sacked and takes revenge by saturating the city with petroleum products and then puts a match to it all. The resulting conflagration is a mighty big one. The personal problems are frantic and *City on Fire* creates its own problems, trying to hold the interest of its audience with the limited variations possible in the grisly spectacle of buildings and people being burned. In the movie disaster genre, *City on Fire* is a minor entry. It required Fonda to do not much more than look concerned. The film ends with him saying, "All it takes is one man to destroy a city." Be that as it may, Vincent Canby in his *New York Times* review couldn't help but point out, "The Japanese do this sort of disaster movie much, much better."

WANDA NEVADA

1979

A United Artists release of a Panda Film, produced by Neal Dobrofsky and Dennis Hackin, directed by Peter Fonda, written by Dennis Hackin, photographed in Technicolor by Michael Butler, music by Ken Lauber, 105 minutes.

CAST:

Beaudray Demerville, *Peter Fonda;* Wanda Nevada, *Brooke Shields;* Dorothy Deerfield, *Fiona Lewis;* Ruby Muldoon, *Lake Askew;* Strap Pangburn, *Ted Markland;* Merlin Bitterstix, *Severn Darden;* Texas Curly, *Paul Fix;* Old Prospector, *Henry Fonda;* Card Hustler, *Larry Golden;* Gas Station Greaser, *John Denas;* Sherman Krupp, *Bert Williams.*

For his third film as a director, Peter Fonda chose an offbeat modern western comedy called *Wanda Nevada,* also giving himself the male lead and hiring the beautiful young Brooke Shields for the title role. The critical concensus was that choosing her was a major mistake because her lack of acting ability undermined the picture. But even with a better actress the film would still have buckled because the story and the characters are not plausible. It concerns a young gambler, circa 1950, who wins an orphan in a poker game and then travels around the West with her. They search for gold in the Grand Canyon and try to avoid the bad guys who also know about the find. They drift around like a whimsical "odd couple" going through improbable adventures.

Wanda Nevada sadly sank from sight shortly after its release. Peter Fonda was too relaxed in his own performance and failed to get any kind of performance from the lovely Brooke. As a lark, father Henry agreed to play a small role. He appears toward the end of the film as an eccentric, grizzled old prospector. But he is so hidden by whiskers and beard and thick goggles that viewers could be excused for not recognizing him. Henry apparently had fun doing it but in a letter to his son he said he would understand if the part was cut out. It wasn't. But since this was the only time father and son had worked together, it is regrettable it could not have been for a better project.

With Peter Fonda and Brooke Shields.

ON GOLDEN POND

1981

A Universal-AFD release of an ITC Films–IPC Films Production, produced by Bruce Gilbert, directed by Mark Rydell, written by Ernest Thompson, based on his play, photographed in color by Billy Williams, music by Dave Grusin, 109 minutes.

CAST:

Ethel Thayer, *Katharine Hepburn*; Norman Thayer, Sr., *Henry Fonda*; Chelsea Thayer Wayne, *Jane Fonda*; Billy Ray, *Doug McKeon*; Bill Ray, *Dabney Coleman*; Charlie Martin, *William Lanteau*; Sumner Todd, *Chris Rydell*.

There could have been no better film with which to conclude Henry Fonda's career on the screen than *On Golden Pond*. There was something almost divine about it happening. A playwright dealing with the career of a veteran actor and ending his story with a final item like this might well be accused of sentimentality. Real life, the critics would point out, cannot be climaxed this neatly and triumphantly. In the case of Fonda, however, this is precisely how it happened.

Ernest Thompson's play opened off-Broadway in 1978 and ran for 126 performances. A nice lit-

tle success for a nice little play. Fonda was in Washington when the play was staged at the Kennedy Center and it was brought to his attention as a likely vehicle for himself. He was unable to see it but asked that a copy of the script be

With Jane Fonda and Katharine Hepburn.

sent to him. He was delighted with it. He had at the same time been told that Katharine Hepburn felt the same way about the script, and so the casting of the two leads seemed a natural consequence.

When Jane Fonda realized how interested her father was in the possibility of making a film of Thompson's play, she not only arranged with her producer partner Bruce Gilbert to raise the production money but offered to play the role of the daughter, even though it was a small part. Hepburn readily agreed to the film and the company went on location in New Hampshire in July of 1980. They worked near the lake-surrounded town of Laconia, with most of the footage being shot on Squam Lake.

The plot of *On Golden Pond* is simple and conventional, and therein lies its beauty. It takes place at the summer home of Norman and Ethel Thayer. He is on the verge of his 80th birthday and she is not far behind. Norman is conscious of his frail health and constantly makes mordant

quips about death. This is their 48th summer in their cottage in the lake district of New Hampshire and Norman fears it will be their last. He has become increasingly irascible with the years, but Ethel keeps up a happy front and joyfully busies herself with fixing up the place.

Norman is a long-retired professor and hides his affections behind a gruff manner. She knows how to deal with him, but others find the going hard. They are expecting a visit from their divorced daughter Chelsea (Jane Fonda), and Ethel is hoping that father and daughter will behave considerately toward each other. The pair have always been at odds and Chelsea harbors

With Katharine Hepburn.

resentment that she did not receive the love and attention she felt due her as a child.

Chelsea arrives with her boyfriend Bill Ray (Dabney Coleman), together with his 13-year-old son Billy (Doug McKeon), who immediately adds to the somewhat tense atmosphere with his flip manner and his profanities. Bill tries to be friendly with the testy Norman but makes little progress. When he asks, "Well, how does it feel to turn eighty?" Norman snaps back, "Twice as bad as it did to turn forty." Things become a lit-

251

With Dabney Coleman, Jane Fonda, Katharine Hepburn and Doug McKeon.

tle more relaxed as the group celebrate Norman's birthday. Then Chelsea leaves for a trip to Europe with Bill, and Ethel breaks the news to Norman that Billy will be left to stay with them. Neither the old man nor the young boy show much enthusiasm for the idea, and after the couple leave Billy warns the elderly pair, "I'm not going to take any crap from you people."

Billy, who feels almost as rejected as Chelsea felt by her perfectionist father, is at first sullen but soon comes to respect Norman as a tough old bird and agrees to go fishing with him. Gradually Billy builds up enthusiasm for the surrounding natural life and finds himself to be a keen fisherman. Norman tells him about a big trout he has been trying to catch for years and that he calls it Walter. Searching for Walter now becomes a cause for the pair and one evening they have an accident while moving their motor boat through a rocky cove. The boat is damaged when it runs on the rocks and Norman and Billy are thrown in the water. As the evening grows darker Ethel

goes out looking and finds the pair clinging to a rock. She does her best to confine them to the house but Norman and Billy, now buddies, do their best to outfox her.

Chelsea returns by herself, Bill having gone back to his home in California, and tells her mother they were married in Brussels. She looks out on the lake and sees Norman and Billy having a good time and comments a little bitterly about not having had that kind of relationship with her father. In anger she refers to him as "a son of a bitch" and Ethel slaps her face. Ethel points out the qualities of this admittedly austere father and that understanding is a two-way thing. Chelsea now makes an attempt to make peace with him. She finds it easier than she thought. Because of his friendly, fatherly rapport with Billy, he has become more tractable. When Chelsea does a backflip off a diving board into the lake, something she was always scared to do as a child, it meets with his applause.

When Chelsea and Billy leave, she and her

With Katharine Hepburn and Doug McKeon.

father finally put their arms around each other. Having always called him by his first name, she says "Goodbye, Norman," and then quietly adds, "Dad." After they are gone Norman and Ethel prepare to make their own departure but Norman strains himself in lifting a box and has a heart seizure. As he lies on the porch, Ethel assumes that the end has come. But with the pill she has given him he slowly rallies and gets up in good humor. They quip about death; and perhaps there might be one more summer together.

On Golden Pond was not a good commercial prospect for the movie theatres of 1981. The idea of a film about an elderly couple near the end of their lives was poles away from the kind of film then in production. With players other than Fonda and Hepburn it probably would not even have come into being. But with these two veterans came a mystique that not even the most flinty Hollywood producer could deny. They had never worked together before, in fact they had barely even met before, and yet the idea of Fonda and Hepburn coming together for this film seemed like fate.

By 1980 hardly anyone else had been stars for as long as these two. Veteran moviegoers had grown up with Fonda and Hepburn—almost a

With Doug McKeon.

half-century of familiarity. Watching them in *On Golden Pond* is like watching beloved grandparents, and not without pain. Both actors were obviously in ill health. Hepburn had been advised by her doctors not to do the film because of surgery to her shoulder, but Fonda kept at her until she agreed. He said he wouldn't do it with anybody else.

254

A vital part of the emotional impact of *On Golden Pond* is due to the fact that Jane Fonda is in the film playing Fonda's daughter. The film public had never seen them on screen before, but they had heard about the difficulties the pair had had in relating to each other in real life—the emotionally inexpressive father and the rebellious daughter. Now the public had the chance to see them play out similar roles on screen. Since this particular father and daughter were expert actors they were able to play upon the situation with skill. The result not only moved audiences but during the filming of the reconciliation scene even the film crew was moved to tears.

Fonda had not enjoyed making most of his films. The stage was always by far his first love. But making *On Golden Pond* meant a lot to him. It was a thoroughly believable role about a kind of man he knew thoroughly well. In his last movie, art and life blended beautifully. No actor could have asked for a better finale. Said Henry Fonda, "I'm not a religious man but I thank God every morning that I lived long enough to play that role."

On Golden Pond not only did well at the box office, it did marvelously well. It proved that the public would indeed support a picture that dealt honestly with the faded glory and the contentment, as well as the pain, of old age. And in observing two obviously aged players performing the material in such a straightforward manner, no sensitive audience could remain unaffected. Fonda was 75 at the time but he looked all of the 80 years of Norman Thayer. There was a general feeling in Hollywood, and probably sensed by audiences, that this would be his last film. Sentiment clearly was a factor in the success *On Golden Pond* found at the Academy Awards in March of 1982. Fonda and Hepburn received Oscars for best actor and best actress, and Ernest Thompson received one for his screenplay. But more importantly, this beautifully photographed (by Billy Williams) story of an elderly couple coping with the challenge of the years struck a responsive, and no doubt lasting, chord with people of all ages everywhere.

Jane Fonda and Katharine Hepburn.